Beyond the Control of God?

Bloomsbury Studies in Philosophy of Religion

Series Editor:
Stewart Goetz

Editorial Board:
Thomas Flint, Robert Koons, Alexander Pruss, Charles
Taliaferro, Roger Trigg, David Widerker, Mark Wynn

Titles in the Series

Freedom, Teleology, and Evil
by Stewart Goetz

Image in Mind: Theism, Naturalism, and the Imagination
by Charles Taliaferro and Jil Evans

Actuality, Possibility, and Worlds
by Alexander Robert Pruss

God's Final Victory: A Comparative Philosophical Case for Universalism
by John Kronen and Eric Reitan

The Rainbow of Experiences, Critical Trust, and God
by Kai-man Kwan

Thinking Through Feeling: God, Emotion and Passibility
by Anastasia Philippa Scrutton

Philosophy and the Christian Worldview: Analysis, Assessment and Development
edited by David Werther and Mark D. Linville

Goodness, God and Evil
by David E. Alexander

Well-Being and Theism: Linking Ethics to God
by William A. Lauinger

Free Will in Philosophical Theology
by Kevin Timpe

The Moral Argument (forthcoming)
by Paul Copan and Mark D. Linville

Beyond the Control of God?

Six Views on the Problem of God and Abstract Objects

Edited by Paul M. Gould

B L O O M S B U R Y

NEW YORK • LONDON • NEW DELHI • SYDNEY

Bloomsbury Academic

An imprint of Bloomsbury Publishing Inc

1385 Broadway	50 Bedford Square
New York	London
NY 10018	WC1B 3DP
USA	UK

www.bloomsbury.com

Bloomsbury is a registered trade mark of Bloomsbury Publishing Plc

First published 2014

Library of Congress Cataloging-in-Publication Data
Beyond the control of God? : six views on the problem of God and abstract objects / edited by Paul M. Gould.
pages cm.– (Bloomsbury studies in philosophy of religion)
Includes bibliographical references and index.
ISBN 978-1-62356-541-1 (hardback : alk. paper)– ISBN 978-1-62356-365-3 (pbk. : alk. paper)
1. God. 2. Abstraction. 3. Object (Philosophy) I. Gould, Paul M., 1971- editor of compilation.
BL473.B49 2014
212'.7–dc 3
2013046264

ISBN: HB: 978-1-6235-6541-1
PB: 978-1-6235-6365-3
ePDF: 978-1-6235-6748-4
ePub: 978-1-6235-6937-2

Typeset by Fakenham Prepress Solutions, Fakenham, Norfolk NR21 8NN
Printed and bound in the United States of America

For Ethel
… a loving wife who exemplifies in excelsis the property being patient.

For J. P. Moreland
… it is his fault I am a platonist regarding abstract objects.

For Michael Bergmann and Jeffrey Brower
… who introduced me to the problem of God's relationship to abstract objects while in graduate school.

Contents

Acknowledgments   ix

Introduction to the Problem of God and Abstract Objects *Paul M. Gould*   1

1.   God and Propositions *Keith Yandell*   21

     Response to Keith Yandell   36

        Paul M. Gould and Richard Brian Davis   36

        Greg Welty   38

        William Lane Craig   39

        Scott A. Shalkowski   42

        Graham Oppy   44

     Response to Critics *Keith Yandell*   46

2.   Modified Theistic Activism *Paul M. Gould and Richard Brian Davis*   51

     Response to Paul M. Gould and Richard Brian Davis   65

        Keith Yandell   65

        Greg Welty   66

        William Lane Craig   68

        Scott A. Shalkowski   70

        Graham Oppy   72

     Response to Critics *Paul M. Gould and Richard Brian Davis*   75

3.   Theistic Conceptual Realism *Greg Welty*   81

     Response to Greg Welty   97

        Keith Yandell   97

        Paul M. Gould and Richard Brian Davis   99

        William Lane Craig   100

        Scott A. Shalkowski   102

        Graham Oppy   104

     Response to Critics *Greg Welty*   107

4.   Anti-Platonism *William Lane Craig*   113

     Response to William Lane Craig   127

        Keith Yandell   127

    Paul M. Gould and Richard Brian Davis   128

    Greg Welty   130

    Scott A. Shalkowski   132

    Graham Oppy   134

    Response to Critics *William Lane Craig*   137

5.   God with or without Abstract Objects *Scott A. Shalkowski*   143

    Response to Scott A. Shalkowski   155

    Keith Yandell   155

    Paul M. Gould and Richard Brian Davis   156

    Greg Welty   158

    William Lane Craig   160

    Graham Oppy   162

    Response to Critics *Scott A. Shalkowski*   165

6.   Abstract Objects? Who Cares! *Graham Oppy*   169

    Response to Graham Oppy   182

    Keith Yandell   182

    Paul M. Gould and Richard Brian Davis   184

    Greg Welty   186

    William Lane Craig   187

    Scott A. Shalkowski   189

    Response to Critics *Graham Oppy*   192

Bibliography   197

Contributors   205

Index   207

Acknowledgments

Parts of this book draw from previously published works. The Introduction and the Yandell, Gould/Davis, and Craig lead essays appeared in earlier form in a symposium on "God and Abstract Objects" within the pages of *Philosophia Christi*, the journal of the Evangelical Philosophical Society (www.epsociety.org). I am grateful to the Editor of *Philosophia Christi* who has granted non-exclusive, global rights for materials by Gould, Craig, Davis, and Yandell (vol. 13, no. 2, Winter 2011) to appear in this volume.

I am grateful to all the contributors for their hard work, collegiality, and insight, as we have grappled together with the knotty question of God's relationship to abstracta. This project is not for the faint of heart, and I have benefitted greatly from the vigorous yet irenic spirit of all participants in this book. I personally have learned a great deal, and have been challenged and pushed further than I could have hoped for at the outset in clarifying and defending my own preferred view (along with Richard Brian Davis) of God's relationship to abstracta. I am grateful to Professor J. P. Moreland for first introducing me to metaphysics; it is his fault that I am a platonist regarding abstracta. I am also grateful to Michael Bergmann and Jeffrey Brower, two members of my dissertation committee, who presented a tight argument in the literature for the incoherence of the conjunction of two things I hold dear—traditional theism and platonism. Their sober argument provided the perfect target for me to begin exploring the problem of God and abstract objects. I am especially grateful to my friend Richard Brian Davis, my co-defender of modified theistic activism in this book. Rich has been a constant source of encouragement and joy. Finally and above all I am grateful to my wife Ethel; without her patience and support I cannot imagine this work, or much else I do, coming to completion.

Introduction to the Problem of God and Abstract Objects

Paul M. Gould

The problem of God and abstract objects did not make the cut in Bertrand Russell's 1912 *The Problems of Philosophy*. The Lord Russell knows that abstract objects are problem enough by themselves.[1] Of course, Russell did not believe in God, so it goes without saying that there is no problem of God and abstract objects for him.[2] It is only a problem for those philosophers who are also theists. Minimally, the problem is one of specifying the relationship between God and abstract objects. But, as we shall see, the problem runs much deeper. In this introduction, I shall attempt to bring clarity to the debate related to God and abstract objects by first explicating as precisely as possible the problem of God and abstract objects and then by imposing some order into the debate by classifying various contemporary answers to the problem, answers that are rigorously set out and debated in the interactive format of this book.

Statement of the problem

What exactly is the problem of God and abstract objects? The term "God," as traditionally understood, signifies a personal being who is worthy of worship. Stipulate that terms and predicates such as "property," "proposition," "relation," "set," "possible world," "number," and the like belong to the class "abstract object." Suppose there are objects that satisfy the above terms and predicates. God exists and so do abstract objects. *Prima facie*, there is no problem here. So, we dig deeper: As a being worthy of worship, God's non-existence is reasonably thought impossible. That is, God is best understood as a necessary being. But, it is natural to think of abstract objects as necessary beings as well. Again, no obvious problem here—God is a necessary being and so are the members of the platonic horde.

But, as we dig deeper problems begin to surface. As a being worthy of worship, God, a necessary being, is typically thought to exist *a se*. That is, God is an *independent* and *self-sufficient* being. Further, God is typically thought to be supremely sovereign over all distinct reality in this sense: All reality distinct from God is dependent on God's creative and sustaining activity. Thus, a *traditional theist* will endorse the following aseity-sovereignty doctrine AD:

AD: (i) God does not depend on anything distinct from Himself for his existing, and (ii) everything distinct from God depends on God's creative activity for its existing.[3]

But the view that there are abstract objects that also exist necessarily seems to be a repudiation of AD. The reason is this. It is natural to think that if something exists necessarily, it does so because it is its nature to exist. Thus, abstract objects exist independently of God, which is therefore a repudiation of AD and traditional theism.

Call the view that there exists a realm of necessarily existing abstract objects *platonism*. For many contemporary analytic philosophers, platonism offers a theoretically attractive way to understand the relationship between mind, language, and reality. Interestingly, platonism also continues to be the ontology of choice among many contemporary analytic representatives of traditional theism. Yet, as we can now see, there is a tension between traditional theism (which includes AD) and platonism, a tension that has been noticed since at least the time of Augustine.[4] To state the tension explicitly, consider the following three jointly inconsistent claims (setting aside sets with contingent members):

INCONSISTENT TRIAD
(1) Abstract objects exist. [platonism][5]
(2) If abstract objects exist, then they are dependent on God. [from AD]
(3) If abstract objects exist, then they are independent of God. [platonist assumption]

All three claims can be independently motivated, but they form an inconsistent set. At most only two of the three claims in INCONSISTENT TRIAD can be true. Which claim should go? This question is difficult because the rejection of any of (1)–(3) leads to further problems. If (1) is rejected, the best solution (to many) to the problem of universals is abandoned and the age-old nominalism-realism debate ensues. All is not the same however. With the inclusion of God as an entity on the ontological books, the debate is pushed further along and familiar objections to either view lose some of their original force. Brian Leftow, who defends a view he calls theist concept nominalism, argues "if there were a God, this would have dramatic implications for the problem of universals. In particular, it would (I believe) blunt the force of all standard arguments for realism" (2006, 325). Others are not so sure. Professor Weaver blames the fourteenth-century theist, William of Ockham and his nominalism as the root of contemporary culture's decline: "the defeat of logical realism in the great medieval debate [on universals] was the crucial event in the history of Western culture; from this flowed those acts which issue now in modern decadence" (1984, 3). So, the rejection of (1), that is, platonism, is difficult for many contemporary analytic philosophers of religion: Platonic entities do all sorts of work and (to many) seem to be required for the best theory of the mind-world-language relationship. Thus inclined, the theist will want to be a platonic theist. Thus, the platonic theist can either reject the common understanding of traditional theism (that is, reject (2)) or reject a common platonist assumption regarding abstract objects (that is, reject (3)).

Claim (2) is well motivated given AD. If abstract objects exist and God is not an abstract object (that is, God is distinct from abstract objects), then it is natural to think

God is the creator of abstract objects as well. And if God is the creator of abstract objects, it follows that abstract objects are dependent on God. Claim (2) also allows for abstract objects to exist as uncreated yet dependent entities, as long as they are not "distinct from" God. If "distinct from" simply means something like "not external to God's borders," then one might consistently endorse (2) and argue that abstract objects are uncreated entities that are somehow part of God. Such abstract objects would be dependent on God in some way, (say) perhaps a kind of constituent dependency, and AD is preserved. Alternatively, the platonic theist can reject claim (2) by arguing that traditional theism does not require the strong aseity-sovereignty doctrine AD. Perhaps the notion of God creating abstract objects is incoherent or impossible. Or perhaps AD is not entailed by the teachings of Scripture, or it does not apply to abstract objects. Of course, the platonic theist could simply opt to be a nontraditional theist as well in her rejection of claim (2).

But, if claim (2) is rejected, the platonic theist runs into another problem, call it the *ultimacy problem*. Consider one kind of abstract object, property. If properties exist independently of God, and God has properties essentially, then God's nature is explained by some other entity, and God is not ultimate.[6] But, as Leftow states, "theists want all explanations to trace back *to* God, rather than *through* God to some more ultimate context" (1990, 587; cf. Plantinga 1980, 31–3). The same problem surfaces when considering other platonic entities as well. On the platonic story (for example), possible worlds exist independently of God and God's existence is necessary because in each possible world, God exists. But then "this threatens to make God's existence derive from items independent from Him: The worlds are there independently, that He is in all of them entails God's existence" (Leftow 2009, 27). It seems that the platonic theist must bite a bullet and admit that God is not ultimate in explanation or existence if claim (2) is denied, yet this thesis appears to be a core intuition of the theist's conception of God.

What about a rejection of claim (3)? Perhaps platonic entities depend on God in some way for their existence and nature. If so, a question that naturally arises is, How is the dependency relation to be understood between two kinds of necessary beings? The dependency relation cannot be mere logical dependence, where the existence of x entails the existence of y, but not vice versa. To see why, consider two necessary beings, x and y. Given that necessary beings could not fail to exist, then (necessarily) x exists and y exists are mutually entailing, in which case it is impossible for y to asymmetrically depend on x (again, if the dependency relation is merely a logical relation). Rather the relation between x and y is one of mutual logical dependence. Call this the *dependency problem*.[7]

The dependency problem has led some contemporary philosophers to the view that it is logically impossible for any necessary being to asymmetrically depend on another.[8] But, asymmetrical dependence need not be cashed out solely in terms of logical entailment. Taking our cue from AD, perhaps abstract objects are created by God.[9] The fact that creation is a causal relation suggests the following dependency relations: Abstract objects are *causally* dependent on God. This causal dependency between God and abstract objects seems to be just what we are looking for—an ontologically significant, asymmetrical or one-way relation of dependence running from each nondivine object to God. So, the platonic theist can maintain that God, as the creator of all distinct reality, eternally creates (that is, causes) abstract objects to exist and does so of necessity. Of course, in making this move, a hornet's nest of issues arises: Is it metaphysically possible for God, or anything else, to create abstract objects? Assuming that abstract objects are everlasting, is the notion of eternal causation coherent? Does co-eternality render God somehow less ultimate? What sense can be given to the notion of one necessary being (God) creating another necessary being? What analysis of causation is required to give sense to the notion of God creating abstract objects?

Worse, even if the above questions could find acceptable answers, it appears that the resultant platonic theism, as many have suggested, is hopelessly incoherent, succumbing to the *bootstrapping worry*. Typically, the worry is advanced as follows: "God has properties. If God is the creator of all things, then God is the creator of His properties. But God cannot create properties unless He already has the property of *being able to create a property*. Thus, we are off to the races, ensnared in a vicious explanatory circle."[10] These questions and worries, and many more, reveal the apparent intractability of the dependency problem specifically, and the problem of God and abstract objects in general.

The problem of God and abstract objects is multilayered. Philosophy pushes many to platonism regarding abstract objects. Theology pushes many to endorse a strong reading of the aseity-sovereignty doctrine AD. The conjunction of platonism and traditional theism results in the tension described in INCONSISTENT TRIAD. Attempts to resolve the tension of INCONSISTENT TRIAD lead to additional problems:

- Reject claim (1) and the *problem of universals* is of central concern;
- Reject claim (2) and the *ultimacy problem* is of central concern;
- Reject claim (3) and the *dependency problem* and *bootstrapping worry* are of central concern.

Thus, the deliverances of theology and philosophy threaten to wreck the (would-be) traditional theist, or alternatively, the (would-be) platonist, on the shoals of unorthodoxy or anti-realism. For the traditional theist, it seems that realism must be rejected. For the platonic theist, it seems that theistic orthodoxy must be redefined or rejected. It is not clear that anyone will be happy in the end. Still, hope dies hard. There have been a number of prominent contemporary attempts to navigate the waters of the problem of God and abstract objects. In the next section, I shall survey the contemporary literature and highlight recent efforts to place a stake in the sand on our central problem and its ancillary issues.

Some contemporary answers to the problem

Depending on which claim of INCONSISTENT TRIAD is rejected at least four views can be discerned and advocates of each view ably defend themselves in this book. The first three views are realist (maybe even platonist if abstract object realism is endorsed), although for clarity, I shall only label the first view as platonism proper. The fourth view is nominalistic and anti-realist.

According to (the view I shall call) *platonic theism*, at least some abstract objects exist wholly distinct from God and are independent of God. Keith Yandell and his defense of theistic propositionalism is in this category, hence Yandell rejects (2). The defender of *theistic activism* argues that the platonic tradition can accommodate abstract objects being necessarily created by God, and thus dependent on God. Paul Gould and Richard Davis argue for a version of theistic activism, called modified theistic activism (MTA), and thus reject (3). The defender of *divine conceptualism* identifies abstract objects with various constituent entities of the divine mind which are uncreated yet dependent upon God. Greg Welty defends a version of divine conceptualism called theistic conceptual realism (TCR), and also (along with the theistic activist) rejects (3). The defenders of *nominalism*, in this book, William Lane Craig and Scott A. Shalkowski, reject claim (1)—there are no abstract objects, only concrete objects. Of course, one may argue, as Graham Oppy does, that the existence or nonexistence of abstract objects is irrelevant—it makes no philosophical difference—to God's existence. If abstract objects exist, they do so independent of God (and claim (2) is rejected). If they do not exist, then there are no abstract objects (and claim (1) is rejected). Either way, there is no problem of God and abstract objects.

In order to provide as broad a framework as possible for the reader to navigate the contours of the debate, I shall survey the contemporary literature with respect to these four views, highlighting arguments in their favor and attempts at resolving the resultant problems. Once completed, I shall describe in more detail the position of each of our six lead essays, thus setting the stage for what follows.

Platonic theism

The distinguishing feature of platonic theism is that there is a realm of abstract objects that exist independently of God. Some also exist wholly apart from God. Consider properties. Assuming an abundant theory of properties and a unified theory of predication (where all atomic sentences of the form "*a* is *F*" denote a particular "*a*" and a property "*F*") then there will be two domains, or realms, of abstract objects: (Within the) divine substance and Plato's heaven. Or again, consider propositions. According to the platonic theist, propositions exist wholly apart from God and are not to be identified with ideas in the divine mind. On this picture, to have a propositional thought, say a belief, is to stand in a certain special relationship to a specific proposition (Jubien 2001, 47). The platonic theist rejects claim (2) of INCONSISTENT TRIAD and those abstract objects wholly distinct from God are understood as independently existing beings.

Arguments against claim (2) and in support of platonic theism fall into three broad categories: (a) attempts to identify a token abstract object that *in fact* exists distinct from and independently of God; (b) attempts to show the impossibility or undesirability of created abstract objects; and (c) attempts to undercut the motivations for AD and thus show that the traditional theist is within the bounds of orthodoxy in denying claim (2).

In his 1970 book, *On Universals*, Nicholas Wolterstorff attempts to motivate the view that some properties must be excluded from God's creative activity. He suggests that there exist properties such as *being either true or false* that are neither possessed by God nor created by God (that is, a category (a) type argument). And if so, there are (at least some) abstract objects that exist distinct from God and independently of God and claim (2) ought to be rejected. Wolterstorff begins:

> Consider the fact that propositions have the property of *being either true or false*. This property is not a property of God. But is it presupposed by the biblical writers that not all exemplifications of this property were brought into existence by God, and thus that it was not brought into existence by God. For the propositions 'God exists' and 'God is able to create' exemplify *being true or false* wholly apart from any creative activity on God's part; in fact, creative ability on his part presupposes that these propositions are true, and thus presupposes that there exists such a property as *being either true or false*. (1970, 292)

Thus, alethic properties are, according to Wolterstorff, problematic for the defender of claim (2)—they are distinct from God and exist apart from God's creative activity. It seems the defender of claim (2) is not without a response. It could be argued that propositions (the possessors of alethic properties) are either uncreated but not distinct (from God) or distinct (from God) but created. Either way, claim (2) is upheld. On the first story, alethic properties are uncreated, yet always and only possessed by propositions, now identified as divine thoughts. If so, then alethic properties (at least) are not distinct from God's being.[11] As Plantinga puts it: "truth is not independent of mind; it is necessary that for any proposition *p*, *p* is true only if it is believed, and if and only if it is believed by God" (1982, 68). So, even if the properties had by propositions (now construed as divine thoughts) are uncreated, they are not distinct from God. On the second story, it could be argued that alethic properties are distinct from God, yet eternally created by God. If so (and assuming the notion of eternal causation coherent), then it seems reasonable to think that the truth of *God exists* and *God is able to create* is necessarily coextensive with the existence of the properties *being true* and *being either true or false*. But then it is not clear that we have a clear case of a property (or abstract object) that requires the denial of claim (2).

More recently, Peter van Inwagen (2009) has argued for the stronger (and more general) claim that God, nor anyone else, can create abstract objects (that is, a category (b) type argument). Thus, if abstract objects are dependent upon God, it can't be because God creates them. Abstract objects, says van Inwagen, are not the kind of things that can enter into causal relations. Thus, the quantifier "everything" in the statement "God is the creator of everything distinct from himself" should be restricted to things that can enter into causal relations and the traditional theists need not endorse AD (or claim (2)). van Inwagen insists that abstract objects cannot enter into causal relations because no *sense* can be made regarding the notion of divinely created abstract objects. What he is after is the completion of

(*S*) For all x, if x is an abstract object, God caused x if …

in order to show what makes the causal fact both true and accessible enough for us to understand. van Inwagen considers two possible completions of (*S*), the so-called Aristotelian view, which endorses the claim that all abstract objects exist *in rebus* and are created when God creates the concrete object in which they are a part; and the theistic activist view, which endorses the claim that abstract objects are caused by the divine activity of thinking. Since, according to van Inwagen, neither of these completions are successful, there is no acceptable completion of (*S*).

Is it the case that there is no acceptable completion of (*S*) or that abstract objects cannot enter into causal relations? Plantinga thinks that abstract objects can enter into causal relations. When considering the epistemological objection to abstract objects, Plantinga suggests that if "propositions are divine thoughts," then

> these objects can enter into the sort of causal relation that holds between a thought and a thinker, and we can enter into causal relation with them by virtue of our causal relation to God. It is therefore quite possible to think of abstract objects capable of standing in causal relations. (1993, 121)

Still, it is one thing to suggest how abstract objects could possibly stand in causal relations and quite another to provide an adequate completion of (*S*). Yet, even *that* seems possible, and the defender of created abstracta, such as the theistic activist, is prepared to argue that it is in fact actual. For if causation is fundamentally about production, then God's production of abstract objects is no more mysterious than God's production of the concrete universe, or so it seems.[12]

Finally, need the traditional theist accept AD? Does Scripture, and because of Scripture, tradition, require the traditional theist to endorse AD? Wolterstorff provides arguments for thinking that the biblical writers did not endorse a wide scope reading of the doctrine of creation, where God is the creator of everything distinct from himself full-stop (that is, a category (c) type argument). Wolterstorff advances two lines of thinking to undercut the motivation toward a wide scope reading of the doctrine of creation. First, he suggests that it cannot "plausibly be supposed that the biblical writers … had *universals* in view in speaking of 'all things'" (1970, 293). He rhetorically suggests that were universals in view, then they would have been mentioned. Wolterstorff's second approach is to claim that the creator-creature distinction is invoked in Scripture for religious reasons and not theoretical, or metaphysical, reasons and thus it does not rule out a narrower understanding of the doctrine of creation.

How strong are Wolterstorff's arguments? Regarding the first, I have some sympathy with the suggestion. But, as Matthew Davidson (1999, 278–9) puts it, the biblical writers probably did not have quarks (or to use the most recent example, the strings of string theory) in mind when they addressed the subject of divine creation, still no traditional theists denies that quarks, or strings, if they exist, are distinct from God and created by God.

But does such reasoning require that the theist ought to think the biblical writers had a wide scope in view, or merely that they *may* think it in view? Scott Davison thinks that this stronger (ought) claim is problematic since all the entities mentioned by Davidson are contingent physical things and we know how the biblical authors would respond if asked whether they should be included, but with respect to abstract objects, "there is no way to know exactly what they would say in response to this query" (1991, 488).

Davison's agnosticism might be a bit too convenient. A look at the article "all" (Greek: *panta*) in Kittel's *Theological Dictionary of the New Testament* shows that while the meaning of "all things" is indeed religious, as Wolterstorff thinks, still its religious meaning seems to be dependent on the complete inclusion of all things whatsoever (1967, 5: 886–96). Thus, *prima facie*, the most natural, simple, and theoretically unified reading of the all things passage seems to favor a wide scope reading and AD.[13] Still, I do not see how the relevant Scripture passages require such a reading.[14]

Theistic activism

Theistic activism locates the platonic horde within the mind of God as created, and thus dependent, entities. Properties and relations are identified with divine concepts, and the rest of the platonic apparatus is built up from there. Propositions are just divine thoughts. Numbers, sets, and possible worlds are also explicated in terms of properties and relations (that is, divine concepts) and propositions (that is, divine thoughts). Importantly, God creates all reality distinct from God, including the entire platonic horde.

The most prominent version of theistic activism is that of Morris and Menzel. In their view, called absolute creationism, "all properties and relations are God's concepts, the products, or perhaps better, the contents of a divine intellective activity... . Unlike human concepts, then, which are graspings of properties that exist ontologically distinct from and independent of those graspings, divine concepts are those very properties themselves" (1986, 166).[15] Thus, divine creation of abstract objects is understood as eternal, necessary, and absolute: God necessarily and eternally creates all abstract objects whatsoever. Further, since God exemplifies a nature, understood as a bundle of essential properties, absolute creationism entails that God creates His own nature.

Not many have been willing to follow Morris and Menzel down the activist road, or at least completely down the activist road. Perhaps the closest thing to an endorsement of theistic activism is from Plantinga, a theist and platonist *par excellence* who has cautiously endorsed the view hinting that if something like it were true, then "abstract objects would be necessary beings that are nevertheless causally dependent upon something else" (1992, 309). More recently, David Baggett and Jerry Walls (2011) have appropriated the insight of the activist to specify God's relationship to goodness, and Paul Gould and Richard Davis argue in this book for a kind of limited activism with respect to concepts and propositions, but not properties and relations. Most who consider it seem to think that theistic activism suffers from at least two minor problems and one major problem.

The first minor worry relates to the notion of creating eternal beings. Intuitively, creation seems to involve bringing something into being, and bringing something into being seems to involve temporal becoming, or an absolute beginning of existence. Plantinga shares this intuition: "a thing is created only if there is a time before which it does not exist" (1974, 169). I too share this intuition when contingent beings are in view. However, my intuition is not as clear when considering necessary beings, which, if they exist, exist at all times (or timelessly exist). In general, to prove that one necessarily existent being could not asymmetrically depend on another would be a difficult task (van Inwagen, 1993, 108). Perhaps there are two notions of creation that need explication: One for contingent beings and one for necessary beings. An explication of creation for necessary beings should not concern itself with issues related to coming into being (since God is not temporally prior to abstract objects and vice versa), but rather it should be causal or explanatory: For example, God is the eternal generating cause of abstract objects. For the activist, God is the eternal generating cause in virtue of the divine intellect.[16] This first worry can be set aside.

The second worry for the activist concerns the *necessity* of creation. It is argued, for example by Bill Craig, that if

> we expand the meaning of creation so as to make any dependent being the object
> of God's creation, then we have radically subverted God's freedom with respect
> to creating... . His freedom is restricted to creation of the tiny realm of concrete
> objects alone. The vast majority of being flows from him with an inexorable
> necessity independent of God's will. (Copan and Craig 2004, 175–6)

Simply stated, the objection is that if we expand our explication of creation to include necessary beings, then God's freedom in creation is *seriously* hindered. But this is not so clear. Perhaps, as Gould and Davis argue in their defense of modified theistic activism (MTA), God freely (and eternally) thinks up all possible creatures and all possible states of affairs. In this creative act, God delimits all modal facts—all possible individuals and possible worlds are set—in virtue of God's intellectual activity. Concepts are divine ideas; propositions (and possible worlds) are divine thoughts. Here is the interesting part: In addition to God's spontaneous creation of all possible creatures via His producing divine concepts and thoughts, God creates, of necessity, a platonic horde of properties and relations that will play the role of structure making in any actual concrete universe God creates. This creating of the platonic horde is logically posterior to the Biggest Bang, and sets the stage for the Big Bang (that is, the creation of the actual contingent universe). If so, divine freedom is preserved (or so it seems) since in the first logical moment of the Biggest Bang, God spontaneously creates all possibilities even if He creates the corresponding properties and relations of necessity in virtue of the divine will.

Alternatively, the activist could maintain that God is *not* free with respect to the creation of abstracta, and argue that, still, this is not a problem the traditional theist should care about. Morris states, "the traditional view is that God is a free creator of our physical universe: He was free to create it or to refrain from creating it; he was free to create this universe, a different universe, or no such universe at all" (Morris and Menzel 1986, 170). Craig assumes without argument that the traditional account of divine freedom to create extends to all existent entities other than God, not just contingent entities. It should be no surprise that divine freedom is interestingly different than human freedom, and perhaps one of these interesting differences is that God is not free with respect to one aspect of His creation, that is, the neces-- sarily existing abstract objects. God is not free with respect to the creation of abstract objects, but as creator, He is responsible for their existence. Still, Craig's claim that these beings flow with an "inexorable necessity independent of God's will" does seem problematic since it is natural to think that the causal buck in creation stops with the divine will, not the divine intellect. This worry does not appear insurmountable for the activist—for the intellect and will are tightly integrated in God—still, it might serve to steer the theist toward other accounts of divine creating (e.g. where God is the creator of abstract objects in virtue of the will)[17] or divine conceptualism (where abstract objects are uncreated yet dependent on God).

The main problem with Morris and Menzel's theistic activism is that it appears logically incoherent. In short, it succumbs to the bootstrapping worry. Many (including myself) think this problem fatal for the absolute creationism of Morris and Menzel. But I am baffled by their failure to take an obvious way out of the incoherency charge. Why not hold that it is only properties distinct from God that are created by God? On this suggestion, all of God's essential properties (that is, divine concepts) exist *a se* as a brute fact within the divine mind, and it is only those properties that are not essentially exemplified by God (that is, necessarily satisfied in God) that are created by God. Morris's answer is that "aside from the fact that no such selective exclusion would work in the first place, this move would amount to scrapping the whole project of theistic activism and abandoning the view of absolute creation" (1986, 172). But, why would no such selective exclusion of God's properties work in the first place? Craig makes this objection a bit more perspicuous when he claims that the move under consideration "would introduce an ad hoc selectivity concerning what properties are or are not created by God (especially evident with respect to properties shared by contingent beings)" (Copan and Craig 2004, 176).

Yet it seems that this move would be *ad hoc* only if there were no independent motivations for thinking abstract objects exist. Now, if there are independent reasons to think platonism true and one is also a traditional theist, then it is not *ad hoc* to modify one's account of platonism (that is, platonic theism) in light of problems that arise in an initial formulation of the theory (nor is it *ad hoc* to modify one's understanding of traditional theism either). This move is similar to those made in theory construction in science where new evidence leads to theory modification. Usually, the newly modified theory is isomorphic to some part of the original, modified in such a way as to maintain the virtues of the old (often the bulk of the old theory) while still accommodating the new evidence. At any rate, it is certainly not *ad hoc* to think that God does not create His own nature given the commonsensical assumption that no being is, or can be, responsible for the nature it has (Rowe 2004, 151–2). As I have argued elsewhere, the bootstrapping worry can be avoided for the platonic theist (who is a theistic activist) if the following two claims are endorsed: (a) God's essential Platonic properties (that is, divine concepts that necessarily apply to God) exist *a se* (that is, they are neither created nor sustained by God, yet they inhere in the divine substance, the divine mind even); and (b) substances are Aristotelian (Gould 2011, 56–7).

In summary, while the activist view has few adherents, it is still a viable option as long as the position of absolute creationism is abandoned. And it was never required, even for Morris and Menzel—as they repeatedly (and rightly) noted—it is only everything "distinct from" God that exists as a result of God's creative activity.

Divine conceptualism

According to divine conceptualism, abstract objects are identified with various constituent entities of the divine mind and are uncreated yet dependent upon God. Just how the dependency relation is to be understood is an open question. As uncreated, abstract objects do not depend on God for their existence or nature. Still, taking our cue from what has been said above, it could be argued that the divine substance is the final cause of its constituent parts and thus abstract objects do causally depend (in one sense) on God. Or alternatively, abstract objects (understood as divine ideas or whatever) could simply be understood as constituently dependent on God.

One interesting version of divine conceptualism is the theistic conceptual realism (TCR) of Greg Welty.[18] According to Welty, abstract objects are those constituent entities of the divine mind that perform a certain function within the created order. For example, the concept of a "universal" is the concept of a thing that plays the ontological role of explaining attribute agreement and grounding the truth of atomic sentences of the form "*a* is *F*" (Welty 2004, 57). The concept of a "proposition" is the concept of a thing that plays the role of bearer of truth values and is what is asserted by the standard use of declarative sentences. Thus, realism holds at the human level and conceptualism at the divine level. That is, relative to finite minds, abstract objects exist as realistically as any platonic entity—they exist apart from us and enjoy multiple-instantiability. But abstract objects do not exist realistically for God, in the sense that they exist apart from or over and above God. Rather, their existence is purely conceptual.

Considerations related to some kinds of abstract objects seem to push the theist toward endorsing divine conceptualism, whereas consideration of other kinds of abstract objects seem to push in the direction of platonic theism. As noted above, a common intuition is that truths are somehow connected to minds, and this fact pushes in the direction of thinking that propositions and possible worlds are best thought of as divine thoughts (or groupings of divine thoughts). As Plantinga says, the idea that abstract objects exist independently of minds and their noetic activity is "realism run amok" (1982, 68). Perhaps numbers and sets too are best thought of as the product of God's (mental) collecting activity (Menzel 1987). Considerations related to these kinds of abstract objects push the theist in the direction of divine conceptualism.

On the other hand, considerations related to the nature of properties and property possession push toward a kind of platonic theism. Consider that a primary role of platonic properties is that of *making* or structuring reality. As George Bealer observes, "[properties] play a fundamental constitutive role in the structure of the world" (1998a, 268). Alternatively, concepts are typically thought to play a *mediating* role between mind and world (Willard 1999). If this picture is correct, then the defender of divine conceptualism (and theistic activism) calls upon divine concepts to play at least two roles: that of mediator and maker. For the created realm, this does not appear problematic. But, when considering the divine substance, the needed account of how God both exemplifies the property *being divine* and possesses the (same) concept/property as a constituent of the divine thought that He is divine appears unlovely and forced.[19] Perhaps considerations of elegance, if nothing else, serve to push the theist toward platonic theism (or MTA as Gould and Davis argue in this volume) over divine conceptualism when properties are in view. And the dialectic continues. The defender of divine conceptualism could, in turn, cry:

> *Tu quoque!* Consider the picture as a whole. On divine conceptualism, the divine substance (and all its constituent metaphysical parts) exists *a se*, within the borders of God, and brings into being the entire created order at the "moment" of creation. Such a picture is theoretically simpler and more elegant than the platonic view of reality in which the platonic horde exists co-eternal and distinct from God (created or not) *sans* contingent creation.

Perhaps the lesson is a familiar one: When working out one's mature metaphysical theory, a cost-benefit analysis will be required and each view will enjoy particular benefits and swallow particular costs.

Nominalism

According to nominalism, there are no abstract objects, only concrete objects. There are brown dogs, but not the *abstract* property *being brown*; there are tables and chairs with the same number of legs, but not *abstract* numbers; and so on. Nominalism is not to be understood necessarily as the rejection of properties, relations, propositions, possible worlds, and so on, rather, what is required of those who believe in such entities is that they think of them as concrete objects.[20] Thus, on nominalism, the problem of God and abstract objects is dissolved—there are no abstract objects (that is, claim (1) of INCONSISTENT TRIAD is rejected). God alone exists *a se* and creates all concrete reality distinct from Himself (and the concrete reality is all the reality there is).

Nominalism's appeal is readily seen—it apparently offers a quick and happy solution to the problem of God and abstract objects. Peter van Inwagen goes so far as to argue that there is a presumption of nominalism and thus one should be a nominalist if one can get away with it.[21] So, *can* one get away with being a nominalist? And further, is it really the case that if one can, one *should* to be a nominalist? I say, a traditional theist *can* be a nominalist—this much seems clear. What is not clear by my lights, is whether she *should* be a nominalist. Specifically, it is not clear that nominalism offers the best theory of the mind-language-world nexus.

Consider the case of divine predication. How is the atomic sentence "God is divine" nominalistically understood? One nominalistic friendly answer, articulated by Bergmann, Brower, and Leftow, is to endorse the doctrine of divine simplicity. The predicate *being divine* does not refer to an attribute that God exemplifies, rather it is truly ascribed to God on some other grounds.[22] But the nominalist need not endorse the doctrine of divine simplicity to account for divine predication. For example, in this volume, Bill Craig argues that there are a number of nominalist options that can do the trick (without appeal to divine simplicity). The choices, argues Craig, center around the acceptance or rejection of Quine's metaontology, specifically Quine's criterion for ontological commitment—roughly, that one is ontologically committed to the value of any variable bound by the existential quantifier in a first-order symbolization of a true, canonically-formulated statement. If one accepts the Quinean criterion, then the nominalist can endorse fictionalism (in this volume Shalkowski and Oppy think this an attractive option). On the fictionalist story, "abstract objects are more or less useful fictions" (Copan and Craig 2004, 180) and "God's concrete condition [is] accurately described by the Platonist's ascription of various properties to God" (ibid., 185) without admitting abstract objects into one's ontology. If the nominalist rejects the Quinean criterion, then there are a number of options (noneism, neutral logic, substitutional quantification, figuralism)[23] that can be employed in explicating the existential quantifier and divine predication can (again, says Craig) be safely analyzed without postulating abstract objects.

Assume that a traditional theist can be a nominalist along the above lines (or something like it). Ought she be a nominalist? Arguments in support of this stronger claim fall into two broad categories: (a) theoretical considerations related to ontological economy (and often an appeal to Ockham's razor); and (b) the claim that there is a presumption of nominalism and thus nominalism wins by default if one can get away with it.

Leftow (2006, 2012) has advanced an argument that nominalism is the most attractive position for the theist since it allows her to economize on kinds of entities (that is, an argument from category (a)). Leftow thinks that nontheistic versions of nominalism (for example, trope theories, human concept-nominalism, human predicate-nominalism, likeness-nominalism and set-nominalism) are either obviously false or less plausible than platonism. Platonism is a better theory—still, it is a strange theory, one that Ockham bids us to avoid if possible. Thus, if divine concepts are already within one's ontology, as they are for the theist, she ought, in light of Ockham's razor, allow them to do as much work as possible before introducing other entities into her ontology. If it can be established that divine concepts, understood as mental particulars, can do the work typically ascribed to platonic entities, then "it is simple parsimony to let divine concepts do as much work as they can once they're in one's metaphysic" (Leftow 2006, 326). Thus, it is in virtue of *ontological* economy that Leftow thinks theistic concept nominalism better than platonism.

Assume Leftow's theistic concept nominalism is in fact as explanatorily adequate as platonism. Does it follow that (because of Ockham's razor) theists ought to be nominalists? Not obviously so. *Ontological* economy (in terms of number of *kinds* of entities) would need to be balanced with *ideological* economy (in terms of the number of *primitive facts* within one's theory). Further, theoretical virtues other than economy—accuracy, scope, fruitfulness, and perhaps more—need to be taken into consideration in theory construction (Shalkowski 1997). Thus, at the end of the day, it could turn out that Platonism, on balance, comes out ahead of Leftow's nominalism. With respect to economy, it could turn out that platonism's explanatory simplicity (in terms of less primitives) outweighs any (putative) gains in ontological simplicity on nominalism.[24]

Craig has recently advanced arguments of the category (b) type. Craig provides two reasons why there is a presumption of nominalism (over platonism) for the traditional theist. First, Craig exposits (and endorses) van Inwagen's argument from queerness:

> For it is very puzzling that objects should fall into two so radically different and exclusive categories as abstract and concrete. It would be much more appealing to suppose that one of the categories is empty. But concrete objects are indisputably real and well-understood, in contrast to abstract objects. So we should presume that abstract objects do not exist. (Craig 2011b, 49)

Secondly, an argument from theology:

> The chief theological failing of Platonism and therefore the reason for its unacceptability for orthodox theists is that Platonism is incompatible with the doctrine of *creatio ex nihilo* and so fundamentally compromises divine aseity.... . An orthodox Christian theist, then, cannot be a Platonist ... . [Thus] we have very strong incentives, indeed, for rejecting [the claim that there are abstract objects] in favor of some sort of Nominalistic view of abstract objects. (ibid., 47)

Thus, Craig thinks there is a presumption of nominalism (in philosophy in general) and certainly for the traditional theist.

One is not sure what to think about Craig's argument from queerness against abstract objects. Certainly such arguments can go both ways: Concrete objects such as trees, dogs, and chairs might not be queer to the man on the street, but they certainly can begin to sound queer in the hands of the metaphysician. Questions that quickly arise include: Do physical objects perdure or endure? Are they three-dimensional or four-dimensional? How does one solve the problem of material constitution? Attempts to provide a metaphysical assay of concrete objects quickly reveals that, *contra* Craig's claim, even concrete objects are not "indisputably real and well-understood." They might turn out to be rather queer themselves. Craig's first reason in favor of a presumption of nominalism does not appear persuasive to the anti-nominalist.

The antinominalist would also push back on Craig's second argument. It could be argued that the presumption is not for nominalism. Rather, the biblical evidence (and the Nicene tradition) motivate, or provide *prima facie* support for, or entail a presumption for, AD. As we have seen, theistic activism and divine conceptualism can accommodate AD. Thus, there is no presumption in favor of nominalism. Nominalism does not win by default. It must be shown superior on other grounds. The open question then is this: Is nominalism explanatorily superior (not merely equal) to realist accounts of various phenomena? It is not clear that it is and thus it is not clear that nominalism represents the best option for the traditional theist, and certainly not the only option.

The essays, the authors

The stage is now set. My goal has been to provide a framework and whet your appetite for the discussion that follows. Our authors include some of the leading thinkers and young rising stars in metaphysics, philosophy of religion, and philosophical theology. They have published many technical books and journal articles on this topic and related topics. I can't think of a more qualified group of people to address this topic. Each author will present an essay in which he argues for his view of the relationship between God and abstract objects. Each essay is followed by a brief response from each other author. Finally, each author will have a chance to respond to the criticisms of his view that the five coauthors raise. The format of the book allows for a substantive interaction between philosophers holding various positions—realist/nominalist, theist/atheist/agnostic, perfect being theologians, and nonperfect being theologians—on God's relationship to abstract objects, if there be any (or, alternatively, if there be any God). All that is left is for me to introduce the authors and their essays.

In the lead off essay, Keith Yandell argues for a kind of platonic theism. His essay focuses on one kind of abstract object—propositions—and argues that, if they exist at all, they exist of necessity regardless of God's modal status. If God necessarily exists, and since, according to Yandell, theistic activism turns out to be untenable, either theistic ideaism is true, the view that propositions are to be identified with the content of God's thoughts, or theistic propositionalism is true, the view that there are propositions but they do not depend for their existence upon God (and neither does God depend for existence on propositions). If God contingently exists, then theistic propositionalism is true. Neither the Biblical evidence nor an appeal to our modal intuitions will do anything to resolve the question of which view is true—still, Yandell claims, either view is perfectly compatible with theism.

Next Paul M. Gould and Richard Brian Davis argue that abstract objects distinct from God exist and are the product of God's creative activity. Some abstract objects are to be identified with various constituents of the divine mind that are produced via intellectual activity: Concepts are divine ideas; propositions are divine thoughts. Hence, Gould and Davis argue for a kind of theistic activism. But it is a *modified* theistic activism (MTA) in two ways. First, some abstract objects—namely, properties and relations—are *not* to be identified with constituents of the divine mind. Rather, these abstract objects exist wholly apart from God's being, in Plato's heaven even, yet are created by God in virtue of the divine will. Second, God's essential properties exist within the divine (Aristotelian) substance *a se*. In this way, Gould and Davis think they have successfully avoided the bootstrapping worry, addressed the dependency problem, and upheld AD.

Greg Welty argues that divine thoughts "play the role" of abstract objects with respect to created reality yet exist as uncreated entities within the divine mind. In order to motivate his preferred version of divine conceptualism, which he calls theistic conceptual realism (TCR), Welty focuses on propositions and possible worlds and identifies six conditions for a successful ontological account of abstract objects. Given the *objectivity* of abstract objects, realism is true. Given the *intentionality* and *simplicity* of abstract objects, conceptual realism is true. Given the *necessity*, *plenitude*, and *relevance* of abstract objects, theistic conceptual realism is true. Since no other theory of abstract objects satisfies each of these six conditions except TCR, as an added bonus, we have an argument for God from the reality of abstract objects.

The remaining three authors are less enthusiastic about the possibility of a realist theory of abstract objects. Next, William Lane Craig argues that realism regarding abstract objects (what he calls platonism) is neither theologically tenable nor philosophically required for the traditional theist. Theologically, the postulation of infinities of uncreated, co-eternal abstract objects that exist independently of God violates God's sovereignty and aseity. Philosophically, the main argument in support of abstract object realism, the so-called Indispensability Argument, is plausibly false. Thus, the anti-platonist perspective on God and abstract objects is a viable contender for truth, and it warrants further investigation on the part of the traditional theist.

Scott A. Shalkowski picks up where Craig left off by first arguing that there are insufficient reasons for thinking that there are abstract objects. He parts company with Craig, however, in arguing, secondly, that even if there are abstract objects, there are no theological problems that arise as a result. Necessities are the end point for explanation and if there are necessarily existing abstract objects, it makes sense to suggest that God somehow explains them or that they impose "limits" on God. Hence, God sovereignly exists whether or not abstract objects do.

In the final essay, Graham Oppy approaches the question of God and abstract objects from a slightly different vantage point than the other contributors. Instead of trying to understand how God might be related to abstracta, Graham is interested in whether the reality of abstracta provides differential support, one way or another, to decide between theism and naturalism. His conclusion is that it matters not; plausible accounts of abstracta, whether realist or fictional, favor neither theory. If correct, then theists who think there are straightforward arguments from abstracta to God are mistaken—abstract objects exist necessarily—it is impossible that anything be their creator, or ground, or source. Abstract objects exist, if at all, with or without God, it makes no difference.[25]

Notes

1 Russell endorses platonism in his 1912 work, arguing that "all truths involve universals" and even if qualitative universals are denied, relational universals must be admitted. In fact, he argues that it is the failure of many philosophers to realize that verbs and prepositions (in addition to substantives and adjectives) denote universals that has led to much confusion over the debate. See Russell (1997).

2 In his preface, Russell notes that he will confine himself to those problems of philosophy about which he thinks it "possible to say something positive and constructive, since merely negative criticism seemed out of place" (ibid., 5). Undoubtedly, given his belief in God's noexistence, the problem of God and abstract objects in not a problem in which it is possible to say something positive and constructive (for Russell).

3 Why think AD true? There are at least four sources of motivation to cull support for AD: (1) Perfect Being Theology, (2) Scripture, (3) tradition, and (4) the notion of worship worthiness.

4 When considering the nature of creation, Augustine notes "God was not fixing his gaze upon anything located outside Himself to serve as a model when he made the things he created, for such a view is blasphemous" (*On Eighty-Three Diverse Questions*, question 46, "*De Ideis*," quoted in Wolterstorff 1970, 280). Aquinas nicely states this tension between platonism and the Christian faith as well: "it seems contrary to the faith to hold, as the Platonists did, that the Forms of things exist in themselves" (*Summa Theologiae* 1.84.5).

5 Henceforth, the term "platonism" shall be used to refer to the view that abstract objects necessarily exist (and have objective ontological status). Many platonists understand their position to entail that such objects enjoy independent existence as well. I hope to show that such independence need not be thought to follow from such abstract object realism. Thus, as INCONSISTENT TRIAD makes clear, I draw a distinction between platonism (that is, claim (1)) and a common platonic assumption (that is, claim (3)).

6 According to Plantinga (1974, 70–7) and Plantinga (1980, 7), an entity x's nature just is the conjunction of x's essential properties.

7 For more on the dependency problem, see Richard Brian Davis (2001, 1–6).

8 See e.g. Keith Yandell (1984, 49–55) and Yandell (1993, 343).

9 Other alternatives are that abstract objects are uncreated yet sustained by God in existence or uncreated yet constituently dependent on God.

10 I think the most rigorous argument against the compatibility of platonism and traditional theism is Bergmann and Brower (2006). Other incompatibility arguments can be found in William Lane Craig and Paul Copan (2004, 167–95); Matthew Davidson (1999); Scott Davison (1991);and Brian Leftow (1990). For detailed responses to such incompatibility arguments, see Gould (2010). Bootstrapping worries can be generated when considering abstracta other than properties as well. See e.g. Paul Gould (2011a), where the bootstrapping worry surfaces when divine concepts (understood as abstract objects) are employed.

11 That is, assuming divine thoughts are essentially possessed by God, then properties of divine thoughts are also essentially possessed by God.

12 For a robust defense of the claim that God can create abstract objects, see Gould 2013.

13   See also Leftow (2012, 61–5).

14   Other relevant passages include Jn 1.3, Rom. 11.36, Eph. 3.9, Col. 1.16–17, Rev. 4.11, Ps. 103.19–22, and 1 Cor. 8.6. For an excellent discussion of theory construction in theology, see Shalkowski (1997), where it is argued that the Biblical text is often underdetermined and the theoretician must employ other criteria in constructing a mature theological (or philosophical) theory, including accuracy, scope, simplicity, fruitfulness, and more. Thus, it is open to the platonic theist to argue that her theory, while (say) light on scope and simplicity is heavy on accuracy and fruitfulness and thus is a live contender for an acceptable theory of God and abstracta. In fact, something like this dialectic is typical of the case provided for platonic theism.

15   There is some confusion in the literature about just what the theistic activism of Morris and Menzel is and is not, as the following sampling makes clear. First, a proposed description of theistic activism:

> Theistic Activism (TA) = the view that (1) necessary abstract objects exist; (2) depend on God's creative activity and; (3) are identified with various constituents of the divine mind.

The question is whether or not (3) holds true. Next, a sampling of quotations from the literature regarding theistic activism, in addition to the quotation cited in the body of the text:

> [A] From Menzel: "PRPs [properties, relations, and propositions], as abstract products of God's 'mental life,' exist at any given moment *because* God is thinking them; which is to just say that he creates them" (1987, 368).

> [B] From Copan and Craig: "Morris and Menzel present their view as an updated version of the Augustinian theory of divine ideas and, hence, as a version of what we (below) call conceptualism. Nevertheless, although that is their intention, they continue to speak of the products of God's intellectual activity as abstract entities, which suggests the interpretation that abstract objects are created things external to God and caused by divine intellectual activity" (2004, 174–5n. 10).

> [C] From Bergmann and Brower: "Contemporary philosophers now typically refer to this Augustinian view as 'theistic activism,' since according to it, the existence of properties and propositions is due to the *activity* of the divine intellect: properties are divine concepts resulting from God's acts of conceptualizing and propositions are divine thoughts due to God's acts of thinking or considering" (2006, 363).

> [D] From Matthew Davidson: "Some have contended that (necessarily existing) abstracta depend on God for their existence and natures (their essential properties). Let's call such a view 'theistic activism'" (1999, 277).

The quote from Morris and Menzel cited in the text above, as well as [A] and [C], seem to support (1)–(3). [B] suggests that (3) is not actually the view of Morris and Menzel, and [D] restricts TA to (1)–(2) only and not the conjunction of (1)–(3). What this reveals is that there is some inconsistency in how TA is defined and utilized in the literature. For our purposes, we shall mean by TA the conjunction of (1)–(3) as this seems to most fully represent the views of Morris and Menzel.

16   But it need not be. It seems possible to argue that God is the eternal generating cause of abstract objects in virtue of the will, in which case theistic activism would be

abandoned, but not the notion of God creating abstract objects. Or alternatively, it could be argued that abstract objects emanate from the divine being, in which case they are still the product of God, but not (obviously) in virtue of His intellect or will.

17 As Bergmann and Cover (2006) suggest, it is plausible to hold that God is not free, nor forced, but still responsible for His actions (and hence thankworthy) in virtue of being an agent cause.

18 See Greg Welty (2004) and (2006). The former applies TCR to properties, the latter to propositions and possible worlds.

19 See Gould (2011a) for an account of how this (unlovely) assay of the divine substance would be understood.

20 See Rodriguez-Pereyra (2011) for more on the realism/nominalism and abstract/ concrete distinctions and their relation. As Rodriguez-Pereyra points out, one can be a nominalist in one sense (the denial of abstract objects) and still endorse universals, as the Aristotelian realist does. Unless it is specified as otherwise, in this volume, we shall understand "nominalism" to mean "only concrete objects exist."

21 In Peter van Inwagen (2004). Of course, as a platonist, van Inwagen does not think one can get away with being a nominalist.

22 Bergmann and Brower (2006) opt for a truthmaker theory of divine predication, where divine predications are explained in virtue of a truthmaker (that is, the divine substance), without requiring the positing of an exemplifiable. Leftow (2006) is more sanguine: "I suspect that no theory of attributes [can adequately account for the predicate *being divine*], and the proper conclusion to draw from this is that it is not an attribute at all. Whatever one makes of it, then, it will turn out to be something surprising." In Leftow (2012, 307) the surprise is revealed, and we've seen it before in Aquinas: "God does not have an attribute of deity distinct from Himself, … 'God's essence is His existence'—that is, … what makes it true that God has His essence is identical with what makes it true that He exists."

23 For a more detailed discussion of each of these options, see Craig (2011b).

24 For a helpful discussion of how to balance ontological and ideological economy (with respect to explanatory adequacy) see Loux (2006, 61) and Oliver (1996).

25 An earlier version of this essay can be found in Gould (2011b). Earlier versions of the lead essays by Yandell, Gould/Davis, and Craig can be found in Yandell (2011), Davis (2011), and Craig (2011a).

1

God and Propositions

Keith Yandell

The overall question at hand is how God is related to abstract objects. One answer is that God has no such relation, there being no abstracta to which to relate. This is nominalism and for the sake of the argument, I will simply assume that it is false. One reason for a theist to accept nominalism is that if there are abstract objects of some sort then theism is false.[1] I will argue that this is mistaken. The metaphysical waters are deep and turbulent, and I can only argue that one path through them avoids philosophical and theological refutation. At least three views compete for first place. First, some definitions are needed.

Definitions

By "God" I mean "the omnipotent, omniscient creator of everything that exists and can be created." By "abstract objects" I mean such things (if there are such things) as propositions, states of affairs, universals, properties, numbers, and the like. Each of these things, should there be any of them, cannot not exist, is not in space, is eternal (timeless) or everlasting, and is bereft of causal powers. They are not conscious things, let alone self-aware. God, on the other hand, is self-aware and has causal powers. God is not an abstract object—not even if God cannot not exist.

Three views

At least three views vie for first place. One is *propositionalism*[2]—the view that there are propositions and they have intrinsic necessary and mind-independent existence. Another is that instead of propositions there are ideas in the mind of God that have as their propositional content the necessary truths, and since God has necessary existence and necessarily has these thoughts, they are necessarily true—a view we will call *theistic ideaism*. The third view, *theistic activism*, maintains that God exists and propositions exist, and the former somehow causes the latter.

There is another distinction that is relevant, that between the view that *necessarily, God exists* is true—*necessitarian theism* (NT)—and the view that *God exists* is true and logically contingent—a view we will call *plain theism* (PT). Theistic ideaism, as noted, requires that necessitarian theism be true. Propositionalism is neutral regarding these two types of theism. One could consistently hold that there are both God and propositions, and each has necessary existence, and neither in any fashion depends on the other. This view, for whatever reason, seems to receive little discussion, and without prejudice I will ignore it here. Much of the following discussion regarding propositionalism will treat it on its own terms, and then it will be combined with plain theism—a view we will call (again without prejudice to necessitarian theism) *theistic propositionalism*. So we have these views:

PROPOSITIONALISM (P): there are bearers of truth value (being true or false) that necessarily exist and cannot depend on anything else for existence.

THEISTIC IDEAISM (TI): there are no propositions; what there are instead are the contents of thoughts necessarily had by a necessarily existing God.

THEISTIC ACTIVISM (TA): there are necessarily existing abstract objects that bear truth value and depend for their existence on God.

THEISTIC PROPOSITIONALISM (TP): there are propositions that do not depend on God for their existence nor does God depend for existence on propositions; the proposition *God exists* is true and logically contingent (though it is necessarily impossible that God depends on something distinct from God for existence).

Logical relations

Note, for clarity's sake that, so far as modality goes, there are two kinds of theism, as follows:

NECESSITARIAN THEISM (NT): The proposition *God exists* is necessarily true.

PLAIN THEISM (PT): The proposition *God exists* is contingently (non-necessarily) true.

Since *God exists* cannot have both modalities, at least one is false. In parallel, from the same perspective, there are two kinds of atheism:

NECESSITARIAN ATHEISM (NA): The proposition *God exists* is necessarily false.

PLAIN ATHEISM (PA): The proposition *God exists* is contingently (nonnecessarily) false.

The logical relations among these views is this:

a) If NT is true, then NA (being the denial of a necessary truth) is necessarily false, and PT and PA (since they both get the modality wrong) are also necessarily false.

b) If NA is true, then NT (being the denial of a necessary truth) is necessarily false, and PT and PA (since they both get the modality wrong) are also necessarily false.

c) If PT is true, then NT and NA (since they both get the modality wrong) are necessarily false, and PA (being the denial of a contingent truth) is contingently false.

d) If PA is true, then NT and NA (since they both get the modality wrong) are necessarily false, and PT (being the denial of a contingent truth) is contingently false.

The task

There is a plethora of writings on whether or not God exists, and on whether or not abstract objects exist. Since the issues vary depending on which sort of abstract object is under discussion, I will choose one type—propositions. Propositions are the bearers of truth value and are asserted by the standard use of declarative sentences. They are not sentences, since the same proposition can be asserted by use of more than one sentence in the same language, and by sentences in more than one language. Propositions, according to propositionalism, are altogether mind-independent. The proposition *Unicorns play on the Matterhorn* (eternally or everlastingly) exists, though sadly it is false. It was true long before there were people to believe it that seven is greater than five and it is impossible that anything has logically incompatible properties. I will be concerned with an incomplete conditional: "If God exists, and there are propositions, then they are related such that ... ." The task will be to correctly fill in the blank. Any way in which this is done will be controversial. My purpose is to sketch a position that, like its competitors, requires considerable discussion and defense, which cannot be provided here. The sketch contrasts with an empiricism that explains necessity away or attempts to make something else primitive to it.

An exegetical answer?

Some will want to decide how to fill in our conditional by appeal to Scripture. There seems to be no direct reference whatever to abstract objects in the Christian Scriptures. But there is Col. 1.16–17: "For by him were all things created: things in heaven and on earth, visible and invisible; whether thrones or powers or rulers or authorities, all things were created by him and for him." Are we to take Paul to be including abstract objects? It is quite unlikely that Paul had abstruse metaphysics in mind. It can be replied that neither Paul nor his audience knew about quantum phenomena,

or electricity, but surely a theist is going to think that God created them, so why not abstract objects? This would be a more impressive objection were propositions concrete objects like quantum phenomena or electricity; but they are not. There is the additional fact that abstracta have no causal powers, and so can do nothing. Abstract objects are not in heaven or earth. Paul's point seems to be that God is sovereign over "thrones or powers or rulers or authorities" that might pose a threat; abstract objects have no such possible role.

It may be useful here to consider a different passage. According to Matt. 13.31–2 Jesus claimed that the mustard seed is the smallest of all seeds. Apparently, it is not— the orchid seed is said to be smaller. Was Jesus wrong? That depends on what he was saying. Is he to be understood as teaching a lesson in agriculture, or using information regarding what a local farmer might "sow in his field" to make a point that his auditors would understand (apparently the mustard seed is the smallest seed about which they would know)? I take it that Paul is asserting the ultimate security of believers from destructive powers and Jesus with the significance of even very small faith and its capacity to grow large. The point is: Over-interpretation of either passage seems unnecessary.

Conventional necessity

There are various attempts to show that necessity is not primitive—that it is somehow grounded in something non-necessary. Only a brief review of some attempts is possible. On one account ascriptions of necessity are just the result of, or are just descriptions of, the way our brains work. On another they are just the way our minds work or just descriptions thereof. But as analyses of necessary truths, or accounts of why they are necessarily true, these suggestions are irrelevant. Waiving the fact that often our brains or minds do not work in these ways, the occasions on which they do work in these ways are contingent in two ways. They might not have done so (they often don't) and, more importantly, there might not have been any brains or minds. Necessity vanishes in the "analysis." Evolutionary accounts are equally beside the point. Telling even a true story about how we came to think as we do (sometimes) think will not tell us whether the laws of logic are necessary truths. The claim that the laws of logic *just are* these things tries to explain necessity in contingent terms. The laws of logic, among other things, define the parameters of reasoning that proceeds from true premises to true conclusions. In that regard, we *ought* to think in that way. The supposed brain, mind, or evolutionary account of how we came to think of laws of logic, or in accord with them, is no analysis of the laws.

Another suggestion is that the deep grammar of our language gives rise to there being necessarily true propositions—propositions of a sort that these rules do not allow to be false. But of course the deep structure of the language we use might have been different (we might have come to use a different language) and there might not have been any "us" to use language at all. The early Edmund Husserl offered this view (which he later rejected): P entails Q if and only if most of those who believe that P also believe that Q. On this view, we would have to wait for an unusual sociological survey to discover whether (I) *Every cat is furry and independent* entails (F) *Every cat is furry*. Those who disliked the result could hire a Madison Avenue firm to construct commercials aimed at changing people who accept (I) into rejecters of (F). More fundamentally, the view assumes "Everyone who accepts (I) accepts (F)" is true if and only if "(I) entails (F)" is true, and is false unless there is this logical relationship. But then it assumes a logical relationship—that of mutual entailment (in the old sense)— that has not been analyzed away. Necessity cannot be grounded in, or depend on, non-necessity.

Descartes offered a somewhat more sophisticated view. He located the relevant conventions in heaven, arguing that, since God is omnipotent, God can do anything; God could have made different laws of logic. If (1) Agnes is happy and (2) brooms live in closets then (3) planets are apples, could have been a valid argument—it would be had God so chosen. (If the objection comes to mind that laws of logic are true and rules are neither true nor false, it should be remembered that for every valid rule of inference R, there is the law that R is a valid rule of inference). Descartes offered two arguments. One was an argument from omnipotence, which he defined as the ability to do anything. This assumes that there is such a thing as making a contradiction true. In fact, however, there is no such thing for God to do, or not to be able to do. His other argument was that something is possible only if it is conceivable by us, so since there are lots of things that are true that we cannot conceive, there are lots of "impossible" things that are possible. There are lots of things that are too complicated for us to conceive—that lack "fit-in-the-head-ability": The truth about the whole history of our planet, the current location of every cockroach on earth, and the collective thoughts of all humans, for example. Yet, since they are possible, possibility is not constrained by fit-in-the-head-ability. (There are more sophisticated attempts to ground necessity in empirical matters—for example, by David Lewis and David Armstrong. I think, but cannot argue here, that they too fail.)

Omnipotence

There is no universally accepted characterization of omnipotence—no account of the idea of the form "God is omnipotent if and only if …" that is universally embraced as the truth of the matter. (In case one thinks that this entails that the notion is unintelligible or unusable, note that there is no such analysis of "cause" or "knowledge" either.) But something like this seems right as far as it goes.

God is omnipotent only if for any proposition P, God can make P true unless:

1) P is formally contradictory, or
2) P is informally contradictory, or
3) P can only be made true by the person to which it refers and P does not refer to God, or

4) P's content is such that it would be false if God so acted as to make it true, or
5) P's content is such that God has an essential property incompatible with God making P true.

Here some examples are needed: of (1) *There is a round square*; of (2) *God makes an immaterial squirrel*; of (3) *God writes (as autobiography) the autobiography of William James*; of (4) *There is something other than God that is not created by God*; of (5) *God digests ice cream without becoming embodied.* Considering some such characterization may make us more realistic concerning what divine omnipotence can be.

Creating abstract objects

If propositionalism is true, then God does not create propositions. One argument for the conclusion that God does not create propositions, even if there are such, is this: To create X is to make it the case that X exists rather than X not existing. In the case of propositions, there is no possibility of their not existing. So propositions cannot be created. (Cf. van Inwagen 2009.) An obvious objection is that it is true that, for any contingent being, when one creates something of this sort that makes it the case that it exists rather than there being no such thing, but this does not hold for anything that necessarily exists. The idea is that one necessarily existing being can cause another, and the caused depends for its existence on the causer. I take it that a necessarily existent being is either eternally timeless or everlasting; in either case, there is no time at which it does not exist. So if God creates necessarily existing object N, which would not exist without that divine activity, it cannot be the case that it was possible that God not create N, for then it would be possible that N not exist. Thus since N is both a necessary being and depends on God, the God-N relation must be that of emanation, defined as follows:

> Y emanates from X if and only if Y would not exist were it not for the fact that X engages in an activity, or is in a state, or has a property, such that X's engaging in that activity, being in that state, or having that property, or some combination C thereof, is necessary and sufficient for Y existing, and X engaging in that activity, being in that state, having that property, or C, is essential to X.

Then if X necessarily exists, so does Y. It is true that *if* a necessarily existing being depends for existence on some other, it will depend for existence on another necessarily existing being. This by itself gives no credence to the idea that a necessarily existing thing can depend for existence on something else. It may also be that *not possibly not existing* is a property that prevents its possessor from existing dependently.[3] If it is—and it does not seem to me obvious that it does not—then theistic activism is a nonstarter. Parenthetically, the idea of a being that (1) is not a necessarily existing being, and (2) exists, and (3) cannot be caused to exist, seems coherent. An omnipotent being seems a good candidate for a being of this kind. If so, *being uncausable* is a property even a certain sort of contingent being may have. (It does not follow that more than one such being could have it.) This notion is important for plain theism, since, given it, plain theism can give an account of divine aseity, which includes uncausability.

Necessary truths

Our particular concern is with necessarily true propositions—propositions true in every possible world, true come what may, true in any possible circumstance. These come in two brands. One is formally true—true in virtue of its logical or syntactical form. Any proposition of the form *[P or not-P]*, *[If P and Q, therefore P]*, *[If X is A and B, then X is A]*, or *[(P or Q) and Not-P, therefore Q]* is a formally necessary truth. *Orange is a color*, *No one is taller than herself*, and *No square root is a salamander* are necessarily true in virtue of their meaning, true in virtue of their semantic content. These are sometimes called, respectively, *narrowly logically necessarily true* and *broadly logically necessarily true*. (cf. Plantinga 1974.)

One tradition holds that if one ascribes a property to something that cannot have it—a property possession of which is inconsistent with the thing's nature or essence—the result is not falsehood but nonsense. Thus *The number seven has a silly smile* is neither true nor false, but simply meaningless. Another tradition finds such propositions unusual but false for exactly the reason that leads the other tradition to think them meaningless—they cannot be true, and so are necessarily false. According to the first view, if *God exists and is necessarily (essentially) morally perfect* is true, then *God sins* is meaningless. This would surprise those medieval thinkers who debated it. If (a) *Necessarily, God exists*, (b) *Necessarily, God is essentially morally perfect* and (c) *Necessarily, a morally perfect being will allow no pointless evil* are all true, then, (d) *Necessarily, no pointless evil exists* follows, since it is against God's nature that God allow a pointless evil and such evil can exist only if God allows it. In the perspective of the first tradition, (d)'s denial is meaningless, though the denial of a necessary truth should be a necessary falsehood. The proposition *If God exists, then God is material, and limited in power and knowledge* is false of the Deity of religious monotheism. How can this be the case when *God is material, and limited in power and knowledge*, by virtue of ascribing to God things that cannot be true of God, has no truth value? Reversing the order, among the properties ascribed to God in religious monotheism as essential features are immateriality, omnipotence, and omniscience. On the first tradition, to deny these properties of God is to utter nonsense. But if the claim "X lacks Q" is meaningless, so is "X possesses Q," so the religious monotheist claim concerning God is meaningless. (A similar problem arises for a strict ineffability doctrine, which maintains "God is not ignorant" is true, but "God knows all" is improper.) I take the first tradition to be mistaken, and will follow the second. So it is true that the number two is even, and false that it plays the violin, that not being within its possible repertoire. The range of informally necessary truths (and therefore of informally necessary falsehoods) is very large.

An ontological argument

If what makes necessary truths true is their being the propositional contents of God's thoughts, then God must have necessary existence. The ontological argument endeavors to prove that this is so. The best version goes as follows. It can be stated briefly (see Plantinga 1974, 1978). A possible world is a maximal proposition P, where P is maximal if and only if, for any proposition Q, either P entails Q or P entails not-Q. Alternatively, a possible world is a maximal state of affairs, where A is maximal if and only if, for any state of affairs B, A either includes B or excludes B. (Propositions are either true or false; states of affairs obtain or do not obtain.) For something X to exist "in" a possible world W is for W to contain some proposition that entails that X exists. A being is maximally excellent in world W if and only if it is omnipotent, omniscient, and omnibenevolent in W; a being is maximally great if and only if it is maximally excellent in every possible world. A proposition that is true in every possible world is a necessary truth. Every proposition has its modalities (necessity, contingency, possibility, impossibility) with necessity. Proposition (G) *God has maximal greatness* ascribes to God existence in every possible world. So it is either a necessary truth or a necessary falsehood. Its denial is not formally contradictory so it is necessarily true if it is not informally contradictory. Upon careful examination (G) does not seem to be informally contradictory. If it is not, it is (necessarily) true and so God enjoys necessary existence.

The catch (noted by Plantinga) is this: Consider (G*) *God exists in some possible worlds, but not in all*. This is to say that the proposition *God exists* is contingent (which does not entail that God exists dependently). If it is contingent, it is necessarily contingent, and so not a necessary truth.

We then ask the same question as we did regarding (G): (G*) is not formally contradictory, but is it informally contradictory? It too does not seem to be. If it is not, it is possibly true; then (G) is (necessarily) false. Since every proposition has its modalities with necessity, either (G) or (G*) ascribes the wrong modality to *God exists*, and so is necessarily false, even though neither seems to be.

Remember that (G) (implicitly) ascribes *being necessarily true* to the proposition *God exists*; its truth entails that God exists. By contrast, (G*) ascribes *being logically contingent* to the proposition God exists; its truth does not entail that God exists. Either (G) or (G*) ascribes the wrong modality. (Both do if *God exists* is necessarily false.) As noted, one or the other is (informally) contradictory, and so (informally) necessarily false (or else both are). Setting aside the alternative of it being necessarily false that God exists, still the ontological argument does not show us which of (G) and (G*) is true. So it fails as a proof.

To sum up: If theism is true, either (G) or (G*) is true. If theism is contingent (whether true or false), (G) is necessarily false. Then *God exists* is contingent as (G*) says, and perhaps false. If theism is necessarily true as (G) says, then (G*) is necessarily false. So far as I know, even if we assume that theism is true, we have no good reason to choose (G) over (G*). An appeal to perfect being theology, or to the claim that a necessarily existing being is greater than one who exists but not with necessity, supposes that God's existing necessarily is possible. Thus (G*) is false, and we can dismiss it. But all of this supposes that perfect being theology is correct, and this assumption includes the claim that (G) is consistent (and so true), which is what was supposed to be established. It wasn't. It seems that the best we can do (as Plantinga suggests) is say that the premises of the ontological argument are reasonable to accept and thus it is reasonable to accept the conclusion—that is, (G). The same kind of case can be made for (G*) though this is not the place for doing it. If we call the position that (G) is true necessitarian theism and the view that (G*) is true plain theism, the argument in question does not decide between the former and the latter.

A cluster of ontological arguments

The ontological argument's gist is that if it is possible that *Necessarily, God exists* is true, then *Necessarily, God exists* is true. Plantinga's version of the argument packs the necessary existence into the definition of God by defining God as being maximally great—that is, maximally excellent in all possible worlds. This is not defining God into existence, whatever exactly that might be. The claim is that a certain *proposition* is necessarily true. The standard objection that we can conceive the non-existence of anything that we can conceive as existing is simply a flat denial of the conclusion of the argument. Kant's claim that existence is not a property (linguistically put, "existence" is not a proper predicate) seems false of *necessary existence*. The claim that no existential statement is necessary and that all necessary statements are conditional (and so do not assert the existence of anything) fall prey to the counterexample *Seventeen is prime*. (These remarks concerning standard objections to the ontological argument constitute only the first replying salvo to the claim to which they reply.) The deep problem with the ontological argument is noted above (and was noted by Plantinga when he originally stated the argument).

There are other ontological arguments to note here, each of them also relying on the principle that second order propositions to the effect that some first-order propositions are true in all possible worlds are either necessary truths or necessary falsehoods, so that if they are possibly true, so not necessary falsehoods, they are necessary truths. Among these arguments are ones that begin with (1), or (1*), or (1**):

> (1) If it is possible that *Necessarily, something exists* then it is true that *Necessarily, something exists*.

Note that (1) does not specify what that thing is, or that only one thing can necessarily exist.

> (1*) If it is possible that *Necessarily, something of type T exists* then it is true that *Necessarily, something of type T exists* is true (of some T-type thing or other).

> (1**) If it is possible that *Necessarily, particular item X exists* is true, then it is true that *Necessarily, particular item X exists* is true.

As noted, each of these claims rely on the (correct) rule regarding propositions that are either necessarily true or necessarily false, namely, for any such proposition, if P is possibly necessarily true, P is necessarily true.[4] Consider the following use of (1):

> (A) If it is possible that *Necessarily, there are propositions* is true then *Necessarily, there are propositions* is true.

Then you note that *Necessarily, there are propositions* seems consistent upon reflection, add the premise that it is not inconsistent, and infer *Necessarily, there are propositions.* Formally:

> (A) If it is possible that *Necessarily, there are propositions* is true then *Necessarily, there are propositions* is true.
>
> (B) It is possible that *Necessarily, there are propositions* is true.
>
> (C) *Necessarily, there are propositions* is true.

So now we have an argument for there being propositions that parallels the original ontological argument. Without doubting that the conclusion of the first ontological argument is more important than the conclusion of the (A)–(C) argument, the (A)–(C) argument frankly seems to be at least as plausible as the first. Of course in both cases there is a lot more to be said.

There are less determinate arguments, one goes as follows:

> (D) If it is possible that *Necessarily, something or other exists*[5] is true, then *Necessarily, something or other exists* is true.
>
> (E) It is possible that *Necessarily, something or other exists* is true.
>
> (F) *Necessarily, something or other exists* is true.

and another:

> (G) If it is possible that *Something (some particular thing) necessarily exists*[6] is true, then *Something (some particular thing) necessarily exists* is true.
>
> (H) It is possible that *Something (some particular thing) necessarily exists* is true.
>
> (I) *Something (some particular thing) necessarily exists* is true.

If any of these arguments are sound (they are obviously valid), the claim that there can be no *a priori* proof that something exists is false. Then that objection to the ontological argument would fail, and if the (A)–(C) argument is sound there is a proof that there are propositions.

Theistic activism

Theistic activism views abstracta of some kind or kinds as existing distinct from, but dependent for their existence on, God. It posits an asymmetrical dependence relation between God and abstracta. If there are abstract objects, they exist necessarily. Thus anything on which they depend for existence must exist necessarily. Strictly, I take it, whatever abstracta exist should be held to *emanate* from God. God is held to necessarily exist, as are abstracta. As noted above what this means, I take it, is something like this: Y emanates from X if and only if Y would not exist were it not the case that X engages in an activity, or is in a state, or has a property, such that X's engaging in that activity, being in that state, or having that property, or some combination C thereof, is necessary and sufficient for Y existing, and X engaging in that activity, being in that state, or having that property, or C, is essential to X. Since God cannot but emanate the abstracta and the abstracta cannot not exist save given the emanative activity, the (*per impossible*) nonexistence of either would be sufficient for the (*per impossible*) nonexistence of the other.

God has no choice but to create something (the abstracta) distinct from God. So it is necessary that God exists "in" every possible world, since abstracta do, so in none of them does God exist alone. Libertarian freedom to create does not belong to God, at least regarding God's inevitable impersonal cohorts. At least often, if a particular sort of abstract object exists—numbers, sets, propositions, properties—there are an infinity of them. If one simply means by free creation by God that nothing external to God brings God to create—nothing not part of God's nature moves God to create anything—then that sort of freedom exists even though God by nature cannot not emanate abstracta. Roughly, God has only compatibilist freedom regarding creation of at least abstract objects. But it is a freedom that removes any chance that God not be emanatatively active. (I think this tells us something about how significant compatibilist freedom is, but that is another paper. Further, God's having compatibilist freedom would not even begin to entail that God was forced to do anything by anything external to God.) *Perhaps* on this view God freely (categorically, and not just conditionally) may create concrete items—the view seems not to require taking sides on this matter—but inherently creates (emanates) abstracta. On this view it is not only the case that God cannot fail to emanate anything that it is God's nature to emanate, but also that God cannot destroy anything that it is God's nature to emanate.

If we consider theistic activism regarding propositions, the view is puzzling. God emanates the proposition (L) *Nineteen is less than forty.* In order to do so, God must have in mind that very proposition—God is not an unconscious proposition producer, even with respect to producing propositions. God must have necessary existence in order for theistic activism to be true. So the God of theistic activism must be a necessarily existing being who, in order to emanate (L), must have a thought the content of which is (L)—a necessarily omniscient being will have such a thought. *Then* God creates or emanates proposition (L). But what is the point? If (L) needs grounding, it already has that in virtue of being the propositional content of a thought that a necessarily existing God necessarily has. What role do propositions play in the metaphysical view with which we are presented? They seem explanatorily unnecessary. Some reason should be given for positing both the relevant divine thoughts and the distinct-from-God propositions. The lack of such a reason regarding the emanation of propositions counts against theistic activism. Further, we have noted that possession of the relevant thoughts is a condition of the production of the propositions. There is also the controversial claim that logically necessary things can depend on anything at all, all this raises doubts concerning the viability of theistic activism.

Perhaps the view fares better with some other type of abstract object. Consider theistic activism concerning properties. If a little rough and rapid history of philosophy be allowed, Augustine was influenced in various ways by Plato but emended at least one platonic doctrine. According to that doctrine, properties are abstract objects. For an item X to have a property Q, there must be an abstract object Q* such that X has Q in virtue of instantiating, exemplifying, or participating in Q*. If there is no Q*, no X can have Q—having a concrete property requires instantiating an abstract object property.

Transferred into a theistic context, this entails that God can possess the property of *being omniscient* only if there is the abstract object property omniscience* for God to instantiate. So it is metaphysically impossible that God exist without there being abstract object properties (properties that are abstracta). God cannot create abstract object properties because in order for God to have the powers (if there are such) that God needs to do so, God must already be participating in them. For God (*per impossible*) to destroy them would be an act of deicide, since then for every essential property that God has, God must exemplify an abstract property in order for God to have its concrete version, and without there being the relevant abstract properties this cannot be done—not even by God. So, as the textbooks say, Augustine put the platonic ideas in the mind of God. He was at least an early theistic ideaist. By avoiding theistic activism, he thereby avoided the inelegance of God having to create God from nothing, a neat trick even for a deity. At least within the conceptual context of his time, Augustine offered an escape from this nasty dilemma. But theistic activism does not do so regarding properties. What God supposedly emanates is something that is a necessary condition of God's essence being instantiated. The dependence is not asymmetrical after all.

The question naturally occurs as to whether propositionalism does not face the same dilemma. If there are propositions, will they give rise to the same problem? Perhaps in this manner: For any proposition P, if P is true, then God knows that P; God has omniscience as an essential property. Consider the set S of all necessarily true propositions. God knows the members of S only if there are the members of S. For propositionalism, there are the members of S only if there are uncreated propositions. The issue is not whether necessary truths are true, or whether God has control over this. As we noted, for theistic ideaism, if what there is rather than propositions is the propositional contents of God's thoughts, God has them necessarily; God's having these thoughts is part of God's nature. The issue is whether what propositionalism thinks of as propositions *are* propositional contents of divine thoughts.

There is a pine tree in my backyard. An omniscient God knows that. Had there not been one there, an omniscient God would know that instead. For any contingent truth that an omniscient God knows, God might not have known it, since it might not have been true. If God creates libertarianly free agents, then God knows what they do without determining that they do it. (This is independent of whether or not

open theism is true.) So there are things an omniscient being knows that it might
not have known, and can be things that an omniscient (and omnipotent) creator
knows that it did not cause to be true. If propositionalism is true, then some of the
propositions God knows are true without God having made them true, but the same
holds for propositions true of what agents do freely. True, in the latter case, the truths
in question depend on items created by God, but why, exactly, should this matter?
Further, whether propositionalism is true or not, God knows exactly the same propositions. Whether necessary truths are the propositional contents of divine thoughts,
or are abstract object propositions, an omniscient God knows all of them. God has
no more control over their being true on one view than on the other. For propositionalism the truths are there to be known in virtue of the existence of propositions.
For theistic ideaism, the truths are there to be known as propositional contents of
ideas that a necessarily existing God necessarily has. In fact, on both views God has
ideas with those propositional contents. There is likely to be a temptation to appeal to
parsimony here—to sharpen Ockham's razor and wield it on behalf of theistic ideaism.
I see no reason to suppose that it applies here, but let that pass. The central fact is that
the assumption of theistic ideaism that the conclusion of the ontological argument is
true is either possibly true or not possibly true, and we do not know which. Appeals
to parsimony, in the light of that fact, are moot.

Theistic ideaism and theistic propositionalism

Thus far we have dealt with propositionalism. It is now time to point out that there is
also theistic propositionalism (TP), which not surprisingly is the conjunct of theism
and propositionalism. It may be helpful to see a bit of the conceptual neighbor-
hoods in which TI and TP dwell. No truth over which God has control given TI is a
truth over which God lacks control given TP. For on neither view is it possible that
a necessary truth has been false, nor a necessary falsehood has been true. (Theistic
activism agrees.) Both TP and TI agree that there is nothing that can fail to exist and
actually exists that does not depend for its existence on God, and nothing that could
fail to exist would fail to depend for its existence on God were it to come to exist. Both
views can consistently claim that in no possible world is there anything that is present
but might have been absent that exists independent from God. TI and TP differ in that
the latter thinks that there exists one world (indeed, one part of every possible world)
that God could not create—a world of only abstracta (or the abstracta that exist in
every possible world). It won't do to say that this world multiplies into many, since all
abstracta that can exist, do exist.

   All along I have been arguing that it is quite unclear that TI has any real advantage
over TP. If it is so much as possible that there are propositions, then there are. Theistic
propositionalism need not deny necessitarian theism, nor is it incompatible with plain
theism (setting aside that one of these sorts of theism is necessarily false). It does not
follow from necessitarian theism that abstract objects depend for their existence on

God. It is rather that the view that they depend for their existence on God presupposes necessitarian theism, lest one hold that necessarily existing abstracta depend on
a non-necessitarian God.

Conclusion

Propositionalism, so far as I can see, is perfectly compatible with theism. Theistic
activism seems mistaken for the reasons noted. A central claim of theistic ideaism
remains unproved. One consideration for it—that a necessarily existing God is greater
than one that lacks necessary existence, or the equivalent claim that it comports
better with theism that God exists in all possible worlds—assumes that necessitarian
(Anselmian, perfect being) theism is logically consistent. In spite of strong efforts,
this remains unproved. (It also remains unproved that plain theism is consistent.)
Under these circumstances, it seems to me that to claim that theistic ideaism is true is
altogether premature. To claim that it (or plain theism) is exegetically required is false.
Both propositionalism plus plain theism, and theistic ideaism, which requires necessitarian theism, seem perfectly coherent, though surprisingly one is not. The claim that
every nondivine thing exists dependent on, and can be destroyed by, God assumes
that propositionalism is false without proving this claim. Appeal to omnipotence or
sovereignty settles nothing, since whatever the truth is concerning omnipotence or
sovereignty, it must be consistent, and whether it is (G) or (G*) that has that advantage
remains undecided. Neither view is compatible with conventionalism concerning
necessity. It is compatible with both views that nothing contingent can exist apart from
creation, and that the only possible world "in which" God would not exist (if there is
any) is one "inhabited" only by abstract objects. Plain theism does not entail that God
is, or can be, dependent on anything else.

Appeals to intuitions in contemporary philosophy are largely fancy ways of saying
that one finds a claim clearly true without being able to offer an argument for it. Once
upon a time, it had a stricter use, limited to a comparatively small range of claims,
namely claims that one could "just see" that some proposition—for example, that
modus ponens is a valid rule of inference, or that the principle of noncontradiction—is
true. I do not see that appeal to even the stricter sort of intuitions will do anything to
resolve the question as to whether theistic ideaism or plain theism is true, assuming
that one is.

Notes

1   See William Lane Craig, this volume.
2   Combined with non-necessitarian plain theism.
3   One might, for example, hold that concrete items cannot have necessary existence,
    and that privilege belongs only to abstracta.

4   Relative to (1*) and (1**), their use requires that the antecedent of (1*) or (1**), with the variable appropriately instantiated, be used as a second premise; then make the obvious inference.

5   That is, for any possible world W, if W exists, it is not empty. This would not defeat the cosmological argument since, compatibly with this claim, our world contains particular things that lack necessary existence.

6   That is, there is something X such that, for any possible world W, X exists in W.

Response to Keith Yandell

Paul M. Gould and Richard Brian Davis

According to Keith Yandell, it is a "controversial claim that logically necessary things can depend on anything at all" (32). Now Yandell embraces propositionalism—the view that propositions are necessary beings. Coupled with plain theism, it isn't difficult to see why he thinks propositions can't depend on God. In worlds where God doesn't exist, he can't ground the existence of propositions by thinking them. Still, if propositions are divine thoughts, why think they couldn't depend on a God who *necessarily* thought them? Why not concede that if necessitarian theism *were* true, some propositions would exist necessarily, and so depend on God as thoughts on a thinker? What exactly is the problem?

There are two worries. First, if theistic activism (TA) were true, says Yandell, propositions would be "explanatorily unnecessary" (31). For suppose God decided to create a proposition, say, (L) *Nineteen is less than forty*. He would first have to form the *thought* of (L) before creating it, in which case (L)—the proposition—looks like a superfluous add-on. Here Yandell is right: "Some reason should be given for positing both the relevant divine thoughts and the distinct-from-God propositions" (31). But that's no strike against our view, since (on MTA) propositions aren't distinct from God's thoughts; they *are* God's thoughts. No extra baggage.

A second worry: Yandell thinks it might be "that *not possibly not existing* is a property that prevents its possessor from existing dependently. If it is—and it does not seem to me obvious that it does not—then theistic activism is a nonstarter" (26). This *might* be, he says. But why think that? In a note, he remarks: "One *might* ... hold that concrete items cannot have necessary existence" (34n. 3, my emphasis). Perhaps so; but apart from an argument that we *should* hold this, the conclusion here can only be that TA *might* be a nonstarter. In any event, on MTA, divine thoughts aren't concrete objects; they are multiply-instantiable (abstract) types. So the worry is misplaced.

Yandell does say something, however, that points to a reason for thinking that necessarily existing abstracta cannot depend on God:

> Since God cannot but emanate the abstracta and the abstracta cannot not exist save given the emanative activity, the (*per impossible*) nonexistence of either would be sufficient for the (*per impossible*) nonexistence of the other. (31)

Take any proposition P. According to Yandell, if P did depend on God—and given MTA—we would expect the following to hold:

(1) If God did not exist, then P would not exist; and
(2) If P did not exist, then God would not exist.

But here's the rub. Given MTA, the antecedents of these conditionals are impossible, so ⟵ that (1) and (2) are *counterpossibles* (CPs). And the fact is: On the standard semantics for CPs, they're true alright—but *trivially* so, as are all CPs.[1] Roughly, this is because for any impossible proposition P, P vacuously entails *any* Q at all, since (i) P entails Q just in case ~ ◊ (P & ~ Q), and (ii) the conjunction of an impossible proposition with ⟵ any proposition is impossible. That means not only that (1) and (2) trivially true, but also

(3) If God did not exist, then P would still exist

which suggests that P does *not* depend on God, since it would exist even if God did not. ⌐

Here we note the following. First, as Zagzebski and others have shown, the standard ⌐ semantics gives us the wrong (intuitive and metaphysical) results for a host of CPs, including the ones we're considering.[2] Second, Yandell's own work on nonvacuous entailment actually provides a basis for assigning nontrivial truth to (1) and (2), and nontrivial falsity to (3), which enables us to make sense of how one necessary being might depend on another. For any necessary propositions P and Q, says Yandell, P relevantly or nonvacuously implies Q if and only if Q's truth-conditions constitute all or part of P's truth-conditions.[3] Thus consider

(4) Three is the sum of two even numbers.

Though necessarily false, (4) nevertheless has (not possibly obtaining) truth-conditions—the states of affairs that would have to obtain to make (4) true—for example, *Three's being evenly divisible by two*. We can therefore say that (4) *relevantly* implies

(5) Three is evenly divisible by two

but not

(6) Plantinga is a prime number.

For of these latter two propositions, only (5) expresses the (*per impossible*) truth-conditions for (4). ⌐

Yandell can therefore think of MTA this way. For any proposition P, the nonex- ⌐ istence of P constitutes part of the truth-conditions for God's nonexistence (since God, by hypothesis, thinks P necessarily). This underwrites (1). Further, if P didn't exist, then (given MTA) this could only be because God didn't exist to cause it. So we also have reason to affirm (2). Still further, (3) is surely false, since P's *existence* is scarcely a truth-condition for God's *nonexistence*. ⌐

So MTA does seem to be in order. But now consider Yandell's claim that "plain ⌐ theism does not entail that God is, or can be, dependent on anything else" (34). This is questionable. For how can Yandell deny that God depends on propositions? To say that God does so depend is to say that (2) is true: If propositions didn't exist, neither would God. But surely Yandell *should* say that; on his view, for example, (2) is a counterpossible whose consequent—*God's nonexistence*—is a truth-condition for ⟵ there being no propositions. For of course if God *did* exist, there would be a world in which He existed, and therefore propositions, since that's what platonists like Yandell tell us worlds are: maximal *propositions*.

Greg Welty

Theistic propositionalism (TP)—the view that propositions necessarily exist, God contingently exists, but there is no dependence relation between them—seems unworkable to me. This is because Yandell adds: "the proposition *God exists* is true and logically contingent (though it is necessarily impossible that God depends on something distinct from God for existence)" (22). Given this view, if God were not to exist then the proposition *God exists* would still exist. But if the proposition *God exists* were not to exist, then it would not be true that God exists, and so God wouldn't exist. So if we grant with Yandell the contingent existence of God but the necessary existence of the proposition, then it certainly *seems* as if God's existence would be asymmetrically dependent on the existence of this proposition. Thus TP seems to require that "God depends on something distinct from God for existence" after all. Like *theistic activism* (TA), "it posits an asymmetrical dependence relation between God and abstracta." Except that here it goes in the wrong direction!

In addition, there remains a conflict between TP and *divine sovereignty and aseity* (DSA), even though Yandell repeatedly qualifies his position to remove this apparent conflict: "both (TP) and (TI) [*theistic ideaism*] agree that there is nothing *that can fail to exist* and actually exists that does not depend for its existence on God" (33, my emphasis). Likewise, he elsewhere says DSA is only of relevance to entities "that could fail to exist," that "might have been absent," etc. But this merely says that all *contingent* existence depends on God. Why is it not relevant whether any *necessary* existents, existing distinct from God, depends on God as well? Why is necessary existence automatically exempt from the demands of DSA? It's not as if the threat goes away once we confess that abstract objects (AOs) necessarily exist. Indeed, the threat is *generated* by confessing their necessary existence, for it is in virtue of their *necessary* existence that we have a realm distinct from God over which He has no control and on which He depends. Repeatedly stating these qualifiers seems to highlight the problem, not solve it.

On Yandell's view the necessary truths known by God "are there to be known in virtue of *the existence of propositions*," whereas on TI "the truths are there to be known as *propositional contents of ideas* that a necessarily existing God necessarily has" (33, my emphasis). Isn't this difference between mind-independent existence, and ideational contents, a crucial difference? The ideas posited by TI are not a necessarily existing realm existing distinct from God and over which He has no control. They constitutively depend on God, and therefore pose no challenge to His sovereignty or aseity. But the propositions posited by TP exist distinct from God, do not depend upon God, and God wouldn't be omniscient if this infinite number of entities distinct from God didn't exist. Thus it seems that God *depends* on the existence of this realm to be omniscient. That compromises aseity. And God has no control over this realm which is distinct from Him. That compromises His sovereignty.

To this Yandell would say that AOs cannot "pose a threat" to God because of "the additional fact that abstracta have no causal powers." But is this "additional fact" required by any of the traditional arguments for abstracta? (For one challenge to this "additional fact," see Plantinga (1993, 121).) And why would having causal powers be the *only* threat to DSA? Suppose there is a brute fact, contingently true proposition that God cannot create mountains at least as tall as Mt. Everest. No causal powers here on the part of such a proposition, but the threat to DSA remains.

At times Yandell seems to equate truth value with existence, for the purposes of assessing threats to DSA. In adjudicating between TI and TP he says, "No truth over which God has control given (TI) is a truth over which God lacks control given (TP)" (33). Likewise, "on neither view is it possible that a necessary truth has been false, nor a necessary falsehood has been true" (33). And with respect to necessary truths, "God has no more control over their being true on one view than on the other" (33). But these parity arguments are misleading, true but irrelevant, focusing as they do on truth value rather than truthbearers. Necessary truths grounded in God's nature pose no problem for divine aseity or sovereignty. But necessary truths that require *necessarily existing truthbearers* do pose such a problem. If propositions are in fact necessarily existing entities existing distinct from God, then there is an infinite *ontological realm* distinct from God over which God has no control, upon which He depends for omniscience. This seems to compromise DSA in a way that mere acceptance of necessary truth does not. There is a distinction between truth value and truthbearers, the threat to sovereignty comes from the latter, and on TP (unlike TI) there is an ontological realm distinct from God over which God has no control.

Finally, the ontological argument material, while very interesting, seems misplaced. Yandell stresses our inability to *prove* that God's existence is necessary by way of a modal ontological argument. He seems to think such proof is prerequisite to affirming the kind of divine necessity implicit in TI. I think this is a mistake. It might be that the challenge of coherently relating God to AOs is a *reason* to affirm divine necessity, whatever the fate of the traditional ontological arguments. In my chapter the argument is from realism to conceptualism to theism. Several realist arguments for AOs seem successful, six conditions on any successful theory of AOs emerge from these realist arguments, and these conditions are best satisfied by a theistic conceptualism that identifies AOs with divine ideas. No ontological arguments needed. If AOs *are* best understood as the thoughts of a necessarily existing God (where "best" is defined as satisfying these six conditions), then my version of TI gives us an *argument* for God's necessary existence, rather than presupposing it.

William Lane Craig

In the second line of his essay, Keith Yandell says of the position which I defend in this symposium, "for the sake of the argument, I will simply assume that it is false" (21). Oh, well, so much for my writing a response—!

Seriously, Yandell's procedure makes his paper massively question-begging with respect to nominalism (or anti-realism). Contemporary anti-realism is a rich cornucopia of different views defended by prominent exponents (Figure 1). No responsible discussion of God and abstract objects can just assume the falsity of anti-realism.

Fortunately, Yandell does interact with the theological warrant for nonplatonist views and does, in fact, give us an anti-nominalist argument to consider. Before I respond to these, however, I want to say a brief word about terminology. Readers who are new to this subject will be confused if there is not a uniformity of labels for various positions. In the interests of clarification, let me say that what Yandell calls propositionalism is just platonism, theistic ideaism is conceptualism, and theistic activism is often called absolute creationism. What Yandell calls theistic propositionalism is just the combination of theism and platonism, a view I take to be theologically unacceptable.

How does Yandell respond to classical theists, who maintain that platonism is theologically unacceptable? He says that in Col. 1.16–17 it is unlikely that Paul had abstruse metaphysics in mind. I think we should agree that Paul did not have abstract objects in mind. But in all probability he did mean to make a sweeping metaphysical generalization that everything apart from God has been created by God. Agreed, abstract objects are not in heaven or on earth. But as a good Jew Paul probably did not think that there *is* anything other than what exists in heaven or on earth! For a first-century Jew what exists either in heaven or on earth just is the totality of reality. The causal impotence of *abstracta* is irrelevant; unless Yandell is espousing a lightweight platonism, the unfathomable plentitude of platonic objects exists just as robustly and objectively as concrete objects, so that it is false that "from him and through him and to him are all things" (Rom. 11.36).

It seems to me that Yandell's theistic platonism is therefore ruled out theologically. This is the case even if God is conceived to be metaphysically necessary (so-called necessitarian theism). For this view denies *creatio ex nihilo* with respect to *abstracta*. Yandell seeks to salvage the doctrine of creation by introducing into his definition of God as "the omnipotent, omniscient creator of everything that exists *and can be created*" (21) the italicized weasel words, which are an addition to the biblical doctrine of creation

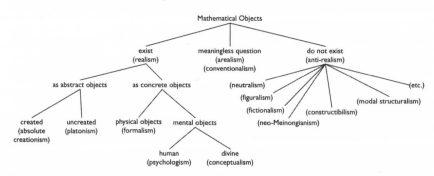

Figure 1: Some options concerning the existence of mathematical objects.

and not to be found in any creed of the church. But it is Yandell's so-called plain theism which is especially noxious theologically, since it holds that God is a contingent being who just happens to exist, so that there are possible worlds in which God does not exist and yet the incomprehensible infinitude of platonic beings does exist.

Therefore, a rationally compelling argument would be required if one were justifiably to embrace theistic platonism. But by his own lights Yandell has no such argument. Look at his argument for platonism (30):

(A) If it is possible that *Necessarily, there are propositions* is true, then *Necessarily, there are propositions* is true.

(B) It is possible that *Necessarily, there are propositions* is true.

(C) *Necessarily, there are propositions* is true.

Yandell concedes that this argument is just as uncertain as is, in his view, the ontological argument. Therefore, it cannot justify platonism in the face of theological objections.

Now I do not share Yandell's skepticism concerning the key premise of the ontological argument

(D) Possibly, a maximally great being exists.

As I have argued elsewhere, the idea of maximal greatness is intuitively coherent, and God's necessary existence is also an implication of other sound theistic arguments such as the cosmological argument and the moral argument. By contrast, if we understand propositions to be uncreated abstract objects, then the theist has solid theological grounds for denying (B). For nothing exists independently of God; it follows that propositions do not exist.

Now admittedly, this creates a problem for the anti-platonist. For if there are no propositions, then Yandell is mistaken in his assumption that "propositions are the bearers of truth value and are asserted by the standard use of declarative sentences" (23). So what are the truthbearers? The anti-platonist can happily admit the existence of sentence tokens as truthbearers, for these are clearly created, concrete objects. But what about a statement like "7>5"? Wasn't that true during the Jurassic Period? But how could it be true if there were no sentence tokens at that time? Indeed, isn't it true in every possible world, even worlds in which God alone exists?

It seems to me that what the anti-platonist should say is that during the Jurassic Period or in worlds in which God alone exists, it is not, strictly speaking, true that 7>5. Rather what we should affirm is simply that during the Jurassic Period, 7>5, and that in all possible worlds, 7>5. This is in line with a deflationary theory of truth according to which the truth-predicate "is true" is simply a device of semantic ascent which enables us to talk about a statement rather than to assert the statement itself. For more on this see Shalkowski's lead essay and my response to Gould/Davis.

Interestingly, Yandell's own anti-nominalist argument illustrates semantic ascent. His premises could have been stated just as effectively by descending semantically and arguing

(A') If it is possible that, necessarily, there are propositions, then, necessarily, there are propositions.

(B') It is possible that, necessarily, there are propositions.

(C') Necessarily, there are propositions.

The semantic ascent featured in his original formulation is a fifth wheel which accomplishes nothing.

As I explain in my response to Gould/Davis, God has no need of a device of semantic ascent and, hence, no need of the truth-predicate—or propositions.

Scott A. Shalkowski

In mapping out some of the relevant intellectual terrain quite usefully, Keith Yandell surveys some proposed reductions of modality. He complains that a satisfactory account of a logical relationship cannot be given in terms of acceptance of the relata (25). He is right to observe that the account is extensionally inadequate. There are (infinitely) many cases where (I) entails (F), but not all who accept (I) accept (F). It is not quite right, though, to say that the account assumes a logical relationship. Merely using "if and only if" is insufficient to sustain this charge. The biconditional states the factually incorrect material equivalence, involving no logical relationship between the left-hand side and the right-hand side. The intended claim, of course, is probably stronger. If the intended relationship is necessary equivalence, then it is false for the same reason. If the biconditional connective is supposed to express mutual entailment rather than necessary equivalence, then Yandell's point is well taken, but then the reductive or analytic claim suffers from being straightforwardly false as well as exhibiting some illicit presupposition. Neither "Everyone who accepts (I) accepts (F)" nor "(I) entails (F)" entails the other. A final option is to treat the biconditional as conveying somewhat confusedly what entailment *is*, to tell us its nature. Kit Fine has defended the view that essence is not even modal, being more fine-grained than necessary coextension (Fine 1994). The claim is still just false because extensionally inadequate. There are, then, options open to one attempting a reductive account of necessity that do not assume logical relations inadvertently.

I agree with what is, in the context of this volume, Yandell's major claim: Propositionalism is compatible with theism. Biblical claims require over stretching to read them as covering the metaphysician's concern about the (in)dependence of abstract objects. Wider theological reflection requiring more than the dependence of contingent existents on God seem to me to falter without the hermeneutic foundations.

While I have no particularly soft spot for theistic activism, I think Yandell's discussion of it merits some attention. It rests on four assumptions: (1) that "… God is not an unconscious proposition producer … ." (31), (2) any additional existence claims require extra justification, (3) the justification for ontological claims regarding propositions is tied to their serving some function, and (4) divine thoughts would already serve any such function. Though some seem to value sparse ontologies over luxuriant, (2) is the better way to articulate a philosophically respectable point. Ontologically speaking, there is no more or less value in (just) more or fewer objects and claims that there are more or fewer objects are, in themselves, of no more or less value, save insofar as they are true and others false, or one is more justified for us to believe than others. To the degree that there is no basis for believing in divinely created propositions, then activism fails.

The activist is entitled to query the work done by (1). If the denial of (1) entails that God does something of which God is unaware, then omniscience is imperilled, one might think. The activist could wonder whether the tricks invoked in the discussion of omnipotence might be relevant here. The nub of each qualification on omnipotence is that it is not possible for even God to do such things (even in some cases, surprisingly, when it is possible for someone else to do them). If it turns out that entertaining a proposition is impossible in the absence of the proposition, then it is not possible to have the thought without the proposition. Of course, were divine creative acts temporal acts, then God could be in the process of creating a proposition without (yet) being aware of what was being created, since until the act is complete (let us stipulate) there is no proposition of which to be aware. Unconscious production of

(L) *Nineteen is less than forty*

is no problem, since prior to the creation of (L), nineteen is neither less than, equal to, or more than forty, one might think. The main problem is avoided so long as God creates many other, related propositions along with (L), such as

(Cr) *God created (L).*

Otherwise, God would know that nineteen is less than forty but not that God had made it so and created the relevant truthbearer.

Activists are entitled to complain that (1) requires a temporal framework for a problem to arise. If there is no process of creation, then there is no time at which God is doing something but—because the relevant proposition is not yet complete—God is unaware of doing it. The activist thesis is that having the thoughts and creating the propositions are not separate divine actions. Thus, activists may either deny (1) or affirm it but deny that it entails the requisite priority of the mental content of the intention over the existence of the ontological unit that is separate from God. The atemporal nature of the case undermines the usual way of thinking of the requirements of creation.

Of course, if all divine creative acts are intentional acts, then there must be the relevant divine thoughts to provide the "propositional content" for those acts. Theistic activism, however, does not require that all divine creation is intentional. In Yandell's terms, God might emanate propositions without intending to do so. The dependence of all on God is preserved. What is lost by "unconscious emanation" that should be retained or what is assumed that is dubious? Unconscious emanation does not entail that God is ignorant, since the proposition is absent, there is nothing to know.

It does not entail that God is not the ultimate ground of all being, since without divine emanation there would be no propositions. Perhaps there is some theological reflection on the divine nature that shows unconscious emanation to be nonsense. A slight expansion is warranted.

Graham Oppy

Yandell distinguishes three views about propositions that "vie for first place" *given* that God exists: (1) There are no propositions but only (propositional) contents of God's thoughts; (2) There are propositions that depend for their existence on God; (3) There are propositions that do not depend upon God for their existence and upon which God does not depend for existence. Yandell notes, further, that at least some of these views can be further divided according to the modal status that they attribute to God's existence (necessary or contingent); he assumes, without further argument, that no similar consideration applies to the modal status of propositions which, if they exist at all, exist of necessity.

Yandell's considered opinion seems to be that the two best views, given that God exists, are (A) that God exists of necessity, and there are no propositions but only contents of God's thoughts; and (B) that God exists contingently, and there are propositions that do not depend upon God for their existence and upon which God does not depend for existence. I think that, if I thought that God exists, I would prefer (C) God exists of necessity, and there are propositions that do not depend upon God for their existence and upon which God does not depend for existence. (Yandell says of this view only that "for whatever reason, [it] seems to receive little discussion, and without prejudice I will ignore it" (22))

I agree with Yandell that there are good reasons to reject (2). Like Yandell, I am unmoved by considerations about Col. 1.16–17. (I see no reason to suppose that, if God exists, God is as Christians suppose, rather than as Jew, or Muslims, or Deists, or others suppose. Setting these considerations aside, I also find Yandell's exegetical proposal congenial.) Like Yandell, I am suspicious of the idea that a necessarily existing being might *depend* for its existence on another necessarily existing being, though perhaps my suspicion goes somewhat further: It seems to me to be *incoherent* to suppose that something that is necessary depends upon something else. Perhaps also following Yandell, I think that there is further incoherence in the idea that God *creates* abstracta whose role is to characterize objects: Propositions, properties, and the like. Creation is a causal process. In the causal order, God would be prior to the abstracta created. But, if so, abstracta cannot be required to characterize God as God was prior to their creation. So why think that abstracta are required to characterize anything else?

Unlike Yandell, I think that there are also good reasons to reject (1). In order to make room for (1), Yandell insists on a distinction between "propositions" and "propositional contents." I do not see what this distinction could be. If there are propositions, then propositions just are the contents of attitudes and expressions of attitudes: beliefs, assertions, desires, statements, wonderings, questions, and so forth. If God exists, and God has attitudes, then, if there are contents of those attitudes, there are propositions—for, on the assumptions in play, the contents of God's attitudes just would be propositions. In particular, if God has thoughts, then, on the assumptions in play, the contents of God's thoughts just are propositions. Here, it is important to remember why we might have been moved to accept that there are propositions in the first place. If we suppose that *our* attitudes—*our* beliefs, assertions, desires, statements, wondering, questions, thoughts, and so forth—require propositions as their contents, then we can hardly suppose that the same is not true for God's attitudes. If, somehow, God could have attitudes that do not require propositions as their contents, then surely the same is true for us, and we have no motivation at all for supposing that there are such things as propositions. (Those who believe in God may also be moved by considerations about the differences between human beings and God. Is it really so, if God exists, that God has attitudes—e.g. thoughts—with the same contents as attitudes that people have? If I have a thought with a particular content, must God have also had a thought with that very same content? If not, how can it be so that the contents of God's thoughts provide all of the propositions that are required to be the contents of our thoughts? Suppose I have a very uncharitable thought about one of the US presidential candidates: Must God also have had that thought, in order to provide the proposition that is the content of my thought?)

There are some minor points on which I disagree with Yandell. For instance: (A) He says that whether propositionalism is true or not, God knows exactly the same propositions. But, in the one case, God knows that propositionalism is true; in the other case, He knows that propositionalism is false! For another instance: (B) Yandell says that, if certain arguments are *sound*, then the claim that there can be no *a priori* proof that something exists is false. This seems wrong; at the very least, we surely require more of a *proof* than mere soundness. Is the sound argument "Something exists therefore something exists" an *a priori* proof of its conclusion? Etc.

Notes

1 See Lewis (1973, 79–83) and Stalnaker (1968) for the standard treatment of counterpossibles.
2 See Zagzebski (1990), Leftow (1990), and Davis (2001, 2006) for examples, along with initial attempts at constructing a theistic semantics for counterpossibles.
3 See Keith E. Yandell (1994).

Response to Critics

Keith Yandell

Paul M. Gould and Richard Brian Davis

My doubt that necessary existents can be created arises from the fact that this would make them dependent and my doubt that they can be, not from TP. I did not offer the redundancy criticism to MTA. I did not claim to prove that necessarily existing things cannot be created, and in developing their MTA Gould/Davis did not show that they can. They offer no reason why my worry is misplaced. Since TA and MTA suppose that they can, both should either grant that this is an unproved assumption or argue for that assumption. For MTA, God's emanating the divine ideas whose propositional contents are the necessary truths is an essential feature of God. Whatever the right analysis of counterpossibles is, it must be compatible with the fact that nothing both exists and lacks an essential property.

Gould/Davis do not mention (4) *If P did not exist, God would exist* which is as much justified by their reasoning as is their (3). (4) would suggest that God does not depend on propositions, contra MTA (given what MTA thinks of as propositions). So they reject the standard treatment of counterpossibles. They do not talk about the fact that if *God exists* or *Propositions exist* is a necessary truth, it is broadly logically necessary. Does the fact that we are dealing with broad logical necessity rather than narrow make a difference here?

They take up a suggestion I once made that we could think of nonvacuous entailment among modal propositions as follows: Modal proposition P nonvacuously entails modal proposition Q if and only if some or all of the truth-conditions of Q are such that if they did not hold, P would be false. So the idea is to show that, given that suggestion, something favorable to MTA follows. Consider the propositions:

(1) *If God did not exist, propositions would not exist.*

(1) follows from MTA, and it is a counterpossible on MTA *but not on PT*. (A counterpossible is a conditional with a necessarily false antecedent.)

(2) *If propositions did not exist, God would not exist.*

For MTA, (2) = (2*) *If God did not think the thoughts whose propositional content is necessarily true, then God would not exist.* For MTA, (2*) is a counterpossible. The same is true for PT on the assumption that omniscience is an essential property of God.

(3) *If God did not exist, propositions would still exist.*
(4) *If propositions did not exist, God would still exist.*

For MTA, these amount to:

(3*) *If God did not exist, God would still have thoughts whose propositional content is necessarily true.*

(4*) *If God did not have thoughts whose propositional content is necessarily true, then God would still exist.*

Gould/Davis then assert that "P's *existence* is scarcely a truth-condition for God's *nonexistence*" (37). It is true that God's having thoughts whose propositional contents is necessarily true is a truth-condition of God's existence. What (3) says amounts to "God's nonexistence would not get in the way of God's having an essential property" and (4) amounts to "God's not having an essential property would not get in the way of God's existing." But consider (3) and (4), read MTAly. The consequent of (3) entails that God would exist, and of course necessarily, and the consequent of (4) also entails that God would exist, again of course necessarily. So the form of (3) is {False then True} and the form of (4) is {False then True} and by standard logic concerning conditionals, both (3) and (4) are true. This follows if we just read (1)–(4) in accord with MTA. At the least, MTA owes us an answer as to why this argument is not correct.

Any maximal proposition will entail the proposition *God exists* or its denial, but will contain both propositions. How to work out the details of this on a possible worlds semantic goes well beyond anything possible here, beyond saying that for TP plus possible worlds theory, every proposition graces every possible world.

Greg Welty

Welty offers an argument that on TP God's existence depends on the proposition (G) *God exists* since God exists only if (G) is true. On any sensible view, (G) is true only if God exists. It is the truth value of (G) that is at stake. God's existence determines (G)'s truth value, not conversely. All of this establishes no dependence of God on propositions. I do not know what "control" *could* be had over necessarily true (or false) propositions. On TP, God's control over contingent propositions concerns determining what their truth value is. If the role that propositions are said to play is played by ideas necessarily had by a necessarily existing God, God has no control over the existence or truth value of those ideas. Having those ideas is part of God's nature and God does not create His nature.

Two central issues are: (a) is (G1) *God exists in all possible world* or (G2) *God exists in many possible worlds* true? (b) is it possible to create a necessary being? Referring to my original essay: Welty needs (G1) but I see nothing in what he says that establishes (G1). Nor is it clear that necessary beings can be created. (Oppy and van Inwagen think not.) If propositions cannot be created and they exist necessarily, then it impossible that they depend on God. What is impossible (e.g. making contradictions true) neither falls within, nor challenges, divine sovereignty. As to confusing truth and existence, for TP, talking about truths is talking about existing truthbearers. Perhaps Welty is confusing truthbearers with truthmakers. The difference between mind-dependence and mind-independence is important but not in relation to sovereignty if the answers to (a) and (b) are as TP asserts. As to the best explanation argument, it assumes that God has necessary existence and that it is possible that necessarily existing things can be dependent without arguing for either. It seems to be easy to forget or ignore that Plantinga (1974), who constructed the best version of the argument for (G1), denies that it succeeds as a proof.

William Lane Craig

As to being "massively question-begging," there is a massive difference between "A is true, so what follows?" (which was not the form of my discussion) and "If A and B, what follows?" (which was that form). Craig mysteriously ignores this. Omnipotence does not include God being able to make contradictions true (there being no such thing not to be able to do). There is disagreement among philosophers over whether it is possible that a necessary existent be caused, and thus dependent. (Oppy doubts it, so do I, and see my reply to Shalkowski.) If not, then the power to create them does not fall within omnipotence. If there are abstracta and they cannot be created, then their existence would not conflict with any noncontradictory doctrine of omnipotence or sovereignty. Abstract ideas are ideas that have been abstracted from experience, not entities that are abstract. Being a mental state rules out being metaphysically abstract, so God's thoughts cannot *be* abstract objects.

The idea that sentences are the bearers of truth values has deep problems. It was true that there were dinosaurs before there were language speakers. This does not merely mean that had someone said "There are dinosaurs" when there were, what they said would have been true. That itself requires that there were in fact dinosaurs then. On Craig's suggestion, it was true that dinosaurs existed only after the dinosaurs were distinct. Incidentally, this runs smack against the deflationist view that "There are dinosaurs" is true if and only if there are dinosaurs—not if and only if there is someone to say there are.

Note that one cannot deflate a modal proposition. *Necessarily, nine is greater than seven* if and only if *Nine is greater than seven, **and things cannot be otherwise***. Without what follows "and" we leave out an essential element. The "necessary" is not redundant, and it is short for "necessarily true." The (A)–(C) argument in my original essay involved no semantic ascent, and Craig kindly points out that it needs none. Essentially, the reason that Plantinga did not think his ontological argument was a proof was that there was no proof that (G1) or (G2) (see my lead essay) is a necessary falsehood, and one must be. Craig says that the idea of a maximally perfect being is intuitively consistent, but so is (G2) and thus exactly what should be included in the notion of a maximally perfect being may or may not include necessary existence. This is different from necessary independence (Yandell 1999, 200).

Scott A. Shalkowski

Shalkowski is right that "if and only if" can be read in ways other that "entails." Since my concern was with necessity, I discussed only that one, and he has no quarrel with my treatment of it. He writes:

> I agree with what is, in the context of this volume, Yandell's major claim: propositionalism is compatible with theism. Biblical claims require over stretching to read them as covering the metaphysician's concern about the (in)dependence of abstract objects. (42)

He adds:

> [T]he theological problems do not arise because even if abstract objects do exist as platonists think they do, they pose no problem for God's sovereignty or aseity.

This puts him in good company. Wolterstorff in *On Universals* held (roughly) that properties exist but cannot be created, and van Inwagen recently wrote "God and Other Uncreated Things" in which he maintains that abstracta cannot enter into causal relations and so cannot be created. Neither rejects the Nicene Creed. van Inwagen writes:

> [T]he Nicene Creed says that God has created all the *visibilia* and all the *invisibilia*. But must a Christian take this creedal statement to mean that God has created … everything *period*? Or is it permissible for the Christian to regard the range of the quantifier 'everything' … as restricted … which is certainly a feature of many "everyday" sentences in which the quantifier occurs, sentences like "I've tried everything, and I still can't persuade Winifred to apologize to Harold"? (2009, 3)

This is no group of heretics, though they differ exegetically, theologically, and philosophically from Craig.

Shalkowski's discussion of theistic activism is clear and helpful.

Graham Oppy

Oppy cannot see what the difference between propositions and propositional contents might be. On one view, I can see why. On that view, if one has the thought *twice two is four*, the content of that thought is an abstract object that exists mind-independently and thus whether anyone has that thought. In other terms, so to think is to be aware of a proposition that exists necessarily—the thinker has the good fortune to be directly aware of an abstract object. On that view, *twice two is four* plays two roles—existing mind-independently and providing content to a mental state. Everett J. Nelson, who taught my metaphysics course, held this view. One might instead hold that in thinking *twice two is four* one has a thought with representational content properly expressed in English by "Twice two is four," the thought being mind-dependent but corresponding to the mind-independent proposition *twice two is four* which is either everlasting or eternal. I am not defending these views or supposing that Oppy is unaware of them.

But there is a propositional content/proposition contrast. Further, Oppy says that, were he a theist, he would believe that God necessarily exists, there are propositions, and each exists independent of the other. Does that view not require necessarily existing propositions—particularly since he says that this is the view of which I said that so far as I know is not widely held, so without prejudice I will not discuss? That view is that God and propositions exist necessarily and independently. So far as I can see, unwed to the first view mentioned above, the view Oppy would take were he a theist, requires the distinction he says he cannot understand. But perhaps I am missing something here. On Oppy's two "small points," he is of course right. I should have inserted something like "save for propositionalism itself" in the first case and something like "since the arguments are plainly valid" in the second.

2

Modified Theistic Activism

Paul M. Gould and Richard Brian Davis

It is not easy to give an illuminating definition of an abstract object. According to Morris and Menzel, an abstract object is (at the very least) an object "so firmly rooted in reality that [it] could not possibly have failed to exist" (1986, 161).[1] This characterization is not sufficient of course, since if classical theism is true, God is a necessary being; it is not possible for Him not to exist. And no one thinks God is an abstract object. Philosophers working in this area have therefore tended to proceed by giving examples. Abstract objects are said to be impersonal entities: such things as properties, relations, propositions, numbers, sets, and the like. Plantinga expresses the view of many here: An abstract object, he says, is "an object that (like God) is immaterial, but (unlike God) is essentially incapable of life, activity, or causal relationships" (1985, 88).[2]

Of course if you are wondering what nontrivial relationship holds between God and abstracta, this is not the most helpful way to put things. For it implies right up front that God cannot be causally related to abstracta, in which case it is difficult to see how there could be anything but a trivial two-way relation of logical dependence between them. This is just to say that in every world in which God exists (that is, in every world), abstract objects also exist. But there is no deeper (asymmetrical) sense in which abstract objects depend for their existence on God. There are powerful reasons for thinking this sort of "platonistic theism" is incompatible with classical theism, though we will not take the time to survey them here.[3]

Conceptualism is the attempt to identify abstracta with divine ideas or concepts, which by the very nature of the case would depend on God as thoughts on a thinker—that is, causally and asymmetrically. In this respect, so-called theistic activism is simply a strong form of conceptualism: One holding that "*all* properties and relations are God's concepts ... the *contents* of a divine intellective activity" (Morris and Menzel 1986, 166, emphasis added). However, a proper theistic activist also maintains that

> *All* necessarily existent propositions ... can be thought of as "built up" out of properties. Thus, in the way in which we characterize properties as God's concepts, we can characterize propositions as God's thoughts... . And taking numbers to be a variety of property, we thus have *all* necessarily existent abstract

reality, from necessary mathematical objects to haecceities, to nonmathematical universals, to propositions, deriving existence from God. (ibid.)

So the suggestion is that divine concepts are ontologically basic; everything else in the platonic horde is a derivative entity: a complex construction on God's mental concepts.

In what follows, we shall argue two things. First, it is plausible to think that conceptualism holds with respect to propositions; in any event, it does a much better job than its closest competitors (platonism and nominalism) in accounting for the truthbearing nature of propositions. Secondly, it is wholly implausible (so we say) to take the added step and equate properties and relations with divine concepts. Thus, a modified theistic activism (MTA) emerges as the most natural and defensible way for a theist to think about God's relation to abstract objects.

Recipe for a proposition

Let us begin with propositions. What *are* they? Here we can do no better than to begin with Lord Russell's insight: "The fundamental characteristic which distinguishes propositions (whatever they may be) from objects of acquaintance is their truth or falsehood" (1984, 108). Propositions are truthbearers. We know this (or can at least stipulate it) pretheoretically. So consider the proposition

(1) Quine is wise.

The question arises: How is it that (1) manages to be true? Naturally, the truth-conditions for this proposition must obtain: Quine himself must exist and have the property of being wise. But surely there are conditions to be met on the side of the proposition as well—truthbearer conditions, as we might call them. Surely (1), to have a truth value at all, whether true or false, has to be a claim or an assertion of some kind. It must represent reality as being a certain way. Thus Alvin Plantinga:

> Propositions are *claims*, or *assertions*; they *attribute* or *predicate* properties to or of objects; they *represent* reality or some part of it as having a certain character. A proposition is the sort of thing *according to which* things are or stand a certain way. (1987, 190)

Similarly G. E. Moore:

> propositions, in the sense in which I have been using the term, are obviously a sort of thing which can properly be said to be true or false.... . Every proposition is, as we constantly say, a proposition *about* something or other. Some propositions may be about several different things; but all of them are about at least one thing. (1953, 62, 68, emphasis added)

In short, propositions (again, whatever they are) are intentional objects; they are *of* or *about* things. And this is an essential property of propositions; for if they lacked this property, they could not possibly be claims or assertions of any kind, they could not

represent anything, in which case they could not be true (/false). Regardless of how
things stood in the world, propositions just would not have anything to say about
those states of affairs. How then could we say of them that they were true (/false)? For
surely a proposition is true only if it represents the world as it is. And just as surely the
way things stand in reality is depicted as being thus and so only if something is being
claimed about the way things so stand. We do not say that Ayer's memoir *Part of My Life*
accurately represents his life—or rather, part of his life—if he is not mentioned, nothing
is claimed about his person, and no comment at all is made about his comings or goings.

A puzzle about parts

Well then, what does it take to be a truth-claiming proposition? According to one
venerable tradition—represented by Bertrand Russell (1903, §47–8), David Kaplan
(1989), and others—a proposition is a complex whole; it has internal constituents
(parts), and those constituents have a specific arrangement. This thesis can be
developed along platonist or nominalist lines.

Consider, first, a broadly platonist approach to the situation. Here, we suppose,
things could go in a couple of directions. Following Russell, we might see (1) as an
admixture of concrete particulars and abstract objects.[4] On the concrete side of things,
(1) would contain *Quine himself* as a constituent. But its other ingredients would
include the (abstract) property of wisdom, along with the (abstract) exemplification
relation Quine stands in to that property. This is a familiar story. The question, though,
is whether it even slyly suggests that (1) might be about Quine. And it is hard to see
that it does.

Note first that whatever intentionality this proposition enjoys is inherited or
derived; it will be a function of (1)'s parts, each of which is essential to it. If (1) is a
Russellian proposition, for example, then if Quine had failed to exist, there would
have been no such proposition as *Quine is wise*. Moreover, if any of the constituents
of (1) were different than they are—say, if we substituted Obama for Quine—then an
entirely different proposition would have resulted: certainly not one about Quine, and
perhaps even with a differing truth value. So clearly, on the Russellian view, if (1) is
about Quine at all, it can only be because it *contains* him as a constituent.

But here, we think, there is confusion. Although it is not uncommon to see
Russellian propositions presented as "complex abstract entities" (Pelham and Urquhart
1994, 307), the fact is they are neither abstract nor even propositions (at least as we
are thinking of them). They are not claims or assertions that represent certain states of
affairs; they *are* states of affairs. As the Russell scholar Anssi Korhonen notes:

> there is no condition in the world whose obtaining would be necessary for the
> truth of a [Russellian] proposition. Or, at any rate, this condition cannot be seen
> in any way distinct from the proposition itself. And this means that there is no gap
> between a proposition's being true and something's being the case: facts simply *are*
> (that is, are identical with) true propositions. (2009, 165)

In other words, Russellian "propositions" are actually the truth-*conditions* for what we are thinking of as truth *bearers* (propositions). On the Russellian view, (1) is not the *claim* that Quine has the property of being wise; rather, it is a concrete *state of affairs* that we can represent as follows:

(1*) : Exemplification (Quine, wisdom).[5]

(1*) denotes a certain truthmaking fact, one consisting in the specific way Quine is related to wisdom. But as Vallicella points out, we must not confuse this with either the proposition *Quine is wise* or the state of affairs *Quine's being wise*—both of which are in need of something to make them true (/actual).[6] (1*) simply designates the concrete fact that does that.

This should make it clear that simply "plugging" Quine into a Russellian proposition like (1*) is not going to create a vehicle for representing the way Quine is. For (1*) *just is* the way Quine is. (1) represents the way things are; by contrast, (1*) denotes the things that are that way. Or think of it like this: Since Quine is not *of* or *about* anything, since he does not represent anything (even himself), the mere fact that something contains him will not make that thing about Quine. You might as well argue that Harvard's philosophy department was about Quine because it contained him as a member. The point is: *Just in himself,* Quine, while impressive in many ways, is an intentional flop.

Now here the platonist is not without reply. To avoid collapsing truthbearers into their truth-conditions, while at the same time securing intentionality, she might try removing Quine as a constituent of (1). Why not opt instead for a pure mix of platonic properties and relations? In that case, perhaps (1) would be rendered best as

(1**) *Being Quine* is coinstantiated with *being wise,*

a proposition consisting of two properties standing in the relation of coinstantiation. Since it does not include Quine, (1**) is distinct from the concrete state of affairs it represents—or at least so the platonist might claim. But *does* it represent? Why should we think that? Here we can imagine someone arguing as follows. Since *being Quine* uniquely characterizes Quine, how could it *not* be about him? His having this property guarantees that it is about him. Now of course we can all agree that

(2) An object has the property *being Quine* if and only if it is Quine.

But how does it follow that

(3) *Being Quine* is about Quine?

It does not follow. For the slide from (2) to (3) obviously confuses *being P* (where "*P*" names some property) with being about what has *P*. The two notions are not equivalent. Something could have *P* without *P*'s being about what has it. For example, you could have *being the author of Word and Object* without that property being about you. If you are Quine, that property qualifies you all right; it is predicable of you, but it is not in itself *of* or *about* you; it is not directed upon you. Similarly, *being wise* is neither about nor represents any of its instances. This is especially evident when one considers the fact that, for the platonist, there are worlds in which this property exists but nothing is wise. So we do not secure intentionality for a purely abstract property merely by pointing out that it has instances. Nor can we say *being Quine* is about Quine because it contains something that is: Quine himself. For as we have already noted, Quine is not about anything—even himself. To insist otherwise seems no more than a basic category mistake.

So what is a platonist to say at this point? Here is a final possibility. We treat *Quine is wise* as a simple, brutely intentional Platonic Form—end of story. The problem, though, is that this hardly squares with what we all learned at Socrates's knee. The Forms are not propositional.[7] On the contrary, like the self-thinking Thought of Aristotle, they are wholly indifferent to their concrete instances. A Form—say, Circularity—is not directed toward any of the imperfect circles of the sort we routinely encounter. Rather, the "direction of fit"[8] is entirely the other way around. In order to count as a circle, says Socrates, an object must "imitate" or "participate in" Circularity: *being an enclosed line each point on which is equidistant from a fixed point (the center).* It must possess a world-to-Form direction of fit, so to speak, to qualify as a thing of this kind. As a Platonic Form, however, Circularity is a mere ontological target, a certain standard of perfection to be approximated or achieved. And it can perform this function very nicely without possessing any direction of fit toward the lower world of concrete particulars. As a timeless, spaceless, metaphysical exemplar, Circularity is no more about the crop circle that mysteriously appeared on your front lawn this morning than the number five is about the fingers on your hand.

So whereas we know by introspection that such things as thoughts, beliefs, and desires are intentional, we have no basis at all in reason or experience for thinking that Platonic Forms (including propositions, if we smuggle those in) are about anything. Why then are we tempted to think otherwise? For this reason, we believe. If you start with the idea that truthbearing requires intentionality, then (as Michael Jubien warns) it is very difficult not to

> confer a strictly derivative dose of intentionality upon something that is otherwise intentionally inert [that is, the abstract platonic proposition]. It may be very convenient to suppress this and proceed as if the entity had the intentional feature on its own, but doing so would be a matter of efficiency of thought, not ontology. (Jubien 2001, 53–4)

We need propositions to do a certain amount of philosophical work. For the platonist, their job is to serve as truthbearers and objects of our propositional attitudes. It is therefore a matter of expediency to proceed *as if* they had the requisite intentional properties, but without taking the time to explain how this could be. But this is simply to smuggle intentional propositions into the nonintentional world of abstract Forms—a move that has all the appearance of theft over honest toil.

Suppose we turn, then, to a nominalist approach to these matters; perhaps it will prove more promising. Now there are several varieties of nominalism with respect to propositions, and there is not the space here to deal with all of them.[9] Instead, we will simply make some general remarks about what we take to be the core assumption underlying the approach; and hopefully, this will offer hints about how to think of the versions we do not consider.

Now we are operating, you recall, under the assumption that there is such a thing as truth, that there are truthbearers, and that a thing must have *ofness* or *aboutness* to possess truth. What sorts of things can the nominalist bring forward to fill the role of propositional truthbearer? Here *sentences* stand out as the most likely candidate. In the early Wittgenstein, for example, we are presented with the idea that propositions are sentences or linguistic items of a sort. "The totality of propositions," he says, "is language" (2001, 22). Furthermore, a proposition (sentence) is said to represent reality; for a "proposition shows how things stand if it is true. And it says that they do so stand" (ibid., 25). It makes a claim about things, and it does so in part by virtue of its syntactic and logical form: "there must be exactly as many distinguishable parts [in the proposition] as in the situation that it represents" (ibid., 26).

Let us assume all of this is in order. Then (1) is not an abstract object; it is the concrete sentence inscription "Quine is wise"—a linguistic item with parts (that is, "Quine," "is," and "wise"). And of course these parts have parts of their own (letters). The sentence "Quine is wise" is therefore a concrete particular; it is a string of shapes and characters. Call this string "*S*." Why think that *S* is a primary bearer of truth? A truthbearer must represent things. But neither *S* nor its parts is about anything *just in itself*; shapes (even sequences of shapes) are not about things just by virtue of what they are. Accordingly, it is obvious that if *S* possesses any intentionality, it is borrowed or derived: not of course from its constituent parts, but rather (as Plantinga (2006, 17) notes) from our deciding to use it in a particular way, to express a proposition (that is, (1)) about Quine's being wise. Indeed, Wittgenstein concedes this very point when he remarks, "a proposition is true if *we use it* to say that things stand in a certain way, and they do" (2001, 28, emphasis added). This makes it abundantly clear that the intentionality of a sentence lies outside of it.

But where does this leave us? We have seen that "free-floating" abstract objects, that is, Platonic Forms existing in Plato's heaven, are impotent to account for the intentionality of (1); but concrete objects—ordinary particulars and linguistic entities—are really no better. Does that mean that (1) is not about Quine, that it makes no claim about him, and is therefore neither true nor false? Not at all. Fortunately, there is a better way forward. The problems faced by platonism and nominalism lead us to a third, more compelling view of the matter. The reason for the problems is by now obvious: You cannot force intentionality upon objects whose natures simply defy the imposition. Would it not be better, then, to begin with something known to be intentional, something on which intentionality does not have to be imposed? Indeed, there is a whole class of objects of this sort: *ideas/concepts*.[10] By their very nature, ideas, regardless of who has them, are *of* or *about* things. John Locke actually refers to them as *signs*; and of course signs *point* to things. We speak of Descartes's idea *of* a perfect being, Darwin's ideas *about* Nature, and Russell's idea *of* a proposition. It is incoherent to suppose that there are ideas that are not about anything. If it is not about anything, it is not an idea.

This gives us a very handy solution to our puzzle about parts. That puzzle raised the question of how (1), the complex proposition *Quine is wise*, could be about Quine. On the present suggestion, the answer is embarrassingly easy. (1) is about Quine because it contains a part (the *idea* of Quine) that is essentially about him. Neither a Platonic Form nor a concrete particular can pretend to credentials like this.

A puzzle about arrangement

But now a different puzzle emerges. Locating intentional parts—even the *right* parts—for (1) is crucial. But it does not automatically issue in a truth claim. For while ideas are certainly about things, they do not, strictly speaking, represent anything. Thus we cannot say that propositions are representative truthbearers because they are composed of true or false ideas. As John Locke observes, "truth and falsehood belong, in propriety of speech, only to propositions" (2004, 345), not to ideas. One can easily see why. For until "the mind passes some judgment on" its ideas, until it "affirms or denies something of them" (ibid.), there simply is no claim or assertion, no representation of reality as such. To judge or affirm that Quine is wise, to express that proposition, the ideas of Quine (Q) and wisdom (W) have to be joined to one another. To judge *truly* in this respect is to join Q and W in a way that reflects the actual relation of the things these ideas are about.

So a proposition is far more than an unrelated list of items, as is the case, for example, with the ordered pair <Q, W>. The elements of this pair are indeed intentional objects; they are ideas *of* things. Still, <Q, W> does not represent Quine as being wise. To do that, Q and W must be joined *so that* a specific claim is made. This requires that these ideas be put together in a very precise way. Now <Q, W> is indeed ordered since, by hypothesis, <Q, W> ≠ <W, Q>. But the thing to see is that it is not ordered in the right way. For while there is an asymmetrical "directionality" to the arrangement, it is not *affirmative*; there is not the slightest hint that we have a claim or assertion on our hands. For there is no predicational tie between Q and W. And given that Q and W are *ideas*, is not *that* sort of tie going to require a mental knot?

So what explains this arrangement of ideas? Well, according to Thomas Aquinas,

> Every composition … needs some composer. For, if there is composition, it is made up of a plurality, and a plurality cannot be fitted into a unity except by some composer. (1995, 1:103)

Given this principle of composition, propositions will need a composer, since they are composed entities with an orderly arrangement of parts. But *why* is this necessary? Perhaps it will be helpful to remind ourselves of the obvious. Ideas, as we are viewing of them, occupy neither Plato's detached realm of *abstracta*, nor Ayer's world of empirically verifiable *concreta*. Ideas as such "cannot be seen, or touched, or smelled, or tasted, or heard" (Frege 1997, 224). Locke speaks of "those invisible ideas" of an individual "which his thoughts are made up of" (2004, 363). If we think about it, we can see that an essential property of an idea is that it is *had* or *possessed*. Ideas "need an owner" (Frege 1997, 334); they are ontological parasites on thinkers.

And just as there cannot be thoughts without a thinker, ideas (which are nothing but materials for thinking) cannot exist apart from the minds that have them. But then what better explanation could there be for the orderly arrangement of ideas than the *mental activity* of thinkers? The obvious conclusion to be drawn here is that the things properly said to be true or false (propositions) actually result from mental activity—from the joining or separating of ideas. Thus Locke once more:

> Every one's experience will satisfy him, that the mind, either by perceiving or supposing the agreement or disagreement of any of its ideas, does tacitly within itself put them into a kind of proposition affirmative or negative, which I have endeavored to express by the terms *putting together* and *separating*. (2004, 510)[11]

Thus it follows straight away that propositions are mental effects. For propositions have parts, those parts are best construed as ideas, and their being properly related (that is, "fitted into" truth claims) requires a mental arranger.

An objection and reply

"If *Q* and *W* are just *your* ideas, then the proposition *Quine is wise* is only *your* thought or proposition. Indeed, there is no such thing as *the* proposition *Quine is wise*, in which case (as Frege (1997, 335–6) argues) no two people ever think the same thoughts. They only ever think *their* thoughts; nothing is in common."[12]

Frege is on to something here. Propositions are not simply reducible to *our* thoughts (yours or mine). If they were, they would suffer from a deplorable fragility. And in any event, there just are not enough of *us* to think up all the propositions associated with, say, the natural numbers. Propositions are in some sense objective; even if *we* had not existed, *they* would have been none the worse off. So what is to be done? Frege's way out here was to recognize what he called a "third realm": a realm beyond the world of physical objects, beyond the realm of human ideas—in fact, a platonic realm of abstract thoughts without owners. But as we have already seen, such abstract platonic entities are no truthbearers; they lack all the necessary intentional ingredients.

The proper thing to do, therefore, is to go one step further and recognize a *fourth realm*. Things belonging to this realm would have in common with human ideas that they were intentional objects. But like ordinary particulars, their existence would also be objective; that is, even if there were no human minds, these things would continue to exist nonetheless. Thus, to borrow Frege's example, the Pythagorean Theorem is not just true from the time we discover it. It is more like a planet, which "even before anyone saw it, was in interaction with other planets" (Frege 1997, 337). Here we may happily agree. Propositions are indeed independent of human minds. Where Frege erred, however, was in thinking that propositions do not require owners. This is simply false if they are truthbearing claims composed of intentional parts. In this case, what we must grant, it seems, is a *supra*natural realm of divine ideas and thoughts, not subject to the relativistic vagaries of human mental activity. The best way to look at things, perhaps, is to see we human beings as arranging our ideas—which are sometimes complete, but often only partial graspings of God's ideas—into thoughts which approximate (to varying degrees) those of God himself. We can then reserve the term "proposition" for referring to God's thoughts.

The perils of unbridled theistic activism

Naturally, much more remains to be said. But hopefully this fills in at least some of the details (and motivation) behind Morris and Menzel's brief assertion that "we can characterize propositions as God's thoughts." However, we do not think that the activist project should be extended to properties and relations, thus, in what remains, we shall argue for a *modified* theistic activism (MTA).

The linchpin of theistic activism is Morris and Menzel's principle of *Property-Concept Conflation* (PCP): "All properties and relations are God's concepts." It is easy to see that this principle undermines basic attempts to explain the notion of a substance. Consider, for example, the bundle theory: conjoined with PCP, it leads to a form of Berkeleyan idealism. For suppose a material thing is nothing but a bundle of compresent multiply exemplifiable properties. Then if properties are God's concepts, and if relations are God's thinking concepts together, every material object is a mere collection of divine concepts or ideas, in which case we shall have to say that a substance changes just when God starts or stops "thinking together" His own concepts or ideas. Not only does this eradicate the material nature of reality, it smacks of an objectionable divine determinism (more severe than anything calvinism has to offer).

On a nominalist approach to bundles, things look only slightly better. Instead of bundling platonic properties, we might try tropes or property instances—such concrete entities as *the wisdom of Socrates* or *this spot's redness*. A substance would then consist in a bundle of concrete particulars, thereby sidestepping the reduction of material things to abstract universals (and thus, by PCP, to divine ideas). Still, there is the matter of how these tropes hold together to form one substance. The typical explanation posits a basic, unanalyzable relation of *compresence* or *collocation* that serves as the ontological "glue" for these otherwise disparate tropes. According to PCP, however, this relation is *not* primitive; it is analyzable in terms of God's conceptual activity. The tropes that comprise Socrates hold together because God thinks them together. At first glance, this strikes one as a tidy illustration of Paul's words in Col. 1.17—that "in him all things hold together." Strictly speaking, though, Paul does not say that things hold together because God thinks them together. In fact, would not the explanation go the other way around? God thinks of the tropes comprising Socrates as being compresent because He *causes* them to be so. In any event, it is (almost) trivial to say that God's thinking these tropes together is the cause of their being together. For causation is a relation, and on PCP all relations are divine concepts. Therefore, to say that God causes trope compresence by thinking tropes together amounts to the tautologous claim that God thinks of His thinking tropes together by thinking tropes together. The concept of causation as an extramental relation goes completely by the wayside here.

Next, consider bare particular theory. Following Bergmann (1967, 22–6)—and more recently, Moreland (2001, 148–57), Pickavance (2009), and Sider (2006)—we might hold that a proper ontological assay of a substance (Socrates, let us say) must reference a bare particular, the relation of exemplification, and certain external property "ties." To say that Socrates is human just means that the property of *being human* is "rooted in" Socrates as a constituent, but also "tied to" Socrates's bare particular (call it "*b*") by the exemplification relation. Unlike Socrates, however, *b* has no internal property constituents, and thus counts as a "thin" or "bare" particular. Proponents of this view go on to say that bare particulars have no categorical or kind-defining properties of their own; they only ground the properties of the concrete particulars of which they are constituents.[13] But then given PCP, it looks as though Socrates is the result of God's conceiving of *b* in terms of the divine concept *being human*, which is strange enough. However, matters are even worse; for *b* is a thing with no properties of its own, which (on PCP) simply means that God does not have a concept of it; in which case Socrates is the consequence of God's conceiving of a thing of which He has no conception. It is not a coherent picture.

Someone will object that we need only turn to Aristotelian substances and the problem dissolves. On the Aristotelian view, a concrete particular like Socrates is a basic entity; he is not "built up" from constituent properties "tied to" a constituent (bare) substratum. Rather, as Loux notes, the subject of ontic predication is Socrates himself. This is made possible by the simple fact that he belongs to a natural kind (that is, *being human*) that marks him out as a particular sort of thing, "countably distinct from other members of that kind and from members of other kinds" (2006, 113). Moreover,

> in virtue of being an instance of its proper kind, a concrete particular can be the subject for attributes—properties—that are external to its core being. So concrete particulars do have a structure that the ontologist can characterize: there is a core being or essence furnished by a kind and a host of properties that lie at the periphery of that core and, hence, are accidental to concrete particulars. (ibid.)

Here there is no need to call up an incoherent (explanatorily prior) bare particular for purposes of property support. That has to be an advantage.

The deeper issue, for whatever notion of substance used is that, given PCP, divine concepts are called upon to play a role that seems inimical to their nature. As essentially intentional mental objects, divine concepts (and concepts in general) mediate between mind and world.[14] The primary role for properties, however, is that of making or structuring reality. As George Bealer observes, "[properties] play a fundamental constitutive role in the structure of the world" (1998a, 268). As we argued earlier, properties (that is, Platonic Forms) are intentional flops—they are not *about* anything, and essentially so. But, if divine concepts are called upon to play both the mediating and making role, it seems that they can only do so at a high cost in terms of theoretical economy. To see why consider: Divine concepts/properties are essentially intentional (in their mediating role) and *not* intentional (in their making role). But, this picture seems incoherent. To make sense of this story, the activist employing PCP will need to argue that divine concepts/properties have (exemplify?) the following nature (essential property?): *Being intentional when a constituent of thought, being nonintentional when not.* Such a nature (property?) of divine concepts is surely unlovely (at best) and (at worst) smells of *ad hocness.*[15] We say, best to leave properties and relations alone—they are *sui generis*, and admit their own ontological category.

Can God create abstract objects?

The version of MTA we wish to defend is a kind of modified platonic theism. Thus far we've argued that some abstracta are located within the divine mind (propositions and concepts) and some are external to God (properties and relations not exemplified by God). Thus, abstract objects exist in two realms: the divine mind[16] and Plato's heaven. This picture of the world opens us up to a number of worries, worries that we will attempt to discharge in the remainder of this chapter.

If the existence of abstract objects is admitted into one's ontology, a *prima facie* problem arises for the traditional theist. The problem is this. Abstract objects, it seems, are best understood as uncreated entities. But, if abstract objects are uncreated, then God is not the creator of everything, a view that appears unacceptable to the traditional theist constrained by Scripture and tradition.

Some platonists (e.g. Peter van Inwagen (2009)) argue that theists need not worry—there is no actual tension between traditional theism and the existence of abstract objects since abstract objects are not the kinds of things that can enter into causal relationships. It is our judgment that if sense can be given to the causality by which one necessary being (God) would cause another necessary being (abstract objects) to exist, then there is no good reason to think that God could not create abstract objects and hence, no good reason to think that abstract objects cannot enter into causal relations.[17]

Assume anti-reductionism regarding causation.[18] Anti-reductionism is not the view that causation is primitive. Primitivism regarding causation denies that there are *any* concepts more basic than causation. All we wish to endorse here is that there are no noncausal terms that can adequately explicate the notion of causation. Given anti-reductionism regarding causation, God's creating abstracta can be understood as follows:

> (C$_A$) God caused abstract object P if He brought it about that P exists.

(C$_A$) specifies a plausible account of causation in which such creation is possible (in which a *sufficient*, but not necessary condition for such creation is realized). Still, one might object: (C$_A$) is hardly illuminating in terms of *how* God creates abstract objects. Specifically, the right-hand side of the conditional doesn't explain the left-hand side— as it stands, they are virtually synonyms at face value. Fortunately, we've already seen a more illuminating anti-reductive account of *how* God causes abstract objects, the theistic activism of Morris and Menzel:

(C_{TA}) God caused abstract object P if P is (i) a constituent of God's mind (ii) brought about by the activity of thinking.

We also think that the following is an acceptable understanding of God's creating abstracta:

(C_{MTA}) God caused abstract object P if P is brought about by the activity of divine willing.

(C_{MTA}) allows that God creates abstract objects wholly distinct from His being—existing in a platonic heaven even. And if (C_{TA}) and/or (C_{MTA}) are possibly true, then it is reasonable to think that God *can* indeed create abstract objects. We argue that He has in fact done so.[19]

Divine bootstrapping?

But, can our MTA avoid the charge of incoherence because of divine bootstrapping? Recall that the bootstrapping worry is usually advanced as follows: "God has properties. If God is the creator of all things, then God is the creator of His properties. But God can't create properties unless He already has the property of *being able to create a property*. Thus, we are ensnared in a vicious explanatory circle. God causes His nature to exist—a nature He must already possess to do the causing." We think that the incoherency worry due to divine bootstrapping can be successfully avoided by endorsing the following two claims:

[A] God's essential platonic properties exist *a se* (i.e. they are neither created nor sustained by God, yet they inhere in the divine substance); and

[B] Substances are Aristotelian.

Endorsement of claim [A] allows us to avoid the unwanted view that God creates His own nature; claim [B] ensures that the divine substance is a fundamental unity that is the final cause of its constituent metaphysical parts (including divine concepts and essential properties)—which ensures God's ultimacy. Thus, the divine substance, along with all of its essential properties exists *a se* and everything *distinct* from God (that is, everything external to God's borders) is created and sustained by God.

What about the rest of the platonic horde: numbers, sets, quantifiers, states of affairs, and possible worlds? No doubt each of these alleged abstracta requires a paper in its own right. However, if our discussion of MTA has taught us anything, we should not expect any one approach here to single-handedly resolve the issues raised by the platonic horde and its relationship to God. Still, we have good reason to think that each of these abstracta can be safely brought either into the mind of God or located in Plato's heaven, without violating God's aseity or sovereignty. Thus, one *kind* of platonic theist can have it all: an attractive (realist) theory of the mind-world-language nexus and fidelity to Scripture and tradition.

Notes

1 This is not quite true of course. Sets are presumably abstract; however, arguably, some sets—e.g. Obama's singleton—exist in only those worlds in which Obama does. For more on the contingency of sets, see Alvin Plantinga (1976, 146–7).
2 Plantinga now thinks that abstract objects can enter into causal relationships, see (2011, 32).
3 But see the Introduction where they are nicely laid out.
4 Compare Russell: "Whatever may be an object of thought, or may occur in any true or false proposition ... I call a *term*.... . A man, a moment, a number, a class, a relation, a chimaera, or anything else that can be mentioned, is sure to be a term" (1903, 43).
5 Following D. W. Mertz, we use the colon locution ":" for the operator "The fact that."
6 On the importance of distinguishing between concrete and abstract states of affairs, see William F. Vallicella (2000, 237).
7 As Matthew McGrath notes, if Plato believed in propositional Forms, he could have had Socrates solve the problem of how a false belief (e.g. in Pegasus) could actually be about something by saying that there *is* an object of belief here: the (false) abstract proposition *Pegasus exists*. However, no such proposal is even considered. See McGrath (2012, §1).
8 A term coined by J. L. Austin. See Searle (1998, 101).
9 For an excellent overview of nominalist options, see Michael Loux (2006, 130–9).
10 We shall use the terms "ideas" and "concepts" synonymously.
11 Locke actually distinguishes two sorts of propositions: mental (thoughts) and verbal (sentences). Both are composed of signs, he says: the former consist of ideas, the latter of words. Here we focus exclusively on mental propositions. For as we noted earlier, even if we can speak of sentences as being true or false, it is only in a derivative sense.
12 Thus Michael Jubien: "Somehow or other, [conceptualism] has to make room for the fact that you and I can 'believe the same thing'" (1997, 52).
13 Compare Moreland and Pickavance: "the properties said to be necessary for bare particulars are not genuine properties; these include simplicity, particularity, unrepeatability, and those of the three categories of transcendental, disjunction, and negative properties" (2003, 10).
14 Dallas Willard states, "[concepts] form the 'bridge' that connects a thought and its object" (1999, 13).
15 Part of the *ad hoc* character of the necessary fix is that (as we mentioned earlier) it is typically thought that properties/Forms are wholly indifferent to their concrete instances, but now the activist is forced to admit otherwise. One of us has argued that it *seems* possible for the theistic activist to employ PCP, even if it is unlovely and uneconomical—at any rate, it is not logically impossible. See Gould (2011a).
16 Below we will allow that God exemplifies properties and stands in relations to constituent parts, thus this first realm of abstract objects is best understood as the divine substance (of which the mind is a part).

17 We are not alone in this, e.g. Plantinga thinks that theistic activism gives us good
    reason to think that abstract objects can enter into causal relations: "[if] sets,
    numbers and the like ... are best conceived as divine thoughts ... then they stand to
    God in the relation in which a thought stands to a thinker ... . If so, then [abstract
    objects] stand in a causal relation" (2011a, 32).

18 Anti-reductionism regarding causation is plausible, enjoys independent motivation,
    and has been ably defended recently by *inter alia* John Carroll (2010) and James
    Woodward (1990). Typical arguments for anti-reductionism involve (i) detailing
    the repeated failures of reductive analysis; (2) the fact that there is a sparse base of
    noncausal concepts that can be employed in providing a reductive analysis; and (iii)
    the case of preemption.

19 Granted, there are other issues looming in the background that would need
    to be addressed in articulating a *robust* doctrine of God's creation of abstract
    objects, including providing an explication of eternal creation—for in the case of
    God creating everlasting abstract objects, the cause is not temporally prior to its
    effect. This topic would require another paper, but for now let us state that many
    contemporary philosophers working on the metaphysics of causation agree that
    causation need not involve reference to the relation of temporal priority. Indeed
    contemporary discussions of causal asymmetry deal routinely with cases in which
    cause and effect are simultaneous and, we are told, physics takes seriously the
    possibility of backwards directed time-travel and the accompanying backwards
    directed causation. See John Carroll (2010) and Huemer and Kovitz (2003). For a
    robust defense of the claim that God can create abstract objects, see Gould 2013.

Response to Paul M. Gould and Richard Brian Davis

Keith Yandell

In my first reply, I wish to say something that I will not repeat. It has been a pleasure to read the papers of my colleagues. I have learned from them and respect their positions. However much I sometimes disagree with views expressed, I do not think our discussion concerns a point of Christian orthodoxy. I turn to putting my points briefly, concerning both Professor Gould's fine introduction and the fuller essay by Gould/Davis.

Regarding the Augustine passage quoted by Professor Gould (17, note 4), what he spoke strongly against was holding the view that God has to appeal to Platonic Forms in order to have a recipe for making things. It is no part of propositionalism to say that.

Modified Theistic Activism (MTA) holds that some abstracta (e.g. propositions, concepts, and maybe more) are the product of God's intellectual activity, but others (such as properties and relations distinct from God) are the product of God's creative activity, but not His intellectual activity. MTA is "modified" in another way as well: Those properties (and relations) essential to God exist *a se* within the divine substance as uncreated entities, thus waiving a uniform account of properties (and relations).

Whether God strictly creates propositions is another matter. If propositions are the propositional contents of God's thoughts, then if God is necessarily omniscient, having those thoughts are part of, or at least entailed by, God's nature. If necessary omniscience requires being unrelentingly aware of every truth, then God does not create them; thinking them is part of, or at least entailed by, God's nature. If necessary omniscience permits merely being able to bring every true proposition to mind without always having it "in mind," then without independent abstracta, God must recreate whatever propositions are not "in mind." This of course is not possible if God is eternal rather than everlasting, and the eternalist will embrace an eternal unrestricted attendance of all truths in the hall of divine thought.

Suppose there are abstract objects. Then consider the sovereignty issue. Either it is possible that abstracta are caused, or it is not. If it is, then God created them. If it is not, then it no more restricts God's sovereignty that God did not create them than that God cannot make other contradictions true. Either way, on any logically consistent notion of sovereign creation, God is sovereign regarding creating if and only if, for everything X that exists, is not God, and can be created, X is created by God.

The claim that abstract objects are ideas necessarily had by a necessarily existing God cannot be literally true. Granting that there is an abstract-versus-concrete distinction, abstract objects are not concrete. God is a concrete being. The ideas of a concrete being are concrete, as it is that in virtue of which they have propositional content. Hence abstract objects are not God's ideas. The person who says that abstract objects are ideas in the divine mind is saying that what exists *instead of* abstract objects are ideas necessarily had by a necessarily existing God.

There is a problem with saying that propositions are assertions as opposed to saying that they are what can be asserted. "Blueberries are not moonbeams" is a perfectly fine assertion, but I doubt that anyone (including God) has asserted it.

The idea that God creates abstract objects that are distinct from God and necessarily exist has attracted some. I doubt that a necessarily existing thing can be created by, or be dependent on, anything, but I waive that. Strictly, what must be meant here is that God *emanates* necessarily existing abstracta (see my lead essay for further discussion). To say that God necessarily has some property Q, or necessarily engages in some activity A, or necessarily undergoes some process P resulting in the existence of X, is to say that God does so eternally or everlastingly. Given that abstracta are distinct from God, and exist necessarily, God too must exist necessarily. If God emanates abstracta, God is not free to refrain from so doing. So God cannot fail to be a creator. On this view, divine sovereignty does not allow God to be otherwise than being the maker of one kind of thing. Further, God depends for God's existence on there being the abstracta that God must create. This is not merely a case in which, since any necessary truth entails every other, the denial of any necessary truth entails the denial of any other. If God cannot but produce abstracta, then their absence would entail God's absence without appeal to entailment among necessary truths, even assuming that *God exists* is a necessary truth.

Taking "world" in a very broad sense, propositions represent the way that the world is, and are true if the world is that way. They are thus *about* the world whose content determines their truth value. It is not obvious that propositions are made up of concepts as sentences are made up of words. Consider the claim that S has the concept of *being a cow* insofar as S knows what is true if and only if there are cows. Then concepts are propositional abilities that persons have, or the results of using those abilities, and propositions are primary.

Appeal to tradition is not so straightforward as assumed. MTA is inconsistent with the traditional divine simplicity doctrine. Many contemporary Christian philosophers reject divine eternity. Does this raise questions about MTA and divine everlastingism? Why, and to what extent?

I do not think Scripture is against propositionalism. The question of the existence of propositions is a technical philosophical issue and on one view such things are necessarily not causable. The dispute as to whether that view, combined with the view that there are propositions, can be held by Christians who think consistently is controversial—too philosophically, theologically, and exegetically controversial for any "side" to justifiably claim exclusive exegetical basis for its view.

Greg Welty

Anyone reading the Gould/Davis chapter and my own can see that our respective approaches to these matters have much in common. We have both argued that the intrinsic/derived intentionality distinction is relevant to critiquing nominalism, and that the intrinsic intentionality of propositions is best explained as the intrinsic intentionality of thoughts. In addition (going beyond the scope of my own chapter), I agree with Gould/Davis that the Russellian platonist analysis of propositions fails, that unbridled *theistic activism* (TA) is perilous, and that the "God cannot create necessary beings" objection to TA is bogus. Despite all this, here are a few areas of potential disagreement.

Gould/Davis claim that conceptualism "does a much better job than its closest competitors (platonism and nominalism) in accounting for the truthbearing nature of propositions" (52). While their case against nominalism seems secure, their case against platonism needs some work. First, while I agree that the Russellian analysis fails for the reasons noted, Gould/Davis seem to think that the only platonist alternative to Russell is to "treat *Quine is wise* as a simple, brutely intentional Platonic Form—end of story" (55). They continue: "The problem, though, is that this hardly squares with what we all learned at Socrates's knee. The Forms are not propositional" (55). But this criticism unwarrantably restricts platonist options to whatever Plato actually wrote. Why can't the modern platonist stipulate that *there are* non-spatiotemporal, intentional truthbearing entities—the kind expressed by sentences and serving as the referents of that-clauses, among other things—and be done with it? What, exactly, is the problem here? Platonists simply *infer* that there must be such entities because this ontological specification best satisfies the functional concept of "proposition" that emerges from realist arguments for propositions. What Plato said about "Forms" doesn't matter.

Second, Gould/Davis claim that "whereas we know by introspection that such things as thoughts, beliefs, and desires are intentional, we have no basis at all in reason or experience for thinking that Platonic Forms (including propositions, if we smuggle those in) are about anything" (55). But surely platonists will say that we *do* have reason for thinking that propositions are about things: The realist arguments give us reason to think there are such intentional entities. Following Jubien, Gould/Davis apparently think that platonists *start with* an "intentionally inert" entity, "the abstract Platonic proposition," *and then* they "confer a strictly derivative dose of intentionality upon" (55) it. (They "smuggle intentional propositions into the nonintentional world of abstract Forms" (55). They "force intentionality upon objects whose natures simply defy the imposition" (56). "Platonic entities … lack all the necessary intentional ingredients" (58).) But as far as I can tell, platonists just infer that *there are* these intentional entities, and that is that. Who says these entities must start out "intentionally inert," like bits of graphite or ink, only to be baptized by aboutness *later*?

Third, Gould/Davis claim that "Given [Aquinas's] principle of composition, propositions will need a composer, since they are composed entities with an orderly arrangement of parts" (57). But while this would pave the way for conceptualism, it's not clear *why* we should regard propositions as "composed entities with an orderly arrangement of parts." This is part and parcel of *Russell's* (failed) analysis of propositions. Must it be an element of *any* platonist account? Why? (Propositions *make reference* to entities. But are they therefore composed of parts? One might as well say that since God refers to entities *He* is composed of parts. More argument is needed here, I think.)

Fourth, Gould/Davis claim that platonists don't take the time to "explain how" propositions can have "the requisite intentional properties" (55). This is a worry for platonists, but I wonder how strong it is. I agree that "it is incoherent to suppose that there are ideas that are not about anything. If it is not about anything, it is not an idea" (56). But does stating this "explain how" thought has intentionality? Are we not saying that thoughts are intentional *by definition*? In this respect, do platonists claim any less for their entities?

In contrast to all this, my alternative case against platonism and for conceptualism involves conceding that platonists can *easily* infer their denizens of the abstract realm from the various realist arguments on offer (I canvassed four). The problem is not that their entities are not intentional or are not composed of parts, but that their entities multiply ontological kinds beyond explanatory necessity. This appeal to simplicity is not open to Gould/Davis, as they are happy to posit "Plato's heaven" in addition to the divine thoughts.

About *modified theistic activism* (MTA) I will explain just one worry. MTA is "modified" in order to avoid bootstrapping worries. It retains the characteristic claim of TA that abstract objects like propositions and properties *causally depend* upon God. He "brings about" these things in some sense of nonreductive causation. But MTA exempts God's essential properties from this causal process, so that He is not stuck creating His nature. This is certainly an improvement. But as Matthew Davidson has pointed out (1999, 288–90), even if God only creates propositions the bootstrapping worries remain. If God causes the proposition *God exists* to exist, He causes its essence (which includes the property *being true*) to be exemplified. Thus, in causing this proposition to exist, He makes it true, and thus God causes His own existence. In response, Gould/Davis could further restrict MTA, such that propositions (or at least the troublesome ones) *also* inhabit platonic heaven rather than being caused by God. But then this frustrates their sustained, carefully crafted case that platonic propositions are inherently unworkable. I would make the change in the other direction (surprise, surprise!): The relation between propositions and God is one of constitutive dependence rather than causal dependence.[1]

William Lane Craig

Gould/Davis's modified theistic activism is a hybrid view: Conceptualism with respect to propositions and absolute creationism with respect to properties and relations. Their essay, like Welty's, illustrates the way in which the two different debates over so-called nominalism (see pp. 115–16 of my lead essay) can run together.

Consider first their absolute creationism. They affirm that God causes abstract objects (like properties) that are wholly distinct from His being. The key question in assessing their view is whether they successfully answer the bootstrapping objection. In reply to the objection, they endorse two claims (62):

[A] God's essential platonic properties exist *a se* (i.e. they are neither created nor sustained by God, yet they inhere in the divine substance)

and

[B] Substances are Aristotelian.

Their view seems to be that God does not stand in a relation of exemplification to certain platonic properties existing *extra se*, in virtue of which He is powerful, wise, good, and so forth. Rather God just is a powerful, wise, good substance, and any properties He has are immanent universals. But this Aristotelian view seems to me to yield the palm of victory to the anti-platonist. For this just is anti-platonism with respect to God. But then no justification remains for giving things the "ontological assay" that the platonist wants to give. Things can be powerful or wise or brown without being so in virtue of standing in an exemplification relation to an abstract property. Once the absolute creationist has gone this route, no rationale remains for platonism about properties. If this is not their view, then I frankly do not understand it.[2]

Now consider their conceptualism with respect to propositions. I applaud their emphasis on the centrality of intentionality. Any aboutness associated with either sentence tokens or abstract propositions is derivative, the result of their being used by intentional agents.

Now considerations of intentionality immediately raise the question of the ontological status of intentional objects. It is a datum of experience that we often think about things that do not exist—Santa Claus, the accident that was prevented, the hole in my sock, last summer's vacation, and so on. Gould/Davis tell us, "It is incoherent to suppose that there are ideas that are not about anything" (56). This was a characteristic emphasis of Alexius Meinong's Theory of Objects (*Gegenstandstheorie*). According to Meinong the intentional objects of some of our ideas are nonexistent objects. Do Gould/Davis mean to endorse Meinong's view? If so, then why not say with the neo-Meinongian that abstract objects like propositions, numbers, and properties are nonexistent objects? Then divine aseity and *creatio ex nihilo* remain inviolate.

On the other hand, if they mean to endorse a view of intentionality more akin to Meinong's teacher Brentano, according to which intentionality is not a relation between a mental state and an object, but a monadic property of a mental state (e.g. I have the property *thinking-of-Santa Claus*), then why not say with the anti-realist that our ability to think of propositions, numbers, and properties does not imply that there actually exist such objects?

Gould/Davis would say that we need something more than mere sentence tokens to serve as truthbearers. But why? The truth-predicate "is true" may be seen simply as a device of semantic ascent which enables us to talk about a statement rather than to assert the statement itself. For example, rather than say that God is triune, we can ascend semantically and say that it is true that God is triune. Similarly, whenever the truth-predicate is employed, we can descend semantically and simply assert the statement said to be true. For example, rather than say that it is necessarily true that

God is self-existent, we can descend semantically and simply assert that, necessarily, God is self-existent. Nothing is gained or lost through such semantic ascent and descent.

Why is a device of semantic ascent useful or needed in natural language? The answer is that the truth-predicate serves the purpose of blind truth ascriptions. In many cases we find ourselves unable to assert the statement or statements said to be true because we are incapable of rehearsing them due to their sheer numerosity, as in "Every theorem of Peano arithmetic is true," or because we are ignorant of the relevant statements, as in "Everything stated in the documents is true." In theory even blind truth ascriptions are dispensable if we substitute for them infinite disjunctions or conjunctions like "Either p or q or r or … ." While such infinite disjunctions and conjunctions are unknowable by us, they are known to an omniscient deity, so that God has no need of blind truth ascriptions. Hence, He has no need of semantic ascent and, hence, no need of the truth-predicate.

Finally, I am not convinced that Gould/Davis's conceptualism can avoid collapse into anti-realism. I concur with Oppy (pp. 178–9 that thoughts are not abstract objects nor are they composed of abstract objects (ideas). Otherwise, it seems unintelligible to say that thoughts (abstract objects) exist in God's mind. They are concrete mental events or states. Like psychologism, against which Frege inveighed, divine conceptualism, as Welty rightly sees (p. 90), is really an anti-platonic realism. As different versions of concrete realism (see Fig. 1 on p. 40), psychologism and conceptualism posit mental tokens rather than physical tokens in the place of *abstracta*. But the anti-realist theist also believes that God has thoughts to which truth can be ascribed. So what gain is there in conceptualism? One may as well just rest content with anti-realism.

Scott A. Shalkowski

Gould/Davis begin with the wholly sensible task of asking and answering the crucial, but often overlooked, questions regarding propositions. What are propositions supposed to be? What are they supposed to do? In their critique of platonism, they bring together what philosophers say in its favor, showing that even though it is a highly recommended philosophical view, it cannot perform the central tasks for which it was invented. If one does not accept an identity theory of truth (McDowell 1994; Hornsby 1997), then there must be some distinctions between the ways things are and the ways things are represented to be, even for truths. Their discussion of Russellian propositions containing Quine (himself) and non-Russellian propositions containing *being Quine* highlights the idea that things in themselves do not represent. Purely ontological accounts of representation and truth fail, whether platonist or nominalist.

Their rejection of nominalism, however, is too swift. No concrete item intrinsically represents, but nominalists need not think that they do. All that follows from the intentionality requirement on representation is that there are no unintended claims and, hence, no unintended truths. Nominalists and the divine conceptualists are in league here.

Nominalists might part company when Gould/Davis insist that "propositions are mental effects" (58). The problem is not that propositions are parasites (57). All hangs on the nature of the parasitism. If the extension of "proposition" goes no further than beliefs held, assertions or claims made, then the differences are merely stylistic. Gould/Davis want to make propositions God's thoughts. Nominalists need not object. Insofar as we can make sense of the common philosophical vocabulary, God is neither abstract nor physical but is concrete. So, God's thoughts are no less within the nominalist's framework than are ours.

What separates nominalists from MTAists is whose intentions are relevant to our comprehensive philosophical accounting of things. Nominalists may agree that *if* truths antedate the creatures sufficient to intend the relevant signage, then human signage is insufficient. *If* one can sometimes think the same thought as another, then those thoughts cannot be wholly private and the acts of thinking must have something in common.

Two pauses, though. Why think that we do, as we commonly say, think *the same* thought? Why is it not sufficient that you think that Quine is wise and so do I? Both platonists and MTAists share the idea that besides (a) Quine being wise, (b) you and your thoughts, (c), me and my thought, there must still be an *object*—a representation—to which each of us and our thoughts must be related. Nominalists deny that there are sufficient grounds for thinking this. We can, if we like, say that you and I think the same thing when you think Quine is wise and so do I, but each of us represents things to ourselves—and to others when we decide to go public that Quine is wise. To the extent that we have ideas and we intend to direct them as signs one way and not others, we simply intend the relevant mental state and its public exhibition to be directed toward what is (Quine) and how he is (wise). No grounds are apparent to me for taking "the same" to mean anything more, ontologically speaking, than that you and I each think/speak/write about Quine and, furthermore, that he is wise. If this is what "the same" comes to here, then nominalists agree that there are propositions (though the claim will invite inevitable confusion), but deny that there is another object whether external or internal to the mind of God. If one insists that "the same" requires an object besides Quine and any of our signage relevant to isolating and characterizing him, then nominalists parts company and ask why "the same" signals anything more than what the nominalist already recognizes—you and I agree about Quine's wisdom.

If the nominalist's complaint is answered sufficiently, the identity secured by each of us thinking God's thought that Quine is wise brings with it a new problem. My thought, on this account, is no longer primarily related to Quine (though it may be so directed). Lapsing into metaphor perhaps, my thought must be God's, where God's thought is "in" God's mind. Now, I am no more in God's mind—even when God is thinking of me—than Quine is in mine when I think of him, lest the view lapse into the Berkleyan idealism Gould/Davis seek to avoid (59). How exactly is it that the very same thought that is God's is mine? If my thought is a physical going-on in my brain, I do not see how it can be, but even if my thought is in my mind beyond space and time, I still do not see how my thought can literally be God's. Platonists under-tell the story regarding how we are related to *sui generis* platonic objects and MTAism requires something beyond the assertion that we all think the same (divine) thoughts when we think anything. Since the argument for MTAism begins with the failure of platonists to put the whole of their platonistic picture together into a coherent whole by incorporating it with what we think we know about truth, truthmakers, etc., MTAism must not commit the same error. Since we now have God, Quine, you, and me involved, we require a bit more to put the pieces together. How do I get access to God's thought? How is my getting access to that thought different from when God reveals to me that Quine is wise? How is it different when I falsely (let us say) think that Quine is foolish when God thinks (truly) that Quine is wise? When I think that Quine is wise, I do *not* think that Quine is foolish. If propositions are God's thoughts, then assuming that mistaken beliefs whose contents are propositions are possible, then God must think Quine foolish, since there is no independent proposition for God to entertain, while also thinking him wise. How, exactly, does all of that go, especially the identity claim?

Graham Oppy

Gould and Davis defend a conceptualist account of propositions: They claim (*) that propositions are thoughts in the mind of God. In arguing for (*), they make a number of controversial assumptions, including: (1) that there are propositions; (2) that propositions are claims or assertions; (3) that propositions are truthbearers; (4) that propositions are essentially intentional objects; and (5) that propositions are mind-dependent entities.

Ad (1): In the context of a general inquiry into abstract objects, it cannot just be assumed that there are propositions. After all, we might decide that we should be fictionalists about them. And it is not hard to see the utility that talk of propositions brings even if there are no propositions. In particular, there are various kinds of generalizations that are much more easily stated if we allow ourselves to talk about propositions as objects. Consider for example: *If the Pope says it, then it must be true.* Without the fiction of propositions, we would be left with an infinite conjunction, or an infinite number of instances of a schema, or the like. Or consider: *Mary believes what Tom doubts.* Even if we could have said *Mary believes that so-and-so but Tom doubts that so-and-so*, the wheels of conversation are greased if we pretend that there are propositions over which we can quantify (and, in any case, we can say *Mary believes what Tom doubts* even if there is no sentence of the form *Mary believes that so-and-so but Tom doubts that so-and-so* that is available to us). At the very least, in the light of these observations, a case needs to be made that we should prefer realism to fictionalism about propositions.

Ad (2): If there are such things as propositions, then propositions are the *contents* of claims and assertions. If I assert that it is warm, then the content of my assertion is the proposition that it is warm. If I claim that it is warm, then the content of my claim is the proposition that it is warm. But, equally, if I wonder whether it is warm, then the content of my wondering is the proposition that it is warm. And yet, of course, my wondering involves no claim or assertion. This seems to me to be sufficient to establish that, if there are such things as propositions, then propositions are *not* assertions or claims. Moreover, it also seems to me to be sufficient to establish that propositions do *not* represent reality as being some particular way: rather, someone's taking an appropriate attitude towards a proposition *may* represent reality as being some particular way. If, for example, I assert that it is warm, then my assertion represents (local) reality as being warm; but if I wonder whether it is warm, then my wondering does not represent (local) reality as being any particular way.

Ad (3): If there are such things as propositions, it may be so that there is *some* sense in which propositions are truthbearers. But there are other good candidates for truthbearers, and there are important questions to ask about which candidates are base-level truthbearers. Some truthbearers are verbal tokenings. If I say, at a particular time and place, that it is warm, then, if it is warm at that particular time and place, I speak truly. More carefully: If I produce a verbal token—"It is warm"—at a particular time and place, then, if it is warm at that particular time and place, I speak truly in producing that particular token. Of course, my verbal token must be produced with appropriate intent: If I produce my token while acting on the stage, then, even if it is warm on the stage, I shall likely not have spoken truly in producing my token. And doubtless there are other qualifications that should also be introduced. But, at the very least, it is often so that I speak truly, in producing a particular verbal token, just in case things are as my verbal tokenings represents them to be.

Some truthbearers are other kinds of tokenings. If I produce a written token—"It is warm"—at a particular time and place, then, if it is warm at that time and place, I write truly in producing that particular written token (given the satisfaction of other relevant conditions). If I produce a particular mental token—"It is warm"—at a particular time and place, then, if it is warm at that time and place, I think truly in producing that particular mental token (perhaps given the satisfaction of other relevant conditions). And there may be other kinds of tokenings that are also truthbearers.

On the view that I favor, tokenings are the base-level truthbearers, and—perhaps— tokens and propositions are derivative truthbearers. (Whether verbal tokenings are more basic truthbearers than mental tokenings is a question that need not be decided here.) If there are propositions, then tokenings involve both tokens and propositions— "vehicles" and "contents"—but the base-level truthbearers are the tokenings, and not either the tokens or the propositions. (A view to which I might be forced to retreat is that tokenings, tokens, and propositions are all truthbearers, none of which should be supposed to be more fundamental truthbearers than the others.)

Ad (4): Tokenings are intentional—tokenings are about things. So, for example, thought tokenings are intentional—thought tokenings are about things. If I have a thought that Quine is wise, then I have a thought about Quine. If we think of my thought tokening as being a tokening of "Quine is wise," then my thought tokening is about Quine because it contains a tokening of "Quine" and—in appropriate conditions—tokenings of "Quine" are about Quine (because they refer to Quine). Given that tokenings are intentional, and that propositions are the objects (or contents) of tokenings, we can allow that there is a sense in which propositions are intentional objects—but it seems to me that this intentionality of propositions is clearly "secondary" or "derivative." (If you are worried about talk of thought tokenings, it should be clear that I can run exactly the same line in connection with verbal tokenings. Verbal tokenings are intentional, and their intentionality depends upon the referential properties of sub-tokenings of names, pronouns, and so forth.)

Ad (5): Given the distinction between tokenings, tokens, and propositions, it is, I think, quite clear that, while tokenings are mind-dependent objects, tokens and propositions need not be. Certainly, once produced, written and verbal tokens are not mind-dependent; but, if there are mental tokens then, of course, they are mind-dependent. However, crucially, if there are propositions, then there is simply no reason at all to suppose that propositions are mind-dependent. If there are propositions, then propositions are the contents of tokens involved in particular tokenings—but, as just noted, it is the *tokenings* that are the clearly mind-dependent entities.

Ad (*): As argued in my original paper, the claim, that propositions are thoughts in the mind of God, is ambiguous. Thoughts can be, variously, tokenings, tokens, or contents. For reasons already argued, propositions cannot be tokenings or tokens in the mind of God: Each of these suppositions simply involves a category mistake. But, if God exists, and there are propositions, while propositions will be the contents of divine thought tokenings, propositions simply will not be ontologically dependent upon those divine thought tokenings. After all, propositions could not play the role of being the contents or objects of divine thought tokenings unless they were ontologically independent of those divine thought tokenings.

Notes

1   Davidson's argument (ibid.) seems to preclude a TA account of possible worlds as well. If God *creates* them, He causes *God exists* to be true in all possible worlds. Since this includes the actual world, God causes His own existence in the actual world.

2   Neither do I understand Gould/Davis's claim that "[B] ensures that the divine substance is a fundamental unity that is the final cause of its constituent metaphysical parts (including divine concepts and essential properties)—which ensures God's ultimacy" (62). If by "final cause" they mean a final cause in Aristotle's sense, then I do not understand how God is the final cause of His parts. If they mean by "final" something like ultimate, then they seem to countenance that God is the efficient cause of Himself—the ultimate bootstrapping trick!

Response to Critics

Paul M. Gould and Richard Brian Davis

The Bootstrapping Worry

Craig, Welty, and to a lesser extent, Yandell, press worries regarding MTA's suggested way out of the bootstrapping objection. In our lead essay, we suggest that the bootstrapping objection can be avoided by endorsing two claims:

> [A] God's essential platonic properties exist *a se* (i.e. they are neither created nor sustained by God, yet they inhere in the divine substance); and

> [B] Substances are Aristotelian.

In his reply, Craig suggests "this Aristotelian view ... yields the palm of victory to the anti-platonist" (69) for "things can be powerful or wise or brown without being so in virtue of standing in an exemplification relation to an abstract property" (69). Craig admits that if his characterization is not accurate, then he does not understand our view. We concur—his characterization is not accurate and we welcome this opportunity to further clarify our position.

Minimally, to exemplify a property is to possess or have a property. Broadly speaking, two distinct styles of metaphysical explanation—best explained in terms of the concept of "ontological structure" (van Inwagen 2011)—can be discerned for understanding property possession by ordinary concrete objects. The Relational Ontologist thinks that ordinary concrete objects have no ontological structure; that the only parts an ordinary concrete object has are its everyday mereological parts; properties are possessed/tied-to/exemplified by the substances that have them even as they stand "apart" from them. The Constituent Ontologist thinks that ordinary concrete objects have an ontological structure; that the familiar objects of our everyday experience have constituent metaphysical and physical parts; properties enter into the being of the substances that have them by being nonmereological parts of it (see also Wolterstorff 1991).

Both approaches tell us that substances exhibit whatever character they have in virtue of properties had by it. Properties *characterize* substances. How, on either approach, is property possession assayed? Consider the following sentence:

> (1) God is divine.

On the relational approach, (1) can be further analyzed as:

> (2) God exemplifies *being divine*.

God stands in a relation or tie to the property *being divine*. On the constituent approach, (1) can be further analyzed as:

(3) *Being divine* inheres in God as a constituent.

and

(4) God's individuator exemplifies *being divine*.

Sentences (3) and (4) are understood as follows: the divine substance (that is, God) has as a constituent the property *being divine*. Further, the property *being divine* is exemplified by an individuator that is also a constituent of the divine substance (perhaps a bare or thin particular).[1] The property *inheres* in the substance and is *exemplified* by some individuator (which also inheres in the substance). Thus, Craig is mistaken in his claim that [A] is "just anti-platonism with respect to God" for God (and other substances) exhibit the character they do in virtue of standing in the exemplification relation to the abstract properties they possess.

Still, our parenthetical remark in [A] tips our hat: we are inclined to think the constituent approach is the way to go here. But, we need not limit ourselves to a constituent approach in avoiding the bootstrapping objection. Rather, we could (and perhaps should) have said the following:

[A*] God's essential platonic properties exist *a se* (i.e. they are neither created nor sustained by God, yet they *are exemplified by* the divine substance)

[A*] highlights the fact that both the relational and constituent approach to property possession is open to the defender of MTA: Either God exemplifies platonic properties that exist *extra se* (on the relational approach) or that inhere within the divine substance (on the constituent approach).[2]

Further, on [B], to say that God is an Aristotelian substance is to endorse the claim that God is a final cause of all His parts. As a final cause, the divine substance explains *why* it possesses the essential properties that it does and *why* it possesses the essential properties it does as a deep *unity*. God is not the "efficient cause of Himself" (74n. 2) as Craig wonders, rather the whole—as a final cause—is logically prior to its parts and the fundamental ground of its parts—hence, God is ultimate in explanation.

Welty suggests that God's creating propositions such as (E) *God exists* simply relocates the bootstrapping worry. If propositions are divine thoughts brought about by the activity of thinking, and causing something to exist is to cause its essence to be exemplified, then in bringing about (E), God causes the property *being true* to be exemplified by (E), thereby causing His own existence. Formally stated, the argument seems to go as follows:

(5) If God causes (E), then God causes the property *being true* to be exemplified by (E).

(6) If God causes the property *being true* to be exemplified by (E), then God causes His own existence.

(7) God causes (E).

(8) Therefore, God causes His own existence.

The principle grounding (6) seems to be that "x makes true y" entails "x causes y" or
(more accurately and awkwardly, since y is a proposition) "x causes the object y is
about." Far from it. Socrates' drinking the hemlock makes it true that *Xantippe is a
widow*, but it doesn't follow that Socrates' drinking the hemlock *causes* her to become
a widow (Davidson 1999, 283). Hence, we reject (6), and thus avoid the incoherency
charge in this iteration of the bootstrapping objection. On MTA, God is the creator of
all propositions, and in the Biggest Bang (see Leftow 2012) God freely (and eternally)
thinks up all possible creatures and possible states of affairs thereby fixing all necessary
alethic truths and falsehoods. On this picture, it makes no sense to say that God
thereby brings about His own existence!

Yandell claims that the nontrivial truth of

(9) If abstracta did not exist, then God would not exist

entails that "God depends for God's existence on there being the abstracta that God
must create" (66). In our reply to his lead essay we respond to this worry in greater
detail. Here let us say the following. On MTA, the nontrivial truth of (9) is grounded in
the fact that God is the creator of all abstracta (setting aside His essential properties).
While it is true that the absence of abstracta entails God's absence, it is false that God
thereby depends for His existence on abstracta. The *existential* dependence is the other
way around given the causal asymmetry between God and abstracta. There is no otiose
dependency in view, and no divine bootstrapping on MTA.

Worries regarding divine conceptualism

There are two substantial objections to MTA that remain. Both concern the conceptualist understanding of propositions. A proposition, we say, is a truthbearer. Further,
possessing truth entails being an intentional object: An object that is *of* or *about*
something, that represents the world (or some part of it) as being *thus and so*. This
is precisely what concrete sentence inscriptions and platonic[3] abstracta cannot do—
not *in themselves* anyway.[4] Thoughts, by contrast, are indisputably and essentially
intentional. They are, says the proponent of MTA, composite wholes: specific mental
arrangements of (brutely) intentional parts—Locke's "invisible ideas."

Of course if all we have at our explanatory disposal is human mental activity, the
lifespan of a proposition will be fleeting indeed, lasting only as long as we happen to
be thinking it, and existing in just those worlds where we do so. In short, there won't
be any necessary truths (/falsehoods). The best course is to recognize a *supra*-natural
realm of divine cognitive activity. A Proposition (capital 'P') is a divine thought: an
ordered arrangement of divine ideas. Propositions are abstract in the sense of being
multiply instantiable in human minds; but they're not mind-independent abstracta *of
the platonic variety*. (Thus *contra* Craig and Yandell, there is no incoherence in saying
that God is a concrete being whose thoughts are abstract.) It doesn't follow though,
as Shalkowski fears, that our thoughts are literally identical with God's. Instantiation

doesn't entail identity. Our thoughts, as we say, are mere *approximations* and *partial graspings* of those in God's mind. Now on to the objections.

The Composition Objection. It is "not obvious" (says Yandell) and "not clear" (says Welty) that propositions have parts—namely, concepts or ideas. This may be so. But then again we don't so much as slyly suggest that our "parts proposal" has that irresistible and evident lustre Locke extolled. It's not a deliverance of introspection; it's an inference to the best explanation. That it lacks Lockean luminosity in no way counts against it.

Unfortunately, Yandell and Welty claim that the "parts proposal" isn't even a good explanation. Thus Welty comments: "This is part and parcel of *Russell's* (failed) analysis of propositions" (67). But that's not why Russell's analysis failed: because it held that propositions have parts. It failed because it invoked the entirely wrong *sort* of parts—parts that were painfully nonintentional (e.g. Quine himself), and thus impotent to account for a proposition's being about anything.

Yandell's concern lies elsewhere. We should reject the "parts proposal," he tells us, because "propositions are primary" and concepts are merely "propositional abilities that persons have." This follows if we accept this claim: "that S has the concept of *being a cow* insofar as S knows what is true if and only if there are cows" (66). Here Yandell seems to say that you have the concept *being a cow* only if you know *there are cows* is a true proposition. But surely that is incorrect. Graham Oppy, we may assume, grasps or apprehends the concept of God. But it hardly follows that he knows there is a God. He'll be the first one to tell you that! In general, to grasp the concept of being an F, you don't have to know that there are any Fs. There is no threat to the "parts proposal" here.

The Content Objection. Oppy isn't inclined to think that propositions are truth-bearers; nor are they to be identified with thoughts. Rather, on his favored view, there are *tokens* (e.g. the inscription "Quine is wise"), *propositions* (e.g. the content of "Quine is wise"), and *tokenings* (e.g. my producing the token "Quine is wise"). Oppy's claim is that only tokenings are truthbearers, since only tokenings are intentional.

There are two principal difficulties with this suggestion. First, tokenings aren't truthbearers. A tokening—whether verbal, written, or thought—is an *act* or *event*. However, as C. S. Lewis so aptly put it, "events in general are not 'about' anything and cannot be true or false" (1947, 21). The slamming of a door, for instance, isn't "about" anything. It's the sort of thing that "happens" or "occurs." But it's nothing even remotely like an intentional object that could represent a state of affairs. Thus it couldn't possibly be true or false. The same thing goes for tokenings.

Secondly, why think that thoughts and propositions are distinct? On Oppy's view, a thought tokening is the producing of a thought—a mental token. Suppose we agree. Now consider this token:

(T) The thought that *Quine is wise*.

The propositional content of (T) is presumably

(P) Quine is wise.

Oppy declares that (T) and (P) are distinct. This isn't obvious. If propositions can exist in worlds where there are no human beings, and indeed no concreta at all (as the

proponent of MTA holds), then (P) won't be a physical object. It will be something ⟵
nonphysical: an abstract platonic object, perhaps, or an immaterial thought. Now (P)
is about Quine and represents him as being wise; hence, it can't be a platonic object. QED
Like it or not, then, we must say that (P) is a thought. *Which* thought? Well, obviously, ·
the thought that *Quine is wise*. But notice that's just (T) itself. *Contra* Oppy, therefore, ·
there really is no difference between (T) and (P). At any rate, thus sayeth the modified
theistic activist.   ⌟

Notes

1   There are sophisticated defenses of bare particulars in Moreland and Pickavance
     (2003) and Sider (2006). For those who feel a little queasy, think of an individuator in
     Wolterstorff's (1991, 543) way: a particular that just is a nature.
2   For more see Gould (2011a and 2013) and Moreland (2001 and 2013).
3   The astute reader will notice that we use "platonic" in a more technical sense when   ⌐
     talking about intentionality. In one sense, as Gould makes clear in the Introduction
     (n. v), "platonism" is just the view that abstract objects necessarily exist. In this sense,
     we agree that propositions are in fact platonic. But, we deny that propositions are
     "platonic" in the sense that they exist in Plato's heaven as brutely intentional entities. ⌟
4   Welty asks why platonists can't "just infer that *there are* these intentional entities, ⌐
     and that is that" (67). The answer is that the inferences involved in indispensability ⟵
     arguments simply don't deliver "intentional entities." They give you—at best and if
     they work—only *indefinite* entities that play the role of truthbearers. Intentionality ,
     is "bestowed" after the fact. But simply to *announce* here that platonic abstracta are
     intentional is wholly gratuitous and unsupported. Not so, of course, for thoughts,
     whose intentionality is known by introspection, not indispensability.   ⌟

Theistic Conceptual Realism

Greg Welty

"Inconsistent triads" have been all the rage in analytic philosophy of religion since at least 1955.[1] Here's another one, central to the discussion in this book:

1) Abstract objects (AOs) exist.
2) If AOs exist, then they are dependent on God.
3) If AOs exist, then they are independent of God.

These present an obvious tension for anyone who affirms both God and AOs, for there seem to be extremely plausible intuitions in support of each claim. The traditional arguments for metaphysical realism about AOs support (1). The traditional theological doctrines of divine sovereignty and aseity support (2). The traditional, robust platonistic conception of AOs as necessarily existing supports (3).

Any consistent way of relating God to AOs must therefore explain which of these claims should be rejected and why. As a "theistic conceptual realist" I reject (3), though for a different reason than theistic activists. I argue that the platonistic tradition can accommodate AOs being *necessarily dependent* on God, in virtue of their being uncreated divine ideas that "play the role" of AOs with respect to all created reality.[2] I think there are good reasons for thinking that AOs cannot *causally* depend on God, and so I part ways with theistic activists in this respect. Still, I maintain that AOs are *constitutively* dependent on God, for they are constituted by the divine ideas, which inhere in the divine mind and have no existence outside of it. That these ideas (read: AOs) aren't caused by God doesn't mean that they therefore exist "in themselves," that is, "outside" of the being of God and independent of God.

Theistic conceptual realism (TCR) holds that AOs are necessarily existing, uncreated divine ideas that are distinct from God and dependent on God. Two main arguments can be provided for TCR: a philosophical argument (from AOs to God, showing that realists have good reason to be theists) and a theological argument (from God to AOs, showing that theists have good reason to be realists). Though these arguments have different trajectories, they mutually reinforce a particular relation between God and AOs. Space only permits presentation of the first.

My philosophical argument for TCR contends that AOs exist (realism), that these objects are best understood not merely as ideas (conceptualism) but as divine ideas (theism), and that this twofold conclusion not only relates God to AOs in a consistent way, but also provides materials for a successful theistic argument.

Realist arguments for propositions and possible worlds

The following realist arguments seek to remain neutral, at least to a significant degree, on the kind of entities propositions and possible worlds are (material? mental? a *sui generis* category that is neither material nor mental?). Rather, these arguments merely seek to establish that entities doing the philosophical work of propositions and PWs do genuinely exist.[3]

Propositions

Typical realist arguments for AOs posit the existence of particular kinds of abstract object on the grounds that such objects must exist in order to perform indispensable work in our best philosophical theories. Realists draw attention to various phenomena—grammatical, quantificational, counterfactual, and modal—and argue that positing the necessary existence of *propositions* provides the best explanation of these phenomena.

The *grammatical argument* for propositions takes propositions to be those things which are the objects of propositional attitudes and the referents of that-clauses, things which are intersubjectively available and mind-independent. Crucial to this argument is the assumption that the syntactic properties of verbs are a *prima facie* guide to their semantic properties. This is true whether we are considering cognitive verbs (know, see, smell, taste, feel, hear) or propositional verbs (intend, think, hope, wish, believe, judge, guess, consider). Realists contend that neither the existence of disanalogies between cognitive and propositional verbs, nor an appeal to an adverbial theory of act-content, successfully undermines this grammatical argument.

The *quantificational argument* for propositions is that (at least in certain cases) substitutional quantification is not available as a way to interpret certain obvious truths, such as "there is a speck of interstellar dust that is so small and so distant from us and any other language users there may be that no language user has any knowledge of it." Rather, we must objectually quantify over propositions and thus be committed to their existence as objects (Loux 1986, 508; 1998, 148–51). These entities have the property of being true but lack the property of being expressed in a language.

According to the *counterfactual argument* for propositions, if we take propositions to be contingently existing entities, then there seem to be counterfactual situations that cannot be coherently described, such as "if there had been no human beings, it would have been true that there are no human beings" (Plantinga 1993, 117–20). Thus, it's not merely that propositions exist (the grammatical and quantificational arguments), but that these truthbearers exist *necessarily* (the counterfactual argument).

Likewise, the *modal argument* for propositions contends that a view of propositions as only contingently existing cannot accommodate the obvious modal intuition

that there are necessary truths (Plantinga 1993, 117–20). For if "necessary" means
"could not have failed to be true," then for the contingency theorist *no* propositions are
necessary, since *ex hypothesi* each could have failed to be true, by failing to exist. But
since it is obvious that some propositions are necessary, it follows that the contingency
view is mistaken, and that propositions must necessarily exist.

When these arguments are taken together, a picture begins to emerge of propositions as necessarily existing objects possessing alethicity (capacity to be truth valued)
and doxasticity (capacity to be believed or disbelieved). These four constraints
upon any successful theory of propositions—necessity, objectivity, alethicity, and
doxasticity—will help to ultimately determine what kind of thing propositions are,
ontologically speaking.

Possible worlds

According to the *argument from ordinary language*, we are already committed to the
existence of possible worlds (PWs) by way of our prephilosophical belief in "ways
things could have been." This commitment is expressed in our ordinary language
about the world, and retaining this commitment leads to fewer difficulties than the
attempt to paraphrase it away. Both "abstractionists" (van Inwagen 1983, 80–1; 1986,
185; 1993, 82) and "concretists" (Lewis 1973, 84; 1986, 1–2) about PWs make this
argument.[4] Interestingly enough, the ordinary language argument does not prove that
PWs are either concrete or abstract (in any weighty ontological sense of those terms),
but merely that they are entities that *represent* the world, and therefore could be the
kind of entities that either obtain (correctly representing the world) or do not obtain
(incorrectly representing the world). And for all we know from *this* argument, either
concrete or abstract objects (as traditionally conceived) could play this role.

According to the *argument from explanatory utility*, commitment to PWs illumi-
nates a whole host of philosophical issues, and thus should be retained on the basis
of this explanatory utility. Again, both "abstractionists" (Plantinga 1976, 253) and
"concretists" (Lewis 1986, 3–4, and especially 5–69) about PWs make this argument,
each for their own ontological vision of PWs as either abstract or concrete. In Lewis's
words, "Why believe in a plurality of worlds?—Because the hypothesis is serviceable,
and that is a reason to think that it is true" (ibid., 3). The payoff for concretists like
Lewis is to give nonmodal, reductive analyses of various modal claims in terms of
spatiotemporal PWs as the truthmakers of modal statements. (This increases the
economy of our total ontological theory by reducing the *kinds* of things we must
accept as having existence. We need only allow concrete objects (and sets of such
objects) into our ontology.) The payoff for abstractionists like Plantinga is to posit
PWs as one element in a modally irreducible system that affords insightful analysis of
a wide range of philosophical claims.

One objection to both concretist (Lewisian) and abstractionist (Plantingean)
accounts of PWs is that on either construal PWs seem utterly *irrelevant* to the
phenomenon of modality. As William Lycan puts it in "Possible Worlds and Possibilia,"

even if one throws together a system of actual objects that *ape* the group of 'non-actual' things or worlds we need, in the sense of being structurally isomorphic to that group of things, why should we suppose that real *possibility* and other modalities in this world have anything to do with specially configured sets of items, whether sentences or propositions or matter-elements? It seems unlikely that what fundamentally makes it true that there could have been talking donkeys is that there exists a fabulously complex set of some sort. (Lycan 1998, 92)

The situation seems even worse if we take the "system of actual objects" as abstract simples, each having no internal structure at all. Why think the existence of such abstract simples is what makes modal statements true? This "relevance problem" remains even if we maintain, with the ordinary language argument, that possible worlds are representations of some sort. If "worlds are merely representations," then "the way *representations* can ground the possibility of Socrates' being a carpenter is hard to fathom" (Shalkowski 1994, 685n. 20). High on the agenda then, for *any* theory of PWs, is to give an ontological specification of PWs that somehow solves this "relevance problem."[5]

When these last two realist arguments are taken together, a picture begins to emerge of PWs as necessarily existing objects that *represent* the universe as being such-and-such, and that must be *relevant* in making it the case that the universe could be as they represent it to be. These four constraints upon any successful theory of PWs—objectivity, necessity, representation, and relevance—will help to ultimately determine what kind of thing PWs are, ontologically speaking.

Six conditions on a successful ontological account of AOs

A promising strategy for adjudicating among rival ontological conceptions of AOs is found in John Divers's discussion of "ontological applications" of "possible-world talk:"

> … the conception of an equivalence thesis as grounding an ontological identifi-cation is inevitably informed by some conception of the analysis of the concept. For example, we should expect the analysis of the concept of a proposition (e.g. a specification of the proposition-role) to exert some constraints on the kind of thing that a proposition can be. Such constraints are conditional. They are of the form: if there are things that play the proposition-role then they must be thus and so. (Divers 2002, 32)

Thus what emerges from the preceding realist arguments (granting their *prima facie* plausibility) are several conditions on a successful theory of AOs, and that theory of AOs which best satisfies these conditions is to be preferred to its rivals.

Objectivity—propositions and PWs are objects

Objectivity is a condition on propositions because it follows from the grammatical and
quantificational arguments that propositions are *objects*, entities which are intersubjectively available and mind-independent, existing independently of the subjects who
take up various attitudes towards them.

Objectivity is also a condition on PWs because it follows from the ordinary
language and the explanatory utility arguments that we must posit PWs as entities that
exist independently of us. The ordinary language argument asks us to take PWs with
this kind of ontological seriousness because (*ceteris paribus*) we are to "take seeming
existential quantifications in ordinary language at their face value" (Lewis 1973, 84).
The explanatory utility argument asks us to posit PWs as objects because without this
ontological foundation, we lack resources for explaining modality, either by means of
reducing the modal to the nonmodal (as the concretist would have it), or by means
of clarifying a network of irreducible modal relationships in terms of true counterfactuals about PWs (as the abstractionist would have it).

Necessity—propositions and PWs could not fail to exist

Necessity is a condition on propositions because it follows from the counterfactual
and modal arguments that propositions are *necessarily existent* objects, and thus
entities which cannot be ontologically identified with contingent entities such as
human sentences or thoughts.

Necessity is a condition on PWs because apart from this the realist cannot provide
a theory of modality and modal relationships that secures the claims about modality
that he wishes to make. Abstractionists for their part simply accept that necessary
existence is a defining feature of PWs (Plantinga 1976, 262; 1987, 193), and indeed
the notion that PWs could have failed to exist seems to comport rather poorly with
our modal intuitions. (Note that the necessity of modality is implicit in the characteristic axioms of the S4 and S5 systems of modal logic, systems that seem adequate
to our intuitions.) As for concretists, despite their claim to reduce the modal to
the nonmodal, it certainly *seems* that they implicitly appeal to primitive modality
whenever they characterize their PWs and their features as necessarily existing.[6]

Intentionality—propositions have intentionality and PWs represent the World

Because of the counterfactual, modal, and quantificational arguments, it follows that
propositions exhibit "alethicity," that is, the capacity to be truth valued. The need for
truthbearers in certain counterfactual situations, and in certain modal and quantificational contexts, makes this clear. In addition, because of the grammatical argument,
it follows that propositions exhibit "doxasticity," that is, the capacity to be believed
or disbelieved. The various propositional verbs featured in that argument denote the

attitude of belief (or disbelief) in the entity which is its grammatical accusative. It follows from their alethicity and doxasticity that propositions must have *intentionality* or "aboutness." For it is only if propositions make claims—that is, represent the world as being a certain way—that they can be the sorts of things that have alethicity and doxasticity.

As for PWs, they seem to have a representative capacity as well. If they are (as the ordinary language argument has it) ways *the World* (or universe) could be, then they are *about* the World, representing it as such-and-such, and thus are the kind of entities that either obtain or do not obtain. Only one PW obtains, precisely because every other PW *incorrectly* represents the World. Nevertheless, every other PW represents the World as it *could* be.[7] So in the case of propositions their intentionality explains why they have alethicity and doxasticity, while in the case of PWs their intentionality explains why they represent the universe as being such-and-such.

Relevance—PWs must be relevant to the phenomenon of modality

Relevance is a condition on PWs, this constraint emerging from the attempt to adjudicate the abstractionist/concretist debate by means of the explanatory utility argument. Why should the existence of entities spatiotemporally isolated from me, whether concrete or abstract, have any relevance in making it the case that the universe could be as these entities represent it to be? The challenge is to give an ontological specification of PWs that somehow solves this "relevance problem."

Taking stock, then, of how propositions and PWs *function* in philosophical theory, they must at the very least be necessarily existing objects that have some sort of intentionality/aboutness/representative capacity. An additional condition on PWs is that they must be relevant to the phenomenon of modality (e.g. as truthmakers for modal claims).

Plenitude—there must be enough propositions and PWs

To this list we must add two more constraints on a successful theory. First, there is "plenitude." There need to be *enough* propositions and PWs to do the job, the ontological theory guaranteeing that there are as many AOs as we think there are (Divers 2002, 33). And intuitively, there are an infinite number of propositions. As Plantinga puts it, "For each real number r, for example, there is the proposition that r is distinct from the Taj Mahal" (Plantinga 1998, 91). Or, somewhat less whimsically: "Platonists never tire of pointing out, for example, that there is a nondenumerable infinity of propositions specifying, in turn, that each irrational less than the number one is less than the number two" (Loux 1986, 499).

Likewise for PWs: At the very least, for each real number r there is the PW in which there are two atoms r millimeters apart. (Or, restricting ourselves to the natural numbers, we could say that for each natural number r there is the PW in which there are r atoms.) While no single argument can generate reference to *all* of the PWs which exist, intuitively there do seem to be an infinite number of possible "ways things could be," such that any theory of the ontological status of PWs which cannot supply enough worlds to meet this intuition is thereby a defective theory.

Simplicity—ontological kind-economy as a general constraint on metaphysical theories

A final condition emerges as a general constraint on metaphysical theories. If we are committed not only to realism about AOs but also to a principle of ontological kind-economy, then we are committed to not multiplying ontological kinds beyond necessity. Even as we should not multiply *entities* beyond necessity (say, by positing two planets when one will do), so we should not multiply *kinds* of entity beyond necessity (say, by positing mental and physical events as fundamental categories of being when physical events will do). Therefore, if propositions and PWs can be satisfactorily understood as belonging to an ontological kind we already accept, this in itself is an argument that we should so understand them. In debates over the nature of propositions and PWs, all sides appeal to this principle.

For instance, nominalist theories of propositions seek to avoid multiplying ontological kinds by identifying propositions either set-theoretically (as sets of spatiotemporal wholes spatiotemporally isolated from each other in logical space; cf. Lewis 1986, 5–69 [§§1.2–1.5]) or linguistically (as either linguistic-tokens, or the tokening of sentences in Mentalese; cf. Sellars 1963 and 1975, respectively). Conceptualist theories also seek to avoid multiplying ontological kinds, by identifying propositions with thoughts or mental states of some sort. Realist theories identify propositions with "abstract objects" that inhabit a "third realm" which is neither material (having spatiotemporal location and extension) nor mental (to which a subject has privileged access). It was partly the failure of both nominalist and conceptualist theories of propositions that led Gottlob Frege to posit abstract "senses" of declarative sentences (Frege 1919), i.e. a realist theory of propositions. But while realists do thereby multiply ontological kinds, they contend that this is not done beyond *explanatory necessity*, and the latter is a crucial but often overlooked feature of the principle of parsimony.[8]

Theistic conceptual realism is the theory of AOs that best satisfies these conditions

Conceptualism satisfies these conditions

So which ontological theory of AOs best satisfies these six conditions? It is useful to divide up the field into conceptualism, nominalism, and (platonic) realism, and assess these in turn.

According to Plantinga,

> It is the *intentional* character of propositions that is most fundamental and important. Propositions are *claims*, or *assertions*; they *attribute* or *predicate*

properties to or of objects; they *represent* reality or some part of it as having a certain character. A proposition is the sort of thing *according to which* things are or stand a certain way. (1987, 190)

But the same kinds of things are usually said about thoughts as mental entities. They have an intentional character; they variously claim, assert, attribute, predicate, and represent. Thus they are natural candidates to do the philosophical work of propositions. One aspect of propositional intentionality in particular is that its aspectual shape is very fine-grained, in almost exactly the same way that belief-contents are fine-grained. It is not merely that propositions are about objects and the properties they exemplify. It is also that propositions pick out these objects and properties in a fine-grained way. There seems to be a one-to-one correspondence between thoughts and propositions, with respect not only to directedness but also aspectual shape.[9]

A conceptualist might therefore contend that we not only can but should understand propositions as *thoughts* of some sort, for the intentionality of propositions (presupposed in their alethicity and doxasticity) is best explained as the intrinsic intentionality of thoughts. If we are already committed (as most of us are) to persons as items in our ontology, then being committed to a conceptualism about propositions enables us to be realists about these things while respecting the principle of ontological kind-economy. Simply put, realists about propositions should be conceptualists about propositions.

Unfortunately, it is clear that *human* conceptualism, while perhaps satisfying the intentionality and simplicity conditions in the manner just explained, utterly fails to satisfy the plenitude, necessity, and objectivity conditions. There aren't enough human thoughts to go around (Loux 1986, 499), human thoughts don't necessarily exist, and *whose* thoughts will serve as the intersubjectively available and mind-independent referents of propositional attitudes (referents that are also named by that-clauses)? If I have the thought that the sky is blue, and so do you, whose thought is the "real" proposition, and whose is the impostor? Any answer here looks arbitrary (Gale 1967, 500).

Something similar seems to go for understanding PWs as thoughts, a position considered by several philosophers (Rescher 1973, 179; Loux 1979, 58; Lycan 1979, 303). Like conceptualist accounts of propositions, while conceptualist accounts of PWs seem to satisfy the intentionality and simplicity conditions, they fail to satisfy the plenitude, necessity, and objectivity conditions.[10]

But construing propositions as *divine* thoughts seems to mitigate these deficiencies of human conceptualism. First, a divine mind (being omniscient) can certainly have enough thoughts for all the truths and possibilities we intuitively think there are. Second, if necessarily existent thoughts are required, they must be the thoughts of a necessarily existent mind. "It doesn't require much further thought to see whose mind this must be. A necessarily existent mind must be the mind of a *necessarily existent person*. And this, as Aquinas would say, everyone understands to be God" (Anderson and Welty 2011, 336). Third and finally, objectivity is secured by there being just *one* omniscient and necessarily existent person whose thoughts are uniquely identified as

AOs. These thoughts would have extramental existence, just as on realism. At least, they have it *relative to finite minds*. Propositions would exist independently of any human cognition, although they would not exist independently of divine cognition. Does this crucial qualification pose an insuperable barrier to the claim of objectivity? It doesn't appear to. For example, in the earlier realist arguments propositions were deemed to exist as the objects of *human* propositional attitudes, and to be the referents of that-clauses associated with the propositional verbs *humans* employ. There is no reason why divine thoughts cannot supply the requisite objectivity by being the objects and referents of these human attitudes and verbs. We humans would be taking up attitudes to propositions which exist independently of our cognitive activities. Surely this is sufficient to secure the requisite objectivity demanded by the relevant realist arguments for the existence of propositions.[11]

Likewise for PWs: If construed as divine ideas, then plenitude, necessity, and objectivity seem to be satisfied (as well as intentionality and simplicity). Regarding plenitude, divine omniscience about the range of the divine power would include enough thoughts to cover all of the possibilities that there are. As Loux puts it, we can accommodate "the difficulty presented by [humanly] unconceived possibilia by insisting that possible worlds are grounded in divine conceptual activity, for presumably God's conceptual activity is not subject to the restriction imposed on the thinking of finite intellects" (1979, 59).[12] Regarding necessity, if the divine thoughts which constitute PWs are the thoughts of a divine Person who necessarily exists, and who necessarily knows the range of His own power (which is, in turn, an immutable, essential feature of his divine nature), then there is no counterfactual situation in which any of the PWs fail to exist. (Nor is there a counterfactual situation in which the PWs are different from what they in fact are.) Regarding objectivity, given the ordinary language argument for PWs, there are indeed "ways things could have been," and these ways exist independently of any human cognitive activity. So the divine thoughts which constitute PWs exist independently of human beings and would exist even if there were no humans at all. So PWs-as-divine-thoughts have extramental existence relative to finite minds.

Nominalism fails to satisfy these conditions

Prospects seem less sanguine for the alternatives to conceptualism. Take linguistic nominalism. If propositions and PWs are linguistic tokens of some sort, then with respect to plenitude and necessity, there simply aren't enough human sentences to go around, and human sentences exist just as contingently as human thoughts. With respect to objectivity, not only are there a multiplicity of human persons, but in addition there are a multiplicity of languages. Which is the real proposition that it is raining, the English sentence "It is raining," or the French sentence "Il pleut"? Here we find the reverse of the plenitude problem. It's not that there aren't enough propositions, but that from this perspective there are far too many. (These same points seem to apply to linguistic nominalism about PWs as well.)

Set-theoretic nominalism about propositions fails with respect to alethicity, doxasticity, and plenitude. It supplies candidates for propositions that are "sets" of concrete objects, and these are not the kinds of things that can be true or false, and believed or disbelieved (Plantinga 1976, 267; 1987, 206–7). Nor are there enough of them, since all necessarily true propositions turn out to be the same proposition: the set of all PWs. Likewise for all necessarily false propositions, which turn out to be the null set. Besides failing plenitude, this result secures an additional failure to satisfy intentionality, for set-theoretic nominalism cannot capture the fine-grained nature of aspectual shape, according to which *2+2=4* and *All bachelors are unmarried* are *different* propositions.

Realism fails to satisfy these conditions

Of course, traditional platonic realism posits a sufficient plenitude of propositions as necessarily existing objects which have alethicity and doxasticity. Since the only remaining condition on a successful theory is simplicity, we are faced with a choice. As we have seen, theistic conceptual realism posits a sufficient plenitude of *thoughts* as necessarily existing objects which have alethicity and doxasticity. So are the propositions posited on traditional platonic realism a different kind of entity than thoughts, or are they just thoughts? If the former, then (traditional platonic) realism multiplies ontological kinds beyond explanatory necessity, but if the latter, then this realism isn't an alternative to TCR but merely a restatement of it.

Traditionally, platonic realism *has* been understood as positing a "third realm" of the "abstract" beyond the material and the mental, as a means of overcoming the perceived weaknesses of both nominalism and conceptualism. This realm was "distinct both from the sensible external world and from the internal world of consciousness" (Rosen 2012, §2). Insofar as this is correct, then there is at least one condition on a successful theory of propositions and PWs that realism does not satisfy vis-à-vis its alternatives: ontological kind-simplicity.

Simplicity—a further look

However things turn out with platonic realism, it might seem obvious that any *nominalism* about propositions and PWs surely satisfies the simplicity condition. Is this not one of nominalism's chief attractive features? But whether, say, linguistic nominalism satisfies simplicity deserves a bit more scrutiny. While it is true that linguistic nominalism supplies entities with alethicity and doxasticity (such as concrete human sentences), and these entities belong to an ontological kind we already accept (material particulars), their intentionality is *derived* rather than intrinsic, presupposing entities such as thinkers or speakers that confer intentionality on them. As Tim Crane puts it,

> Words and pictures gain the interpretations they do, and therefore represent what they do, because of the states of mind of those who use them. (1995, 22–3) The intentionality of the book's sentences is derived from the original intentionality of

the states of mind of the author and reader who interpret those sentences. (1998b, §3)

So while written or spoken sentences can represent, their intentionality—the fact that they do represent anything at all—is derived, since the intentionality of sentences presupposes the intentionality that inheres in the mind or minds which interpret and use those sentences. And it appears in turn that this intentionality is *intrinsic* to the thoughts or minds in question. Since at least some mental states can have intrinsic intentionality, while no nonmental states can have it, mental states can alone supply the intentionality from which all other forms of intentionality are derived.[13] Thus propositional intentionality can *ultimately* be accounted for most simply only in terms of mental states, not material objects, since the intentionality of the latter *presupposes* mental states. And this requires linguistic nominalism about propositions to be more complex, other things being equal, than conceptualism about propositions.

The same points apply, *mutatis mutandis*, to linguistic nominalism about PWs: It must posit two different kinds of entities—linguistic descriptions, and the thoughts from which their status as representations is derived—in order to provide an adequate account of what is necessary for a PW to be a PW, whereas conceptualism simply has to posit thoughts. (We might say that the intentionality of the mental is *doubly* primitive: It not only explains other aspects of thoughts (their alethicity and doxasticity), but also the intentionality of other entities besides thoughts.)

Given this reasoning, we now discover something very surprising: Our point seems generalizable to *any* alternative to conceptualism. For instance, set-theoretic nominalism is typically said to satisfy *par excellence* the principle of ontological kind-economy. After all, Lewis reduces PWs to spatiotemporal wholes (and propositions to sets of spatiotemporal wholes, or their parts). So PWs are just more things of the same kind as the actual world, and the latter is nothing more than "me and all my surroundings"—everything which is spatiotemporally related to me. These worlds and their parts have aboutness according to counterpart theory. It is as spatiotemporal particulars that they represent possibilities for us *de re* (Lewis 1986, 194).[14] But in virtue of what do these spatiotemporal particulars represent? If Searle is right about the distinction between derived and intrinsic intentionality—if the nonmental only has its representative status conferred on it by the mental—then the entities posited by set-theoretic nominalism (spatiotemporal wholes), linguistic nominalism (token human sentences), *and* realism (abstract simples) ultimately receive their intentional status as representations in virtue of the intrinsic intentionality of thoughts. The fortunes of these three positions are tied to those of conceptualism itself.

In short, advocates of these three positions—initially advertised as distinct alternatives to conceptualism—are implicitly committed to some version of conceptualism anyway, because in each case the status of PWs as representations (as with the status of propositions as intentional entities) requires the conceptual activity of thinkers. In that case conceptualism would truly be the only game in town, and its chief alternatives would be parasitic upon its adequacy, and therefore superfluous. Failing the simplicity condition is the price they pay for satisfying the intentionality condition. Perhaps one reason why neither nominalism nor (platonic) realism strike many as particularly illuminating on this matter of representation is because something fundamental has been left out: The intrinsic intentionality of thoughts, from which all other intentionality is derived. And this is not some utterly mysterious phenomenon; the aboutness of our thoughts is a reality with which we are intimately familiar, if we are familiar with anything at all.

One could even say that these alternatives to theism presuppose theism, at least if as just argued, they presuppose conceptualism, and as argued earlier, the only conceptualism adequate to the six conditions on AOs is one strengthened by theism.

The "relevance problem"

As it turns out, the above theoretical advantages of TCR are reinforced by way of a sixth and final condition on a successful theory of PWs: that of relevance. A point noted when discussing the explanatory utility argument for PWs was this "relevance problem:" Why should the existence of entities spatiotemporally isolated from me, whether concrete or abstract, have any relevance in making it the case that the universe could be as these entities represent it to be?

To put it crudely, if I draw a stick figure of Socrates pounding nails into wood, I might have *represented* the possibility that Socrates was a carpenter, but it makes little sense to think that a picture on a piece of paper is a truthmaker for certain modal statements about Socrates, such that Socrates *couldn't* have been a carpenter if that picture didn't exist. Likewise if this representation of Socrates takes the form of a counterpart spatiotemporally isolated from Socrates, or a linguistic description, or my (or anyone else's) thought of Socrates, or an abstract simple of some sort. This problem is even more pressing if all of the theories of PWs reduce to or require in some sense the truth of conceptualism, such that the status of PWs as representations must be ultimately derived from the intentionality of thinkers. Why should anyone's *thoughts* about Socrates serve as a real constraint on possibilities for Socrates? Why does Socrates have to answer to *me* (or any other thinker), modally speaking?

But while possibilities for creatures exist independently of human cognitive activity, we may have good reason for thinking they do not exist independently of *divine* cognitive activity. And that is because if God exists, then nothing *can* exist independently of His intentional activity or permission. I want to suggest that TCR, in contrast to typical conceptualist, nominalist, and realist theories of PWs, provides a broader context in which the nature of PWs are relevant to various modal claims. If this is the case, then the relevance condition does have some force in adjudicating among these theories of PWs.

Consider God as an essentially omniscient and omnipotent being who exists *a se* and is an intelligent creator if a creator at all. He not only creates everything that exists distinct from Him, but creates rationally, according to knowledge, realizing His purposes by executing the intentions of His own will.[15] Thus, God's omniscience is comprised by his self-knowledge, since it cannot depend on anything distinct from God. And God's self-knowledge is comprised, in part, by His knowledge of the range of His own power (cf. Aquinas, *Summa Theologiae* Ia, q. 14, a. 5 *respondeo*, a. 6 *respondeo*). But any possible act of divine creation is constrained by the range of the divine power. Therefore, because any act of divine creation will be *intelligent* creation, any act of divine creation will be constrained by the content of these divine ideas. The rational act of divine creation is always *according to knowledge*, in particular, according to God's knowledge of the range of His own power, such that (a range of) the divine ideas constitute all possible blueprints for any act of creation. There is a certain class of divine ideas which represent to God the entire range of ways He could have created.

Because, necessarily, any World which exists is intelligently created via the realization of a divine idea, these divine ideas sustain a unique relationship to any World which in fact exists: The possible features of any World are constrained (quite literally) by the content of the divine ideas. Modal facts about the World—what can possibly be the case in any World you please—are grounded in something which obtains independently of the World: the divine self-knowledge. God's uncreated knowledge of His own power constitutes the "structure which exists in and delimits every possible world ... a structure which would have to be instantiated by any contingent created universe" (Morris and Menzel 1986, 162). It makes sense, then, that whatever is possible for the creature depends upon whatever is possible for the creator. More perspicuously, whether or not Socrates could have been a carpenter depends on (i) whether that possibility falls within the range of the divine power *and* (ii) whether that possibility is represented to God by means of His knowledge of His own power. If, necessarily, any act of divine creation is an intentional act, the realization of a rational purpose, then clause (ii) is crucial.[16]

The preceding picture is a sketch at best, but already we can see the outlines of an answer to the relevance problem. Since any created World must necessarily be the realization of a divine idea which represents to God the range of His own power, the specific content of those ideas constrain possibilities for the World. But this means that a range of the divine ideas not only constitute PWs, but these ideas are *relevant* in making it the case that the possibilities for any World are what they in fact are. If indeed everything in the World (besides God) exhibits a relation of creaturely dependence upon the God who purposefully creates according to His knowledge of what He can create, then it is not hard to fathom how the conceptual life of such a being is modally relevant for that creation. On TCR, worlds are not merely representations. They are representations which function in the context of a divine life which intelligently creates according to self-knowledge of the divine power. It is this creator/creature relation that is missing in the typical nominalist, conceptualist, and realist theories of PWs. It is a relation that sheds light on how the relevance condition could be satisfied, and it emerges in the context of the only theory of PWs that comes close to satisfying the *other* five conditions on a successful theory of PWs as well. Surely this is a significant result.

Conclusion—a theistic argument?

So realism about AOs (objectivity) leads us to conceptualism about AOs (intentionality, simplicity), which in turn leads us to theism about AOs (necessity, plenitude, relevance). One might say that TCR combines theistic strengths with a conceptualist core. Ontologically disambiguating the conclusion of the realist arguments in a conceptualist direction, and then specifying that conceptualism in terms of theism, provides the best way to satisfy the relevant conditions on a successful theory of propositions and PWs. My claim is not that no other theory of AOs satisfies any of these conditions, but rather that only TCR satisfies *all* of them.

In "Divine Necessity," Robert Adams suggests that "Augustinian theism" could provide "an attractive explanation ... [of] the ontological status of the objects of logic and mathematics," by appealing to the plausibility of the following two views:

1) "Possibilities and necessary truths are discovered, not made, by our thought. They would still be there if none of us humans ever thought of them."

2) "Possibilities and necessary truths cannot be there except insofar as they, or the ideas involved in them, are thought by some mind."

Note that thesis (1), at least with respect to possibilities and truthbearers, was argued by means of various realist arguments. And thesis (2), also with respect to possibilities and truthbearers, was argued by way of the six conditions on these entities which emerged from those same realist arguments. Now theses (1) and (2) appear contrary to each other. Plantinga would say that (1) is *realism* and (2) is *creative anti-realism*.[17] But Adams claims that

they can both be held together if we suppose that there is a nonhuman mind that eternally and necessarily exists and thinks all the possibilities and necessary truths. Such is the mind of God, according to Augustinian theism. (1983, 218)

It certainly does look as if we have materials for a theistic argument. To the extent, then, that we have reason to be realists and conceptualists about propositions and PWs, to that extent we have reason to be theists.

Notes

1   Mackie (1955, 200). Of course, the trilemma inspiration here is David Hume, *Dialogues Concerning Natural Religion*, Part X (1779), and perhaps Epicurus (3rd–4th century B.C.).

2   Some might wonder how an abstract object can be a concrete object, such as mental events like divine ideas or thoughts. However, I am prepared to argue (with David Lewis 1986, 171) that the abstract/concrete distinction is in disarray, ontologically speaking. As will be seen shortly, in this essay I operate with a purely functionalist account of "abstract object" that is compatible with a wide variety of ontological specifications. Indeed, I believe I can give my main argument without

ever referencing the term "abstract object." I simply need to refer to objects that are traditionally seen as falling under that category, such as "proposition" and "possible world." I am a realist about these objects, and a conceptualist, and a theist. So if divine ideas are "concrete objects," then my position is that abstract objects functionally speaking are concrete objects ontologically speaking.

3 Space does not permit anything more than these argument *sketches* for two kinds of abstract object. Several of these arguments are developed further in Anderson and Welty (2011), and especially in Welty (2006, chs. 2–3). Neither does space permit addressing a third category of "abstract object": properties. I say some pertinent things about the latter in relation to theistic conceptual realism in Welty (2004).

4 For the terminology of "abstractionist" and "concretist" as applied to the debate over possible worlds, see van Inwagen (1986). In short, "abstractionists" think that possible worlds are non-spatiotemporal and causally inert, whereas "concretists" think that possible worlds are spatiotemporal entities spatiotemporally isolated from us, the same in kind as the universe with which we are spatiotemporally related.

5 Plantinga raises the "relevance problem" for concretist conceptions of PWs, claiming that Lewis "flouts the obvious pretheoretical truth that what is a possibility for me does not depend in this way upon the existence and character of other concrete objects" (Plantinga 1987, 209; cf. Plantinga 1973). But as we have seen from Lycan, this same objection can be raised against abstractionist conceptions of PWs as well.

6 In this regard, cf. Lewis's comments on trans-world causation (Lewis 1986, 80), epistemology (ibid., 111), and ethics (ibid., 125–6, 128). In addition, if the counterfactual and modal arguments are correct that propositions necessarily exist, then if (as Lewis has it) propositions are just sets of PWs, then these worlds must necessarily exist as well.

7 "Like propositions, possible worlds have that intentional property: a possible world is such that things are thus and so *according to* it; a possible world *represents* things as being a certain way" (Plantinga 1987, 212).

8 On PWs, Lewis considers the ontological kind-simplicity of his vision of PWs as spatiotemporal wholes as a theoretical advantage, for in it "we find the wherewithal to reduce the diversity of notions we must accept as primitive" (Lewis 1986, 4).

9 On directedness and aspectual shape as the "two main elements of the concept of intentionality as discussed by recent philosophers," see Crane (1998a, 243; 1998b, §2; and 2001, 13–21).

10 On the plenitude condition, cf. Lycan (1979, 304); Loux (1979, 58); Rescher (1973, 180–1); and Divers (2002, 340n. 30).

11 In his article on "Propositions," George Bealer notes that "conceptualist reductions" of propositions to thoughts—in which "the entities designated by 'that'—clauses are identified with mental entities (mind-dependent conceptual entities)"—are all bound to fail as theories of propositions. However, continues Bealer, "If you knew that, necessarily, God exists and has all the requisite concepts, you might be able to avoid this conclusion" (1998b, 136, 145n. 21). This is precisely the move which is being advocated here.

12 So as not to mislead, it should be pointed out that immediately following this citation Loux raises some difficulties with this move, though I do not regard them as insuperable.

13 For the distinction between intrinsic and derived intentionality, and an argument for the point made in the text, see Searle (1983, 27–9).

14 On Lewis's view, Socrates could have been a carpenter if Socrates has a flesh-and-blood counterpart in another world who is a carpenter. That living, breathing counterpart-who-pounds-nails represents the actual Socrates as being a certain way.

15 A conception of God as "pure limitless intentional power" (Swinburne 1994, 150–8) comes close to capturing what I am saying here.

16 I am using "creation" in a broad sense to include God's permission, since God's permission is always a *willing* permission. It is not that God necessarily intends all that He permits, but that He *intends to permit* anything He permits, and apart from that intention it would not be permitted. (No one forces or coerces God to permit anything. The existential buck, in that respect, stops with Him.)

17 Cf. Plantinga (1982, 70).

Response to Greg Welty

Keith Yandell

Professor Welty is a theistic conceptual realist. There is much about this view that is attractive. If platonism concerning propositions is false, then I think that (slightly revised) it is true. The view that abstract objects are ideas necessarily had by a necessarily existing God, it seems to me, can't be quite right. Without going into the basis of the abstract/concrete distinction, the (correct) consensus is that God is concrete. A concrete being's ideas are concrete—they are mental states of a concrete being. Mental states are concrete. But then God's ideas or mental states are not abstract, and hence are not abstract objects. TCR, a perfectly fine view for one to take, cannot really mean that there are abstract objects, and that they are ideas in the mind of God. Presumably what it means is that, *in place of* abstract objects, there are ideas necessarily had by a necessarily existing God—that these ideas ground necessary truths, constrain the logical structure of possible worlds (and hence of the possible world that is actual), and so on. What is called an abstract idea is abstract in virtue of its content, not in virtue of its not being concrete. On this view, what exists in place of abstract objects can be causally efficacious. If one changes his mind about abstract objects being noncausal, he has changed his mind about what we should be talking about instead of abstract objects rather than changing his mind about what abstract objects are *per se*. That divine ideas play the role for theistic conceptualists that abstract ideas play for the platonist does not entail that divine ideas are abstract objects, any more than that tractors play the role for farmers that horse-drawn plows play entails that tractors are horse-drawn plows.

While I agree that Professor Welty's (1)–(3) is an inconsistent triad, it seems to me we should take seriously the view that (1) and (3) are true—that there are abstract objects independent of God—since we do not know that (G1) *God has logically necessary existence, and the proposition "God exists" is a necessary truth* rather than merely (G2) *God exists, cannot be caused to exist, and cannot be caused not to exist* that is true. I think it is consensus among Christian (and of course non-Christian) philosophers that the ontological argument does not provide us with a proof that (the Anselmian) God exists, at least for the reason that we do not know that it is (G1) rather than (G2) that is true (and the other necessarily false). For reasons given in my original essay, and those given in Professor Shalkowski's, I do not think the view that abstracta were not created by God is anti-Christian.

Professor Welty seems to agree that abstract objects cannot be created, and holds that ideas necessarily had by a necessarily existing God are uncreated, proposing instead that abstract objects are constituted by ideas that God has. His idea is that, as such, they are neither created by, nor independent of, God. If there are, strictly speaking, no abstract objects this seems to be the right view to have.

We are promised an argument that shows that if abstracta exists, then so does God. I do not see how all of this argument can be neutral as to whether Weltian abstract objects are material without being neutral concerning God's being material, since the argument is intended to show that God exists. Having an argument that is neutral concerning whether propositions are material, mental, or some third sort of thing surely must abandon neutrality around the premise that says "since there are things that play the role a platonist ascribes to abstracta, they are ideas in the divine mind." Still, it is worth doing, as Professor Welty does, to remain argumentatively neutral on this point as long as one can.

The essay offers a really excellent survey of types of argument for abstract objects and an interesting critique of accounts that endeavor to explain away the force of these arguments by ascribing the features or roles of abstracta to concrete things. The range covered and the clarity offered is impressive. A clear idea is given of the sources of realism about abstract objects. Realists discouraged by the anti-realist arguments and considerations presented in our other essays can have their courage strengthened by the arguments on realism's behalf. The combination of contention for, and critique of, realism concerning abstract objects is a good introduction to relevant issues and proposals. The references in the bibliographies provide a good reference base for further thought.

The crucial turn in the argument from abstracta to theism is found in the claims that (1) the intentionality of thoughts with propositional content is inherent, that (2) the intentionality of anything that is not a thought is derivative, and (3) a thought exists only if someone has it. These claims unpack at least much of the resistance to the idea that propositions can exist mind-independently and it is easy to feel their pull. The argument depends, or at least is greatly aided by, there being discernibly, irreducibly necessary truths. If there are propositions that are eternally or everlastingly true in virtue of their being necessarily true, then there is no time at which they are false. If these propositions represent some way the world is, they are intentional in the sense of being about something other than themselves. So they are truths no matter which possible world is actual. Thus they are true in possible worlds uninhabited by human (or other creaturely) minds, and thus independently of any such mind. Suppose a theist accepts the view that (G3) *If a concrete item other than God exists in a world, then God created that item.* This view places God "in" all possible worlds that contain concrete items. If there is another world besides these, it contains only abstract items—say, only propositions. Is that world possible? Theistic conceptualists answer negatively.

Waiving (G3), we have a dispute among theist conceptualists versus theistic and nontheistic platonists. Propositions represent things as being a certain way. Necessarily true propositions represent a way in which things must be. Can they do this without someone intending that they do—must their intentionality be derivative? That seems to be the issue at this point of intersection between TCR and (theistic and nontheistic) platonism regarding propositions, and thus the next topic in the argument.

Paul M. Gould and Richard Brian Davis

We find much to agree with in Greg Welty's defense of theistic conceptual realism (TCR). At least *some* abstract objects, propositions and possible worlds, exist and asymmetrically depend on God. As essentially intentional entities, propositions are best thought of as divine thoughts/ideas. As essentially representational entities, possible worlds are best thought of as divine thoughts/ideas. We think that considerations related to propositions and possible worlds do indeed lead us to conceptualism (again, with respect to *those* abstract objects, and perhaps more) and we advanced similar arguments for a kind of limited conceptualism in our own lead essay. Still, even setting aside the fact, as we argued in our lead essay, that it would be unwise to identify all abstracta with constituents of the divine mind, there are significant differences between our modified theistic activism (MTA) and Welty's TCR, differences that provide us with further opportunity to demonstrate the theoretical advantages of MTA (and correspondingly, the weaknesses of TCR).

Uncreated abstract objects?

According to Welty, abstract objects exist as uncreated objects that are constitutively dependent on God. Why think abstract objects (i.e. divine thoughts) are uncreated? The answer has to do with the rationality of creation. Welty states:

> The rational act of divine creation is always *according to knowledge*, in particular, according to God's knowledge of the range of His own power, such that (a range of) the divine ideas constitute all possible blueprints for any act of creation. (93)

Hence, "God's uncreated knowledge of His own power constitutes the 'structure which exists in and delimits every possible world'" (93). We say Welty's TCR begs the question against MTA. As Brian Leftow points out:

> Omnipotence need not have a specific range of effects—what *is* in fact possible— written into itself … . [It is true that] every power has a range of effects it can bring about. But a power's very nature need not determine that range. In fact, it usually does not. (2012, 148)

For example, Michael Jordan has by nature the power to jump, but this power's nature does not determine on its own how high he can jump. Other factors (gravity, the physical conditions in which he jumps, what he ate for breakfast, etc.) are relevant to specifying the range of his power. Granted, in God's case there is no external environment not of His own making, but the conceptual point about powers and ranges stands (ibid., 148–9). It could be up to God to determine the range of omnipotence by freely thinking up what creature-concepts are producible.[1]

We offer three reasons for thinking divine thoughts (i.e. abstract objects) are created. First, the relation between a thought and a thinker is most naturally understood as a *productive* relation: the thinker produces his thoughts. Thus, it is natural to think abstracta are created (Plantinga 2011b, 291). Second, TCR conflicts with God's ultimacy: Since the truthmaker for modal truths, say "water=H_2O" is God's nature, then God's existence depends on facts about water since God exists iff He has His nature. Theories, such as MTA that do not commit us to such dependencies are *ceteris paribus* preferable.[2] Finally, MTA, and not TCR, allows for genuine spontaneity in God's creation of the universe. The idea is that true creation involves creating the plan as well as the end product, and on TCR, the set of prior plans from which God chooses is a brute given independent of God's creative activity. But, if God produces His thoughts, God can be understood as the creator of the plan as well as the end product of creation.

Abstract objects vs. concrete objects

Welty thinks abstract objects exist. But, given his functional account of "abstract object" (94–5n. 2), and his willingness to allow the possibility that "abstract objects" (functional term) can be "concrete objects" ontologically speaking, we think it better to say that Welty is a realist about "whatever plays the role of abstract objects" but he is not a realist regarding abstract objects. Even if the abstract/concrete distinction is in disarray, even if there is no common agreement among philosophers as to the intrinsic nature of abstract objects, we can say *something* ontological about the concept "abstract object," even if only negatively: namely, for any X, if X is abstract, X is not concrete.[3] Thus, "abstract object" is not a *purely* functional concept, we can (again, at least negatively) characterize it ontologically as nonconcrete. For Welty, divine thoughts are not abstract; they are concrete. Therefore, we submit, Welty is a nominalist. By way of contrast, we think being a universal is a *sufficient* condition on being abstract (ontologically speaking),[4] hence it is best to think of divine thoughts (i.e. propositions) and divine ideas (i.e. concepts) as abstract objects.[5]

William Lane Craig

Gregory Welty's contribution is a vigorous defense of divine conceptualism. He therefore risks misleading his readers in affirming that *abstract objects* exist as ideas in the mind of God. For as a form of concrete realism (see Fig. 1 on p. 40), divine conceptualism denies that abstract objects exist. Welty should say, rather, that mathematical objects, for example, are ideas in the mind of God. Only in a note do we learn that Welty is speaking merely "functionally" when he affirms that abstract objects are divine ideas. Properly speaking, there are, according to his view, only concrete objects, some of which are mental, rather than physical, in nature. Like the anti-realist, he therefore denies (1), not (3), of Gould's Inconsistent Triad.

I should therefore be delighted if the divine conceptualist succeeds in formulating a tenable alternative to platonism. The anti-realist also affirms that God has ideas of mathematical objects, propositions, and possible worlds, just as we do; but he does not take divine conceptions to be identical with those objects. Since my claim is merely that anti-realism also affords a tenable alternative to platonism, I need respond only to Welty's critique of anti-realism. Let us consider, then, Welty's arguments for the reality of propositions and possible worlds.

Most of Welty's arguments for propositions and possible worlds are instances of the Indispensability Argument which I have rejected in my lead essay. I therefore ask the reader to consult that essay, if he has not already done so, before continuing, since limitations of space require that my responses below be even sketchier than Welty's admittedly sketchy arguments.

Consider, first, Welty's arguments for the reality of propositions.

The *grammatical argument* is an argument from singular terms referring to propositions. The argument assumes (i) that successfully referring singular terms are ontologically committing and (ii) that that-clauses are singular terms. I have already provided in my lead essay a theory of reference that rejects (i). Now let me explain why I am dubious about (ii) as well. As A. N. Prior observed, when we say, for example, that John fears that he will fail the examination, we do not mean to say that John fears a proposition! This fact strongly suggests that that-clauses are not singular terms having propositions as their referents. Rather when we say, "_____ believes that _____," this expression is, as Prior nicely put it, a predicate at one end and a sentential connective at the other (1971, 16–30).

The *quantificational argument* assumes that objectual quantification is ontologically committing, which I have already rejected in my lead essay.

As for the *counterfactual argument*, the anti-realist position is not that counterfactual propositions exist contingently but that they do not exist at all. A deflationary view of truth according to which the truth-predicate "is true" is just a device of semantic ascent (see my response to Gould/Davis and Shalkowski's lead essay) is free of ontological commitments to propositions. Thus, rather than talk about truth we can descend semantically and truly affirm, for example, that, necessarily, if God had not created the world, human beings would not exist.

As for the *modal argument*, again the anti-realist position is not that propositions exist contingently but that they do not exist at all. The modal argument collapses into the quantificational argument, since it assumes that "Some propositions are necessary" is ontologically committing. If we stipulate that we are speaking in a metaphysically heavy sense, then the anti-realist's denial that there are (necessary) propositions is no obstacle to his truly affirming, for example, that God is necessarily good or that, necessarily, 2+2=4.

Welty's arguments for the reality of possible worlds are even less compelling. Possible worlds are naturally taken to be merely a heuristic device adopted for the purpose of clarifying modal discourse.

The *argument from ordinary discourse* involves the outrageously implausible claim that ordinary language commits us ontologically to such bizarre objects as "ways the world might have been." Even Quine would not have countenanced the application of his criterion of ontological commitment to ordinary language in view of the fantastic objects to which such application would commit us. Note that there is no need to resort to paraphrase to eliminate expressions like "There is a quicker way to Berkeley from Stanford than going through San Jose" if such expressions are not taken to be ontologically committing to ways.

The *argument from explanatory utility* is unpersuasive precisely because possible worlds are plausibly taken to be useful fictions adopted because of their utility in illuminating modal discourse. They are akin to ideal gases, frictionless planes, points at infinity, and other useful fictions employed in scientific theories. Incredibly, Welty seems to think that possible worlds are what make modal discourse true. This seems clearly wrongheaded, since possible worlds semantics presupposes a primitive notion of modality in affirming, for example, that a maximal state of affairs (or world) includes only states of affairs which are compossible. This obviously cannot be explicated in terms of truth in a possible world without vicious circularity. Thus, Alvin Plantinga writes,

> we can't sensibly *explain* necessity as *truth in all possible worlds*; nor can we say that *p*'s being true in all possible worlds in [*sic*] what *makes p* necessary. It may still be extremely useful to note the equivalence of *p is necessary* and *p is true in all possible worlds*: it is useful in the way diagrams and definitions are in mathematics; it enables us to see connections, entertain propositions and resolve questions that could otherwise be seen, entertained and resolved only with the greatest difficulty if at all. (1985, 378)

It is striking how Welty's *prima facie* diverse arguments are actually almost all incarnations of the old Quine-Putnam Indispensability Argument. Since that argument is eminently resistible, the theist has no good reason to become a realist concerning putative abstract objects and, hence, no good reason to become a conceptualist.

Scott A. Shalkowski

Greg Welty provides us with an efficient tour of the primary reasons given for two of the main positions regarding propositions: platonism and conceptualism. Perhaps the most important issue he brings to the fore is one of philosophical method. He is well within the current mainstream of metaphysics to think that "payoff" is an important consideration in constructing a philosophical theory. I demur. At the very least, this method deserves somewhat more scrutiny.

I gather that all contributors to, and most consumers of, this volume think that the discourse we use to frame the positions regarding God and abstract objects should be interpreted realistically. Even if there is no consensus regarding what realistic interpretations are, we can agree that they are something like: taking assertions at face value or taking claims to be true. If this is our business, then we should hesitate to propose a case for our views in terms of "payoff."

Talk of payoff, theoretical virtues, the value of ontological economy, etc., serve as a kind of intellectual duck-rabbit. We are prone to see different things, depending on what we need at any given moment in philosophical discussion. If we want to know whether your theory has more of something than does mine, we see in this talk features that apply to your *theory* and to mine. These are features of representations of the world, of *claims about* how things are. These features of the representations are those we can discern and compare independently of knowing whether the theories compared are true or not. Indeed, this is as it must be, if discerning and comparing the virtues of various theories is to provide any grounds for inferring the relative likelihood of each being true. This is the duck.

In the same way, though, that Welty is rightly puzzled about how ordinary representations could constitute their possibilities, we should be puzzled about how the characteristics of a theory could be evidence for its truth. Clearly some characteristics do not count in favor of it truth, so why these? In many cases, we can quite easily determine that one theory is more economical along various parameters: fewer individuals, fewer kinds, fewer causal or explanatory relations. Were we already in possession of the knowledge that reality is economical along any of these lines, we could justifiably conclude that your theory is more likely to be true than is mine, because yours says (perhaps indirectly) that reality is more economical along the relevant line(s). Absent this prior information, appeals to payoff, economy, simplicity, and the like have force only if question-begging. Forgetting that we are trying to *establish* whether reality is economical leads us to think it legitimate to draw metaphysical conclusions from theoretical characteristics, i.e. it leads us to think that we also see the rabbit that interests us. I suggest that we recognize the deceptive duck-rabbit character of this kind of argument and reject it.

Having said that, for those using this strategy, Welty is right to press it further than most. If the business is to construct a theory according to which more is done with less, then finding the source of objectivity, intentionality, simplicity, necessity, plenitude, and relevance for propositions in the mind of God has no less to recommend it than do similar theories, such as Lewis's Genuine Modal Realism, constructed with the same ends in mind. So far as I can see, the rejection of Welty's TCR tends to be based on a prior rejection of his theistic underpinnings rather than on finding any weakness with his strategy. Many who think the "incredulous stare" was ultimately an unserious response to Lewis persist in using nothing more at the prospects of Welty's argument. For many, his is an effective *tu quoque* that deserves attention.

The primary arguments Welty finds persuasive, I do not. Take that-clauses. They signal "things which are intersubjectively available and mind-independent" (82) without signaling the existence of abstracta. In the usual case, we are concerned to signal that we speak about extra-linguistic reality and we signal that directly by that-clauses. I utter, "I believe that Leo roars." Using our object language, I do indeed speak of what is intersubjectively available and mind-independent. I have seen Leo roar and so can you. I do not ascend into the metalanguage and say "I believe that 'Leo roars' is true" because I want to speak directly and efficiently about Leo and not about a sentence. Treating that-clauses as signaling propositions treats me as (quite ignorantly and in spite of myself) really speaking directly and efficiently about something other than Leo. Bringing propositions into our theoretical picture requires that we silently and obliquely advert to another object whose content is that Leo roars and that it is my right relationship to it and its right relationship to Leo and/or his penchant for roaring that makes my utterance true and it is by getting you to look at/grasp that middle object that you grasp the content of my utterance.

⌐ We are offered a false dilemma in the quantificational argument. Some constructions using "there is/are" can easily be interpreted in ways carrying no ontological commitments. The expressions are ambiguous. Consider: "There are some things that do not exist." This concerns what does not exist and not what does. To treat all uses of language that can serve quantificational functions as if they always/must do so is to ∟ misrepresent some of their crucial uses.

In contrast, the modal argument pays too little attention to linguistic form. Standard uses of "necessarily" permit one to express things about Socrates, not about some bearer of truth. We express how *things* must *be*, not what must be *true*. Claiming that "Necessarily, Socrates is human" entails "Necessarily, 'Socrates is human' is true," either begs the question between nominalists and platonists or else it conflates two quite different claims.

⌐ Similar concerns arise for possible worlds. Those treating modality as primitive do not treat "ways the world might have been" as philosophically serious. Making ontological commitments on its basis ignores the force of the modalist option. Interpreting modal claims realistically is to treat the *modal* claims realistically, not the ∟ claims about representations, whether the representations are concrete or abstract.

Graham Oppy

Welty argues that propositions and possible worlds are thoughts in the mind of God. His case has three main parts. First, he argues for the existence and necessity of propositions and possible worlds. Second, he argues for six "conditions" on successful theories of propositions and possible worlds: objectivity, necessity, intentionality, relevance, plenitude, and simplicity. Third, he argues that only the view that propositions and possible worlds are thoughts in the mind of God satisfies all six conditions.

Much of what I would say in criticism of Welty's views I have already said in criticism of the views of Gould and Davis (and in my initial discussion of Plantinga). I shall try not to repeat that criticism here.

Welty does not spell out his "grammatical" and "quantificational" arguments for the existence of propositions. I do not see how appeal to merely linguistic considerations could favor realism over fictionalism; I am skeptical that there could be a successful filling out of these arguments. I say the same about Welty's "argument from ordinary language" for the existence of possible worlds. Moreover, I insist that his "argument from explanatory utility" for possible worlds is incomplete: Whatever explanatory utility may accrue to the postulation of possible worlds must be balanced against other theoretical costs, and all competing comprehensive metaphysical theories should be weighed. For all that Welty says, it may be that the best comprehensive metaphysical theories are fictionalist about possible worlds (and propositions).

Welty says that possible worlds are "entities that represent the world" and "objects that represent the universe as being such-and-such." These claims don't sound right to me. By Welty's own lights, the second can't be right unless God is part of the universe—but surely Welty thinks that God is the creator of the universe, and hence no part of it. And the first seems to entail that the actual world is merely a representation of the actual world—an unacceptable, because incoherent, consequence. If there are possible worlds, it seems very implausible to suppose that they are merely "representations."

Welty claims that there is no reason why divine thoughts cannot supply contents for human thoughts: we are able to have the thoughts we do because God already has those thoughts. I think that many theists will not be happy with this. On the one hand, it seems to undermine notions of qualitative difference between us and God. On the other hand, it threatens to lead to the attribution to God of inappropriate thoughts: bawdy thoughts, banal thoughts, malicious thoughts, silly thoughts, and so forth.

Suppose that we agree with Welty that propositions and possible worlds are divine thoughts. In order for propositions and possible worlds to be necessary, it must then be that God could not have had different thoughts. But why not? If there is no independent reality to which divine thoughts must conform, why is it the case that God could not have had different thoughts (providing for different propositions and possible worlds)? Moreover, what are we to make of modal claims about God Himself: Does God's necessary omnipotence substantively depend upon His thinking that He is necessarily omnipotent? At the very least, it seems that Welty owes us an answer to these kinds of questions. For an example of one kind of response that might be essayed, interested readers could consult Leftow (2012). By Leftow's lights, Welty is defending a "deity theory:" a theory on which modal truth about all apart from God is written into God's nature. Leftow aims to provide a kind of "conceptualist" theory on which God "makes up" modal truth about everything other than Himself.

Welty says: "Since any created World must necessarily be the realization of a divine idea which represents to God the range of His own power, the specific content of those ideas constrain possibilities for the World" (93). Following Leftow, we might say: If divine ideas are representations of God's creative powers, why not eliminate divine ideas from our ontology in favor of divine creative powers. Why suppose that, in addition to God's power to make cats, there is also a divine conception of cats? God's powers to make different kinds of things can provide all of the ontology that is required for modal truths about those kinds of things. But then consider a version of naturalism which insists that all powers of production of kinds of things belong to the initial natural entity (call it, if you like, "the initial singularity"). If you suppose that the initial natural state and the natural laws are necessary, then you arrive at a version of naturalism that is ontologically leaner than the corresponding (Leftownian) version of theism, which is, in turn, ontologically leaner than Welty's version of theism. So, it seems—despite Welty's explicit arguments to the contrary—that there is no successful theistic argument in the offing. (Of course, theists do not agree that the initial natural state and the natural laws are necessary. But naturalists do not agree that God is necessary either. Outside the view that there is an omnipotent and omniscient creator of the natural world, there is no intuitive support for the claim that the initial nature state and the natural laws are not necessary—or, at any rate, so it seems to me.)

Notes

1   Leftow further argues that any so-called deity theory (such as Welty's) does not
    provide enough resources to yield the full panoply of creaturely kind-concepts in
    which to ground modal truths not about God. See Leftow (2012, 135–74).

2   For an extended discussion of this concern against deity theories, see Leftow (2012,
    209–47).

3   See also Plantinga (1987, 205–13), where he makes a similar point against David
    Lewis. Lewis might be a "realist" in that *something* plays the role of propositions and
    possible worlds, but he isn't a realist about abstracta.

4   We think being a universal, being nonspatial, being nonessentially spatiotemporal are
    sufficient conditions for some object X to be abstract. We do not provide a *definition*
    of abstract objects in terms of their necessary and sufficient conditions.

5   Another worry: Welty uses the terms "divine thought" and "divine idea"
    interchangeably, whereas we do not. A potential problem for Welty then is this.
    Does God have singular concepts of possible creatures before creation? If so, how
    does Welty account for these concepts, ontologically speaking? Further, given the
    uncreatedness of divine thoughts/ideas, it would seem that the range of God's power
    is sufficient to specify only general *types* of individuals, not individuals. Either way,
    further clarification and defense is needed.

Response to Critics

Greg Welty

Keith Yandell

Yandell doesn't think that God's ideas can be abstract objects (AOs), since God and His ideas are concrete. However, as I pointed out in Note 2 of my lead essay, I agree with David Lewis that the abstract/concrete distinction is in disarray, ontologically speaking. There is no consensus on how to *metaphysically* cash out "AO" and this is evidenced by the very contributors to this volume! Since neither Craig, Gould/Davis, Oppy, nor Yandell (not to mention Lewis and Plantinga) agree on whether "AO" precludes mentality, being caused, or having causal efficacy, then I know not how to proceed ... except according to a purely *functionalist* account of "AO" that is compatible with a wide variety of ontological specifications.

I also pointed out in Note 2 that my argument need not refer to "AO" at all, but simply to objects that are traditionally seen as falling under that category, such as "proposition" and "possible world." I am a realist about these objects, and a conceptualist, and a theist.

I agree that "we should take seriously the view that (1) and (3) are true" (97) in the inconsistent triad. But in the end it is my acceptance of the sovereignty-aseity intuition about God, and therefore my acceptance of (2), that ultimately leads me to reject (3). My conviction here has little to do with a sound ontological argument for God being on offer.

My argument from abstracta to God is surely neutral in its initial stages as to whether AOs are material. But given the conditions on AOs that emerge from the best realist arguments, there seems little hope for *material* objects satisfying the necessity, intentionality, and plenitude conditions. Abandoning a materialist conception at this later stage is not so much abandoning neutrality as going where the argument leads.

Paul M. Gould and Richard Brian Davis

In my lead essay I never insist that AOs *must* be uncreated, as if this follows from the realist arguments for AOs that I canvassed. As far as I know, it doesn't. My allusion to Aquinas and creational "blueprints" was not meant to bear that weight; it was *not* intended to answer their question: "Why think abstract objects (i.e. divine thoughts) are uncreated?" So I can hardly "beg the question" in a context where I am not even arguing the thesis in question. My point there was something else entirely: the relevance condition on AOs. (Nevertheless, the thesis that God creates AOs *is* subject to bootstrapping concerns, despite the "modifications" of MTA. I won't repeat that earlier material here.)

As for Gould/Davis's three reasons for thinking that divine thoughts are created, first, these are not reasons for thinking that *AOs* are created, if in fact the latter claim generates the bootstrapping issues I and Craig note in our replies to Gould/Davis. Second, Leftow's criticism of deity theories asks us to "coherently suppose" WATER (the "strong necessity" of water being H_2O) "to be untrue by supposing that logical space so differs that there is in it no … God, able to imagine such a stuff as H_2O" (Leftow 2012, 210). I must confess that I cannot "coherently suppose" this. Third, MTA *doesn't* "allow for genuine spontaneity in God's creation of the universe" (100), since on that view AOs are a necessary emanation from God, which is the antithesis of spontaneity. TCR's holding that God's will is the source of *all* contingent reality whatsoever is all the "genuine spontaneity" one plausibly needs in a doctrine of divine creativity.

I can hardly be a "nominalist" rather than a realist if I *accept* (whereas *others* reject) the soundness of the traditional arguments for realism about AOs. Gould/Davis's conception of "divine-mental-events-as-abstract-objects" pits them against what is *widely* seen as traditional ontological constraints on AOs (as Yandell, Craig, Shalkowski, and Oppy point out). Gould/Davis suggest that "AO" can be characterized "ontologically as nonconcrete," but they cannot tell us what it means to be concrete! How then can they convince us that their entities are *not* concrete? Indeed, Gould/Davis hold that something most everyone else thinks are paradigmatically concrete objects (mental states) are really AOs. If "being nonspatial" is a "*sufficient* condition for some object X to be abstract" (100), then is God an AO? Are Cartesian souls? If another sufficient condition for AO-status is "being a universal," and that means being "multiply-instantiable," that is, "one and the same object would need to be multiply located," then are divine mental events *multiply located*? I can't make sense of this. In the face of these obvious disagreements across our contributors, I abandon any appeal to some mythological uniform ontological concept of "abstract" and "concrete." It doesn't exist, and I don't need it to make my argument.

Plantinga (1987) is right about Lewis because the latter's entities *don't* play the role that AOs must play, since (as Plantinga points out), they fail to satisfy the alethicity, doxasticity, intentionality, plenitude, and relevance conditions. It is precisely because my entities satisfy these conditions that they are not subject to Plantinga's critique.

William Lane Craig

Craig offers no careful, defensible conception of the abstract/concrete distinction according to which I "deny" that AOs exist, "properly speaking" (100). Craig merely refers to but does not interact with Note 2 of my lead essay. I like his Figure 1 in response to Yandell. But while a picture is surely worth a thousand words, a picture is not an argument. My functionalist conception is grounded in the arguments realists *actually give* for AOs. What is Craig's conception grounded in?

I concede Prior's point that fearing is not a propositional attitude. In fact, Trenton Merricks has recently argued (cogently, in my estimation) that while believing, suspecting, thinking, and remembering are propositional attitudes, fearing and desiring are not (Merricks 2009). He develops a twofold test that delivers this result, one aspect of the test being that "if instances of the attitude are true or false, then that attitude is a propositional attitude" (2009, 230). So there is a principled reason for removing "fearing" from the list of these attitudes. Notice that this leaves intact the grammatical argument for propositions from various attitudes. In addition, Prior's nonrelational theory of predicate-forming operators cannot account for unspecified that-clauses ("John believes everything that Jack believes"; cf. Loux 1998, 147–51).

I defended the quantificational argument in Note 1 of my reply to Craig, so perhaps he will take up the issue in his final rejoinder.

Can a "deflationary view of truth" accommodate Ramsey's own example: "He is always right"? Can we rewrite this as "For all p, if he asserts p, then p"? Craig cannot interpret the quantifier objectually (so that it ranges over propositions) so he must interpret it substitutionally (so that it ranges over linguistic expressions). But as Grayling points out, "For all p, if he asserts p, then p" turns into "all substitution instances of 'if he asserts p, then p' *are true*"; and so once again 'true' "remains firmly entrenched in the analysis" (1997, 162). (Gould/Davis ably critique deflationist views in their reply to Shalkowski.)

Craig accepts that "God is necessarily good" and that "necessarily, 2+2=4." But if "propositions … do not exist at all," then what does Craig *mean* by "necessarily, 2+2=4"? Does he offer a linguistic or conventionalist account of necessity (such as that critiqued by Yandell in his lead essay)? Does he offer a fictionalist account of the "necessary truth" of "2+2=4" while arbitrarily refraining from giving a similar account of "God is necessarily good"? Is God's necessary goodness a figure of speech?

The argument from ordinary discourse might strike Craig as less "outrageously implausible" (101) if he were to state the actual argument, which not only says that "prephilosophical belief in 'ways things could have been' … is expressed in our ordinary language about the world," but that "*retaining this commitment leads to fewer difficulties than the attempt to paraphrase it away*" (83, emphasis mine). Alas, Craig doesn't offer us any paraphrases, so we cannot test them for plausibility.

As for explanatory utility, *Lewis's* account of truth-conditions *is* in terms of possible worlds, and the far-reaching utility of that conception within his overall theory gives me pause before labeling it "incredible" or "clearly wrongheaded" (102). I already conceded that primitive modality is not avoided even on Lewis's allegedly reductive theory of modality (cf. Note 6 of my lead essay). So what matters is *where* we locate our primitives, and if worlds just are the divine ideas that represent to God all the ways He could have created, then why not locate modality for our universe exactly there? The fact that theistic conceptualism offers a consideration that intuitively satisfies the "relevance condition" on modal truthmakers is a *substantive* point in its favor (Leftow 2012, 548–50).

Scott A. Shalkowski

I appreciate Shalkowski's nuanced assessment of a "cost-benefits" approach to metaphysical theory. Since I assume rather than seek to establish that ontological kind-simplicity is evidence of truth, I don't see any question-begging there. My approach will have less value to any who reject that assumption.

At one time I believed that "Santa brings presents," and so did my sister, but now I do not, and neither does she. What we believed therefore seems, both at a time and over time, "intersubjectively available and mind-independent," but that is not because I have seen Santa bring presents and so can you. So the example of Leo's roaring only takes us so far in illuminating the phenomenon of belief. Some things are not like Leo, and yet we have beliefs about them.

I am sure there are some uses of language that cannot be pressed into the service of the quantificational argument. I'm not sure I have to appeal to those in order to get my desired conclusion. Can the specific example I gave "easily be interpreted in ways carrying no ontological commitments" (104)?

I agree that appealing to a redundancy or deflationary theory of truth can keep one from inferring "Necessarily, 'Socrates is human' is true" from "Necessarily, Socrates is human." I do wonder whether such theories are adequate to all the contexts in which they need to be deployed, and here I advert to comments made by Gould/Davis and myself on Craig's use of this theory. I don't accept a dichotomy between "how *things must be*" and "what must be *true*," since for the realist a proposition's being true just is how some *things are*.

Graham Oppy

I join Plantinga (1987, 212) in thinking that "a possible world *represents* things as being a certain way." Oppy seems to misunderstand my view of possible worlds (PWs). In my lead essay I distinguished between PWs and what they represent: "*the World* (or universe)." My capital is deliberate, because "it is important not to confuse the actual world with the World" (van Inwagen 1993, 83). So the "actual world" is the one PW which accurately represents the World—it is the *way* the World is (Plantinga 1976, 258). (And I have no problem with God Himself being represented in PWs.)

An omniscient God has knowledge of the full range of thoughts that we humans can have and will have. We don't surprise Him by our "bawdy thoughts, banal thoughts, malicious thoughts, silly thoughts, and so forth" (105). His holiness is assured, as He doesn't intend these thoughts as we intend them. He is like the parent who already knows all the ways the child can go astray.

"God could not have had different thoughts" (105) because, as I said in my lead essay, the thoughts in question are thoughts of His own power. I concede this leaves us with primitive modality, but that is unavoidable on any theory (even allegedly reductive ones), and I think my theory locates it in the right place.

We cannot "eliminate divine ideas from our ontology" (105) because God is an *intentional* creator. "The rational act of divine creation is always *according to*

knowledge, in particular, according to God's knowledge of the range of His own   QED
power" (Welty, 93). Oppy hasn't begun to argue that an "initial singularity" satisfies the
intentionality and plenitude conditions on PWs and propositions. Simplicity says not
to multiply entities beyond explanatory necessity; it adjudicates among explanations,   ←
not nonexplanations. If the realist arguments for AOs have in fact supplied *multiple*   ←
conditions any theory must satisfy, then an "initial singularity" falls pretty short.   ⊥

4

Anti-Platonism

William Lane Craig

Central to biblical theism is the conception of God as the only self-existent being, the creator of all reality apart from Himself. God alone exists *a se*; everything else exists *ab alio*. God alone exists necessarily and eternally; everything else has been created by God and is therefore contingent and temporally finite in its being.

The biblical witness to God's unique aseity is both abundant and clear. Consider the following representative texts:

> there is one God, the Father, from whom are all things and for whom we exist, and one Lord, Jesus Christ, through whom are all things and through whom we exist (1 Cor. 8.6 NRSV).

> For just as woman came from man, so man comes through woman; but all things come from God (1 Cor. 11.12 NRSV).

> For from him and through him and to him are all things (Rom. 11.36 NRSV).

> In the beginning was the Word (Logos), and the Word was with God, and the Word was God.... All things came into being through him, and without him not one thing came into being (Jn 1.1, 3 NRSV).

These texts carry the weighty metaphysical implication that only God and His Logos exist *a se*; everything else exists *ab alio*, namely, through the divine Logos. Even an entity which exists in every possible world does so only through the Logos and so is not, as medieval divines saw, necessary in itself (*per se necessarium*) but has a cause of its necessity in another (*causam necessitates aliunde*).[1] God is thus the ground of being of everything else, as even so-called "necessary" beings are contingent upon God. A second significant metaphysical implication is that there are no eternal entities apart from God, eternal either in the sense of existing atemporally or of existing sempiternally. Rather everything that exists, with the exception of God Himself, is the product of temporal becoming.

Partisans of uncreated abstract objects who would be biblical must therefore maintain that the domain of the biblical writers' quantifiers is restricted in some way, being intended to include, for example, only concrete objects. The question at issue here is easily misunderstood. The question is *not*: Did Paul and John have in mind abstract objects when they wrote the above sentences? They probably did not. But neither did they have in mind quarks, galaxies, and automobiles; yet they would take such things and countless other things, were they informed about them, to lie within the domain of their quantifiers. The question is not what Paul and John thought lay in the domain of their quantifiers. The question, rather, is: Did they intend the domain of their quantifiers to be unrestricted, once God is exempted? It is very likely that they did. For God's unique status as the only eternal, uncreated being is typical for Judaism.[2] John himself identifies the Logos alone as existing with God (and being God) in the beginning. Everything else is then created through the Logos. The salient point here is that the unrestrictedness of the domain of the quantifiers is rooted, not in the type of objects thought to be in the domain, but in one's doctrine of God. It is who or what God is that requires the domain of the quantifiers to be unrestricted, whatever beings might be found to lie in the domain. Indeed, given the striking similarities of John's Logos doctrine to that of the Alexandrian Jewish philosopher Philo (20 B.C.–A.D. 50), it is not all implausible that John thought that the intelligible realm of what we would today call abstract objects was contained, as Philo held, in the divine Logos.[3] Everything that exists apart from God has been created by God.

The biblical conviction that God is the creator of everything that exists aside from God Himself eventually attained credal status at the Council of Nicaea. In language redolent of the prologue to the fourth Gospel and of Paul, the Council affirmed:

> I believe in one God, the Father Almighty, Maker of heaven and earth and of all things visible and invisible;

> And in one Lord, Jesus Christ, the only Son of God, begotten of the Father before all ages, light from light, true God from true God, begotten not made, consubstantial with the Father, through whom all things came into being.

The phrase "Maker of heaven and earth and of all things visible and invisible" is Pauline (Col. 1.16), and the expression "through whom all things came into being" is Johannine (Jn 1.3). At face value the Council seems to affirm that God alone is uncreated and that all else was created by Him.

An examination of ante-Nicene theological reflection on divine aseity confirms the *prima face* reading. At the heart of the Arian controversy which occasioned the convening of the Council of Nicaea lay a pair of terminological distinctions prevalent among the Church Fathers: *agenetos/genetos* and *agennetos/gennetos*.[4] The word pair *agenetos/genetos* derives from the verb "ginomai," which means *to become* or *to come into being*. "Agenetos" means *unoriginated* or *uncreated*, in contrast to "genetos," that which is created or originated. The second word pair *agennetos/gennetos* derives from the verb "ginnao," which means *to beget*. That which is *agennetos* is unbegotten, while that which is *gennetos* is begotten. These distinctions allowed the Fathers to hold that while both God the Father and God the Son are *agenetos*, only the Father is *agennetos*.

Like the Arian heretics, the ante-Nicene and Nicene Church Fathers rejected any suggestion that there might exist *ageneta* apart from God alone.[5] According to patristic

scholar Harry Austryn Wolfson (1966, 414), the Church Fathers all accepted the
following three principles:

1. God alone is uncreated.
2. Nothing is co-eternal with God.
3. Eternality implies deity.

Each of these principles implies that there are no *ageneta* apart from God alone.

But lest it be suggested that *abstracta* were somehow exempted from these
principles, we should note that the ante-Nicene Church Fathers explicitly rejected
the view that entities such as properties and numbers are *ageneta*.[6] The Fathers were
familiar with the metaphysical world views of Plato and Pythagoras and agreed with
them that there is one *agenetos* from which all reality derives; but the Fathers identified
this *agenetos*, not with an impersonal Form or number, but with the Hebrew God,
who has created all things (other than Himself) *ex nihilo*. If confronted by a modern-
day platonist defending an ontology which included causally effete objects which
were *ageneta* and so co-eternal with God, they would have rejected such an account
as blasphemous, since such an account would impugn God's aseity by denying its
uniqueness and undermine *creatio ex nihilo* by denying that God is the universal
ground of being. The Fathers could not therefore exempt such objects from God's
creative power, since He is the sole and all-originating *agenetos*.

Platonism, the view that there are uncreated abstract objects, is therefore wholly
unacceptable theologically for the orthodox Christian and on that ground alone
should be rejected, whatever other philosophical objections there might be to it. One
should like to have one's cake and eat it too, by embracing absolute creationism (see
Morris and Menzel 1986), the view that God has created abstract objects; but the
familiar bootstrapping objection has struck me as an insuperable obstacle to such an
easy solution. Therefore, the Christian theist must, it seems, espouse either conceptualism, according to which abstract objects are replaced by some sort of mental or ideal
objects, or nominalism, according to which abstract objects are just useful fictions.
While conceptualism remains a fallback position should all forms of nominalism fail,
I think that the alternatives afforded by nominalism are far from exhausted and merit
exploration.

Prospects of an anti-platonist solution

Assuming that we are talking about a metaphysically heavy sense of existence,[7] what
are the prospects of the anti-platonist view that abstract objects do not exist? In his
Introduction, Paul Gould claims that if one follows the nominalist in denying

(1) Abstract objects exist

then "the problem of universals is of central concern" and "the age-old nominalism-
realism debate ensues." Here a terminological clarification is vital. The word

"nominalism" is used to denote quite different positions in two distinct philosophical debates (see Rodriguez-Pereyra 2011). The first is the age-old dispute over universals, nominalism being the position that there are no universals. The second concerns a very recent debate, centered in the philosophy of mathematics, which has arisen only since Gottlob Frege's *Foundations of Arithmetic* (1884). In this debate nominalism is the position that abstract objects like numbers do not exist. A nominalist in the context of the first debate is not necessarily a nominalist in the context of the second, and *vice versa*. Moreover, the label "nominalism" has negative connotations in the history of theology as a result of its use in the first debate that are entirely foreign to nominalism in the second debate, which is largely a twentieth-century development that has become widely discussed only since Hartry Field's publication of his ground-breaking book *Science without Numbers* (1980). It is no part of nominalism in this second sense to deny, for example, that God is necessarily good.

It would be helpful, then, to find a label other than "nominalism" for the position I wish to explore. "Concretism," an appellation deriving from the Polish logician Kazimierz Twardowski, is tempting. According to concretism, only concrete objects exist; there are no abstract objects. But it is no part of my project to deny that abstract objects exist; I maintain only that uncreated abstract objects do not exist. Another option is referring to the position I wish to explore as "reism," a view connected to the Polish philosopher Tadeusz Kotarbiński, according to which only things exist. Unfortunately, reists understood things to be only material, spatiotemporal objects, a view inimical to theism. Moreover, it is not evident that abstract objects, if they exist, could not be things or individuals. So I have adopted the rather bland label "anti-platonism" to designate my view.

In identifying the problem of universals as a central concern, Gould is evidently thinking of the first debate. But in the context of the second debate, this problem is marginal.[8] Rather what takes center stage in the second debate is the so-called Indispensability Argument for platonism. Since the challenge of platonism to divine aseity concerns the second debate, I shall ignore the problem of universals to focus on the Indispensability Argument.

Balaguer (2004, §4) formulates the Indispensability Argument as follows:

(I) If a simple sentence (i.e. a sentence of the form '*a* is *F*', or '*a* is *R*-related to *b*', or ...) is literally true, then the objects that its singular terms denote exist. (Likewise, if an existential sentence is literally true, then there exist objects of the relevant kinds; e.g. if 'There is an *F*' is true, then there exist some *F*s.)

(II) There are literally true simple sentences containing singular terms that refer to things that could only be abstract objects. (Likewise, there are literally true existential statements whose existential quantifiers range over things that could only be abstract objects.)

(III) Therefore, abstract objects exist.

Although the Indispensability Argument is widely regarded as the best available argument for platonism, I must confess that I find it eminently challengeable, if not wildly implausible. (I) is a metaontological thesis proffering a criterion of ontological commitment that is far from incumbent upon us. But if we do accept such a criterion, then (II), which seems *prima facie* undeniably true, turns out to be far from obviously true and certainly one that the theist is at liberty to reject.

Challenging the truth of abstract sentences

Since I am inclined to reject (I), let us first briefly consider the prospects of rejecting (II) instead. The principal anti-platonist school rejecting (II) is fictionalism. Fictionalism is the view that statements putatively involving either quantification over abstract objects or singular terms referring to such objects are false, or at least untrue. Abstract objects are merely useful fictions; that is to say, even though no such objects exist, it is useful to talk as though they did. Hence, the name "fictionalism".

Fictionalists may regard abstract object talk, including platonistic mathematics, as either dispensable (Field) or indispensable (Balaguer) to physical science. What unites them is their conviction that mathematical sentences, whether pure or applied, as well as other sentences involving putative quantification over or reference to abstract objects, are not true.

The most evident objection to fictionalism is that some mathematical statements, such as statements of elementary arithmetic like "1+1=2," are just obviously true. Indeed, they seem to be necessarily, even analytically, true. Therefore fictionalism is ruled out *tout court*.

One's attitude toward this objection is going to depend on one's attitude toward the metaontological thesis concerning the ontological commitments of our discourse which comes to expression in (I). If with the fictionalist we are convinced that the customary devices for ontological commitment are correct, then we shall find upon reflection that the sentences of elementary mathematics are anything but obvious.[9] For we shall come to see that statements which we have unhesitatingly accepted as true since childhood are, in fact, radical ontological assertions about the existence of mind-independent abstract objects. "2+2=4" is, in effect, the assertion that there is an abstract object which is the denotation of "2+2" and an abstract object which is the denotation of "4," and they are the same object. Such a recondite metaphysical claim is not at all obviously true.

On the other hand, if we find sentences of elementary arithmetic to be obvious because we do not take them to be ontologically committing, then we shall be led to reject the criterion of ontological commitment which would saddle us with such commitments. After all, the sentences of elementary mathematics are much more obviously true than the metaontological thesis expressed by (I) and so should be more tenaciously held and less quickly surrendered than (I). Since platonists and fictionalists share the same metaontological criterion of ontological commitment, the objection to fictionalism from the obviousness of elementary arithmetic is not, then, one that the platonist could press, since, given that criterion, such statements are not obviously true.

I find a pretense theoretical approach to mathematical statements to be an extremely plausible fictionalist position. Such an approach treats abstract object discourse as a kind of fictional discourse and so analyzable in terms of theories of fiction. Contemporary theories of fiction draw much of their inspiration from the brilliant, pioneering work of Kendall Walton (1990). "The central idea of the make-believe approach," says Walton, "is … that what seem to be commitments, by speakers of theories, to non-existent entities are to be understood in a spirit of pretense or make-believe" (2000, 70–1). Prescribed imagining lies at the heart of Walton's theory of fiction. Fictional propositions are propositions which in certain contexts we are to imagine to be true. There are certain features of mathematics that make it seem a prime candidate for a fictional interpretation. (1) *Axiomatization naturally invites a Pretense Theoretical interpretation.* For example, the axioms of Zermelo-Fraenkel set theory are not intuitively true but may be plausibly taken as prescribed to be imagined as true. Such an attitude toward the axioms of set theory is not uncommon among mathematicians and philosophers of mathematics themselves. For example, postulationalism, which treats the axioms of competing theories as postulates whose consequences may be explored, invites us, in effect, to make believe that the axioms are true without committing ourselves to their objective truth.[10] (2) *The creative freedom enjoyed by mathematicians makes set theory particularly apt for a fictional interpretation.* Just as authors of literary fiction are free to shape their characters as they want, without concern for correspondence with reality, so mathematicians are at liberty to craft and explore different axiomatic systems without worrying that they are misrepresenting reality in doing so. As a result a variety of competing set theories with a plethora of different mathematical objects has arisen. (3) *The incompleteness of mathematical entities makes set theory especially amenable to a Pretense Theoretical interpretation.* One of the most striking features of fictional characters is their incompleteness. Similarly, the mathematical objects of set theory are incomplete in a number of significant ways. The most celebrated example is the Continuum Hypothesis (CH), that χ_1, the successor to χ_0, is $2^{(\Lambda 0)}$, the power of the continuum or the number of real numbers.

Thus, even given the customary criterion of ontological commitment, we can plausibly avoid commitment to mathematical objects if we regard mathematical statements as prescribed to be imagined true. The classical theist who accepts the metaontological thesis which comes to expression in (I) will regard mathematical statements, whether pure or applied, as not merely fictional but false. If that seems a hard pill to swallow, then he should retrace his steps and call into question the inflationary semantics which would force such unwanted commitments upon him.

Let us therefore press on to consider the prospects of challenging (I). Despite my considerable sympathies for a fictionalist perspective on the *abstracta* of set theory and scientific idealization, I think that anti-platonists should challenge vigorously the metaontological claim that comes to expression in (I).

Challenging the criterion of ontological commitment

I must confess that when I first began to read the literature on the Indispensability
Argument, I was astonished to learn that so many philosophers should take us to be
ontologically committed (in a metaphysically heavy sense) to the values of variables
bound by the existential quantifier of first-order logic. It seemed to me that one is free
to quantify over whatever one wishes independent of the question of whether those
things actually exist. For example, it would be extravagant to think that someone who
believes that "There have been 44 US presidents" has thereby committed himself to a
tenseless theory of time![11]

I thus find myself sympathetic with the advocates of neutral logic like Jody Azzouni
(1998) who challenge the assumption that the quantifier of first-order logic implies
an ontology or carries ontological commitments. On their view the purpose of the
existential quantifier is simply to facilitate logical inferences, and it can carry out that
function without making ontological commitments. Azzouni (2004, 54) maintains
that even the objectual (or referential) interpretation of the quantifier, which conceives
it as selecting from a domain of objects, is not ontologically committing until one so
stipulates.[12] The claim that it must be ontologically committing because it has as its
range a domain of objects overlooks the fact that the quantifiers of the metalanguage
used to establish the domain of the object language quantifiers are as neutral as the
quantifiers of the object language. Whether the items in the domain D of the object
language quantifier actually exist will depend on how one construes the "there is" of
the metalanguage establishing D. Even objectual use of the quantifier in the object
language need not be ontologically committing if the quantifiers in the metalanguage
are not ontologically committing.

If, when we say that there is an element in D, we are using ordinary language,
then we are not committed to the reality of the objects in D which we quantify over,
unless quantificational locutions like "there is/are" in ordinary language are ontologically committing. For the meaning of the symbol "∃" is entirely determined by such
ordinary language locutions. Saul Kripke insists,

> We did *not* learn quantification theory as our mother tongue. Somehow or other
> the weird notation '(∃x)' was explained to us, by teachers or books, either by
> such examples as ' "(∃x) Rabbit (x)" means "*there is an x* which is a rabbit" ', or
> by a formal definition of satisfaction, couched in English... . And the quanti-
> fiers will be said to range over a *non-empty* domain *D*, where the technical term
> 'non-empty' is explained by saying that *D* is non-empty if *there is an element in*
> *D*, or the equivalent. *If* the interpretation of the English 'there are' is completely
> in doubt, the interpretation of the formal referential quantifier, which depends
> on such explanations, must be in doubt also; perhaps the explanation the teacher
> used when he taught it to us was couched in a substitutional language, and we
> spoke such a language when we learned his interpretation! ... Nonsense: we speak
> English, and the whole interpretation of the referential quantifier was *defined* by
> reference to 'there are' in its standard employments. (1976, 379)

Kripke thinks "There are rabbits" undoubtedly commits us to the existence of rabbits; but he himself acknowledges that there are [*N.B.*!] English uses of "there is/are" which are not ontologically committing, as in "There is a good chance" or "There are three feet in a yard." Kripke's disagreement is merely with "anyone who doubts or denies that English has any resources for making genuinely existential assertions" (ibid., 380)—a position to which no neutralist ascribes. Kripke and the neutralist concur on the overriding point: The existential quantifier is defined in terms of the ordinary English "there is/are," so that if the latter is not ontologically committing, neither is the former. Since, as Kripke's own examples illustrate, "there is/are" is not ontologically committing, neither is objectual quantification.

Such examples could be multiplied. Consider Thomas Hofweber's (1999, 1–2) list of some of the things we ordinarily say there are:

- something that we have in common
- infinitely many primes
- something that we both believe
- the common illusion that one is smarter than one's average colleague
- a way you smile
- a lack of compassion in the world
- the way the world is
- several ways the world might have been
- a faster way to get to Berkeley from Stanford than going through San Jose
- the hope that this dissertation will shed some light on ontology
- the chance that it might not
- a reason why it might not.[13]

W. V. O. Quine, the fount of the criterion of ontological commitment expressed in (I), recognized that the application of such a criterion to ordinary language would bring with it all sorts of fantastic and unwanted ontological commitments, and so he limited its legitimate application only to an artificial, canonical language involving the formulation in first-order logic of appropriate paraphrases of the sentences of our best scientific theories. The problem with this restriction is that we have no clue as to how to carry out such a prescription successfully.[14] Given the bankruptcy of the Quinean project, the criterion of ontological commitment becomes a wildly unreliable guide.[15]

The failure of (I) as a reliable guide to ontology obviously does not mean that we lack resources for making metaphysically heavy affirmations of existence. It is just that expressions like "there is/are" or even "there exists" in the vernacular do not force ontological commitments.[16] On Azzouni's view ontological commitment is person-relative and context-dependent; hence, "there are *no* words or phrases in the vernacular that—in virtue of their standard usage—convey ontic commitment" (2010, 81–2). It will be contextual factors that will tip us off to whether the locutions are being used in ontologically committing ways. Accordingly, the anti-platonist need no longer be concerned about the indispensability of quantification over putatively abstract objects.

The same goes for singular terms. Again, I am astonished that so many philosophers think that true sentences involving singular terms (like proper names, definite descriptions, and demonstratives) commit their asserter ontologically to real world objects. Far too many philosophers, I think, are still in the thrall of a sort of picture theory of language according to which successfully referring terms have corresponding objects in the world. With respect to ordinary language, at least, such a view seems patently false. Consider the following examples:

- The weather in Atlanta will be hot today
- Sherrie's disappointment with her husband was deep and unassuageable
- The price of the tickets is ten dollars
- Wednesday falls between Tuesday and Thursday
- Napoleon was defeated at Waterloo
- James couldn't pay his mortgage
- The view of the Jezreel Valley from atop of Mt. Carmel was breath-taking
- Your constant complaining is futile
- Spassky's forfeiture ended the match
- He did it for my sake and the children's.

It would be fantastic to think that all of the singular terms featured in these plausibly true sentences have objects in the world corresponding to them. Examples like these are legion. In fact, I have come to suspect that singular terms which refer to real world objects may actually be the *exception* rather than the rule in ordinary language. Consider the following paragraph quoted by Michael Dummett from a London daily:

> Margaret Thatcher yesterday gave her starkest warning yet about the dangers of global warming caused by air pollution. But she did not announce any new policy to combat climate change and sea level rises, apart from a qualified commitment that Britain would stabilize its emissions of carbon dioxide—the most important 'greenhouse' gas altering the climate—by the year 2005. Britain would only fulfill that commitment if other, unspecified nations promised similar restraint.

Nothing unusual about such discourse—but, as Dummett observes, "Save for 'Margaret Thatcher,' 'air' and 'sea,' there is not a noun or noun phrase in this paragraph incontrovertibly standing for or applying to a concrete object ... " (1991, 231). A lightweight platonist, Dummett is unfazed about postulating objects as referents for such terms, but those who have a more robust sense of reality will be very hesitant about augmenting the world's population so profligately.

It might be said on behalf of the customary criterion of ontological commitment that a view of truth as correspondence requires that the singular terms in true sentences have real world objects as their denotations. But this claim seems to presuppose, like the picture theory, that the unit of correspondence is individual words. If we take the unit of correspondence to be the sentence as a whole, not its constituent words, then correspondence with reality does not require objects corresponding to every singular term. This insight is in line with a deflationary theory of truth according to which, for example,

> (T) "Sherrie's disappointment with her husband was deep and unassuageable" is true iff Sherrie's disappointment with her husband was deep and unassuageable.

There is nothing more to correspondence than that, so there is no need to search for mysterious objects like disappointments to make this sentence true.

But what about referring terms? These, after all, appear, not only in true sentences, but also in sentences which are not truth-evaluable, such as questions and commands. Does not successful reference, if not truth, involve the existence of objects which are the referents of singular terms? I think not. Almost all contemporary theories of reference are actually theories about how to *fix* reference rather than theories about the nature of reference itself. The unspoken assumption behind most contemporary theories of reference is the presupposition that reference is a word-world relation, so that terms which refer must have real world objects as their denotations. I am convinced that this assumption is fundamentally mistaken.

It is an experiential datum that referring is a speech act carried out by an intentional agent. Words in and of themselves engage in no such activity. Lifeless and inert, words are just ink marks on paper or sounds heard by a percipient. Absent an agent, shapes or noises do not refer to anything at all. If, for example, an earthquake were to send several pebbles rolling down a hillside which randomly came to rest in the configuration JOHN LOVES SUSIE, the names—if we would even call them names—would not refer to anybody. An interpreting agent uses his words as a means of referring to something. Referring is thus an intentional activity of persons, and words are mere instruments.[17]

One of the great merits of Arvid Båve's (2009) new deflationary theory of reference is that he takes truly seriously the fact, given lip service everywhere, that it is *persons* who refer to things *by means of* their words, so that words at best refer only in a derivative sense, if at all. Båve's theory features a central schema for reference formulated in terms of the referring activity of agents:

(R) *a* refers to *b* iff *a* says something (which is) about *b*,

where "*a*" always stands for a speaker. This account is deflationary because it does not attempt to tell us anything about the nature of reference itself. It leaves it entirely open whether reference is a relation (as Frege and Meinong assumed) or whether it is an intentional property of a mind (as held by Brentano and Husserl). Taking reference to be a relation between a speaker and some object would make (R) ontologically committing to either existing or nonexisting objects. But Båve's theory is ontologically neutral when it comes to the question of whether there must be objects corresponding to the singular terms we use successfully to reference. On his account, if I assert "1+1=2," then I have said something about 2; it follows from (R) that I have thus referred to 2. But it does not follow that there is some such object, existent or nonexistent, as the number 2. One has the option of avoiding the inference to "There is something to which I have referred" by restricting, with the free logicians, Existential Generalization, or the option of granting the inference but rendering it harmless by denying, with the neutral logicians, that the existential quantifier is ontologically committing. Hence, Båve recognizes the neutrality of his theory for the debate between platonists and anti-platonists.

So what does it mean to say that *a* says something "about" *b*, as stipulated on the right-hand side of the biconditional (R)? Båve offers the following schema as implicitly defining "about":

(A) That $S(t)$ is about t,

where $S(\ )$ is a sentence context with a slot for singular terms. Again, Båve's account of aboutness is extraordinarily deflationary. It does not tell us what aboutness is but simply provides a schema for determining what a that-clause containing a singular term (or, presumably, terms) is about.[18] So, for example, that Ponce de Leon sought the Fountain of Youth is about Ponce de Leon and about the Fountain of Youth because the singular terms "Ponce de Leon" and "the Fountain of Youth" fill the blanks in the sentence context "____ sought ____."

There is nothing in the deflationary schema (A) that entails that aboutness is a relation between propositions and objects. So if I assert, "Ponce de Leon sought the Fountain of Youth," I have said something which is both true and about the Fountain of Youth (as well as about Ponce de Leon); but we are not entitled to infer that there is a (nonexistent) object like the Fountain of Youth which this sentence is about. Therefore, I can say things about Pegasus, the accident that was prevented, or numbers and other *abstracta* without committing myself to there being objects of which I am speaking. Accordingly, successful reference does not entail that there are objects to which one is referring. Reference alone will not yield ontology.

Conclusion

I have not tried to argue for the truth of an anti-platonist perspective on abstract objects. Rather I have tried to argue for its viability. I should be delighted if one of my colleagues can succeed in showing the viability of conceptualist or absolute creationist perspectives on abstract objects as well. What we cannot accept is (heavyweight) platonism, for it fatally compromises the doctrine of God. To defeat the challenge to theism raised by platonism all one needs to do is offer a viable alternative that does not involve the existence (in a metaphysically heavy sense) of objects which are uncreated by and independent of God. I hope to have shown that anti-platonism is such a viable alternative.

Notes

1 Cf. Thomas Aquinas, *Summa theologiae* 1.2.3.
2 See the discussion in Copan and Craig (2004, chs 1–3).
3 The doctrine of the divine, creative Logos was widespread in Middle Platonism, and the similarities between Philo and John's doctrines of the Logos are so numerous and close that most Johannine scholars, while not willing to affirm John's direct dependence on Philo, do recognize that the author of the prologue of John's Gospel

shares with Philo a common intellectual tradition of a platonizing interpretation of
the first chapter of Genesis (Leonhardt-Balzer 2004, 309–10, cf. 318–19). A hallmark
of Middle Platonism was Plato's bifurcation between the realm of static being (τί
τὸ ὄν ἀεί) and the realm of temporal becoming (τί τὸ γιγνόμενον μὲν ἀεί) (see e.g.
Timaeus 27d5–28a4). The realm of becoming was comprised primarily of physical
objects, though it would also include immaterial objects like souls, while the static
realm of being was comprised of what we would today call abstract objects. The
former realm is perceived by the senses, whereas the latter is grasped by the intellect.
For Middle Platonists, as for Plato, the intelligible world served as a model for the
creation of the sensible world. But for a Jewish monotheist like Philo, the realm of
Ideas does not exist independently of God but as the contents of His mind (*On the
Creation of the World* [*De opificio mundi*] 16–25). For Philo the divine Logos may
be thought of as either the divine mind which forms the intelligible world (κόσμος
νοητός) by thought or more reductively, as the κόσμος νοητός itself. On Philo's
doctrine, then, there is no realm of independently existing abstract objects. In Runia's
words, while not part of the created realm, "the κόσμος νοητός, though eternal and
unchanging, must be considered dependent for its existence on God" (Runia 1983,
138). John does not tarry to reflect on the role of the divine Logos causally prior to
creation, but given the provenance of his doctrine it is not at all implausible that he,
too, thought of the Logos as the seat of the intelligible realm of what we would call
abstract objects.

4   For a survey of texts see the nice discussion by Prestige (1964, 37–55).

5   Justin, *Dialogue* 5; Methodius, *On Free Will* 5; Irenaeus, *Against heresies* 4.38.3;
    Tertullian, *Against Praxeas* 5.13–15; Hippolytus, *Against Noetus* 10.1; Hippolytus,
    Refutation of All Heresies 10.28; Epiphanius, *Panarion* 33.7.6; Athanasius, *Defense of
    the Nicene Definition* 7: "On the Arian symbol 'Agenetos';" Athanasius, *Discourses
    against the Arians* 1.9.30–4; Athanasius, *On the Councils of Ariminum and Seleucia*
    46–7; Athanasius, *Statement of Faith* 3; Socrates, Ecclesiastical History 2.19;
    Theodoret, *Ecclesiastical History* 1.3.

6   Athenagoras, *Plea for the Christians* 15, 24; Tatian, *Address to the Greeks* 4.10–14;
    Methodius, *Concerning Free Will*; Hippolytus, *Refutation* 6.16, 18, 19, 24, 43.
    According to Wolfson, every Church Father who addressed the issue located the
    intelligible world in the Logos and, hence, in the mind of God. For a discussion of
    texts taken from pseudo-Justin, Irenaeus, Tertullian, Clement of Alexandria, Origen,
    and Augustine, see Wolfson (1970, ch. XIII: "The Logos and the Platonic Ideas").

7   As Robert Adams has observed, "exists" in English is very lightweight. We often say
    that certain things, e.g. holes, exist without thinking to add them to our ontological
    inventory of objects. Accordingly there is a sort of lightweight platonism which treats
    abstract objects merely as the semantic objects of certain singular terms without
    thereby thinking to affirm their being part of reality. Such lightweight platonism
    would not compromise divine aseity or universal creation because abstract objects
    do not really exist on such a view. See Robert Adams, "The Metaphysical Lightness of
    Being," paper presented to the Philosophy Department colloquium at the University
    of Notre Dame, 7 April 2011; and Linnebo (2011, §5.2–3).

8   And the facts which generate the problem in the problem of universals hardly
    supports platonism. If asked (e.g.) to provide an explanation of why John's feet are
    fleet, the nominalist will offer a perfectly plausible and, I think, adequate explanation
    in terms of John's musculature, consistent training, healthy diet, and so forth. By

contrast it helps not at all to explain why John's feet are fleet by saying that John exemplifies the property of fleetness. Indeed, how does being partly composed of or standing in relation to a static, nonspatial, causally effete, abstract object make an otherwise motionless person fleet? Platonism enjoys no explanatory advantage over nominalism.

9 See Field's reaction to the objection that it is unintelligible to deny the truth of mathematical assertions like "2+2=4," since it is simply a consequence of the meaning we have assigned to "2," "4," "+," *etc.*, that this and similar assertions hold. He says that this objection cannot be right because analytic truths cannot have existential implications. He grants that the claim "If there are numbers then 2+2=4" has some claims to count as an analytic truth, indeed one so obvious that its denial is unintelligible.... But ... it can't be an analytic or purely conceptual truth that there *are* objects 1, 2, 3, 4 etc. obeying such laws as that 2+2=4. An investigation of conceptual linkages can reveal conditions that things must satisfy if they are to fall under our concepts; but it can't yield that there are things that satisfy those concepts ...." (1980, 5)

10 See Michael Potter (2004, 6–11). Since Potter takes postulationism to be a species of formalism rather than realism, it is plausibly interpreted as an expression of pretense theory. One imagines certain objects to exist as prescribed by the axioms, and then one explores what is (unconditionally) fictional in that world. It is the fictionality of the theorems that enables them to be unconditionally asserted without ontological commitment.

11 As asserted, e.g. by Theodore Sider (1999). It is astonishing that such theorists never think to challenge the criterion of ontological commitment that would have such an untoward result, nor do they argue for it; it is just assumed.

12 In substitutional quantification, by contrast, we take the variables as dummy letters which may be replaced by linguistic expressions in order to form sentences; no domain of objects is presupposed. Whether a substitutionally quantified statement is ontologically committing will therefore depend on whether the ordinary language expression "there is/are" is ontologically committing.

13 See also Gerald Vision (1986). We say there are, e.g., shades of grey, differences in height, angles from which something can be seen, principles, hostilities, prospects for success, primes between 2 and 12, hours before dawn, dangerous excesses, drawbacks to the plan, etc.

14 As Chihara (1973, ch. 3; 1990, ch. 2) points out, Quine gives not even a hint as to how we are to put the sentences of ordinary language into canonical form, nor any argument at all that so doing will rid them of all unwanted commitments of ordinary language, nor any guarantee that our best scientific theories can be successfully put into first-order logical notation.

15 Platonists who want to persist in using the customary criterion of ontological commitment as a guide to ontology—unless they are using "exist" in a metaphysically light sense—face two daunting and uncompleted tasks: (i) to provide a general, universally applicable way of paraphrasing ordinary sentences which carry unwanted ontological commitments and (ii) to show that nominalistic paraphrases cannot similarly be found for sentences involving commitment to *abstracta*. The anti-platonist need not lose sleep that either of these tasks will be completed any time soon.

16 See Azzouni (2007).

17 For a nice statement of this point see Alvin Plantinga (2006).

18 For reasons which I have not the space to explain, I think it preferable to provide an account of aboutness that is cashed out, not in terms of linguistic expressions, but in terms of the speaker's intentions. What is wanted in place of (A) is something along the lines of

    (A′) a says something S about b iff in saying S a intends b,

where "a intends b" means something like "a has b in mind." In accordance with (R) I refer to b because I say something about b, and in line with (A′) I say something about b because in making my utterance I intend b. On such an account what some theorists have called "speaker's reference" becomes paramount.

Response to William Lane Craig

Keith Yandell

Early in Professor Craig's essay, he quotes four biblical passages, including 1 Cor. 8.6 and Jn 1.1, 3. He remarks that they "carry the weighty metaphysical implication that only God and His Logos exist *a se*; everything else exists *ab alio*" (113). Given Trinitarian doctrine, these Scriptures are not exhaustive regarding *a se* reality. To read "God and His Logos" as meaning "The Trinity and the Son" would be to make the reference to the Word (Son) redundant. Their scope is more limited, even though this is not specified. There can be good reasons to think that their scope is limited without this being expressed. The same may be true of the "all things" in the other two verses. Do 1 Cor. 11.12 and Rom. 11.36 teach that temptation comes from God? That sin comes from God? There are scriptural reasons for restricting the scope of all these passages. It does not follow that every good reason must be scriptural.

Professor Craig himself seems to be doing with Scripture the same sort of thing he says cannot be done properly with ordinary, everyday language—requiring that every time the word "all" appears in Scripture we must think of it as being properly captured, not of course by "there is an x" but by "for all x." Given the examples above, this would hardly be an exegetical rule it is wise to follow.

Professor Craig's central strategy is to spell out philosophical alternatives that have plausibility to interpret statements that realists appeal to as support for their position. On the nominalist account, these statements involve no reference to abstract objects. The idea is that there are sufficient alternatives to realism regarding abstracta so that there is no need for the theist to worry that there may be a proof, or very strong reasons, to think that the sort of entities Professor Craig finds unwelcome exist. Thus there is not the deep clash between philosophy and Christianity to which there being abstracta would, in his view, give rise. It is not part of his program to show that one of the alternatives presented is correct. The overall strategy is appropriate, though of course proving that one of the nominalist perspectives was correct would serve his purposes better. I do have doubts regarding the overall success of the strategy. I can only raise a couple of issues here.

It is interesting to see favorable reference to Professor Mark Balaguer's fictionalism. His book *Platonism and Anti-Platonism in Mathematics* (1998) has three sections. The thesis of Part One is that there are no good arguments against full-blooded platonism in mathematics—every item in mathematics that possibly exists does exist. Part Two's thesis is that there are no good arguments against fictionalism (see Professor Craig's account thereof). Part Three contends that there is no fact of the matter as to whether platonism or anti-platonism is true. Further, since the sentences we use are our sentences, we decide what their truth-conditions will be. Since abstract objects, were there any, would be "outside" space and time, and we don't know what it would be like to be "outside" space and time, claims about abstracta have no truth-conditions. It does not take philosophical genius to see the implications for the claim that God exists. (In addition, in a lecture at the University of Wisconsin Professor Balaguer noted that his actual position is that there is no fact of the matter as to whether there is a fact of the matter about this sort of issue.) How far should one take the "sentences are our sentences so we determine their truth-conditions" line? To what degree is it possible, in a principled way, to constrain a fictionalism one has begun to embrace if one wants to do so? Perhaps Professor Balaguer is not the source for a kind of fictionalism that will serve Professor Craig's overall purposes.

In this connection, what are we to say regarding logic? Is it also to receive a fictionalist treatment? Consider such propositions as *[A or B, and not-A, therefore B] is a valid argument form.* This is a necessary truth. That fact, along with a great many others, seems to be one that hold no matter what possible world is actual, because the proposition expressing it is "true in all possible worlds." Are we to fictionalize this so that the necessary truth of the proposition tells us nothing that is mind-independently so—perhaps it is merely a product of our linguistic choices and habits? What about *Metaphysical identity is necessary,* a broadly necessary truth? What is the principled stopper where you say that fictionalism is mistaken? What grounds *There is no possibility that there be a proposition P such that P is true and false at the same time and in the same respect?*

Suppose there is a discerned general disproof of all the varieties of nominalism concerning math and logic. Then assuming that *Either nominalism or realism is true,* contrary to Balaguerism, one can infer to the truth of realism. Then it is plausible to think that if something necessarily exists, it is either God or abstract objects (I would read the "or" as inclusive). This would seem to be a perfectly fine route—generally speaking—for a theist to take (though I think not the only one). It would not require embracing nominalism. Indeed it would require realism. But what would be bad about that?

Paul M. Gould and Richard Brian Davis

William Lane Craig's main quarrel is with theists who endorse the reality of uncreated abstract objects. We allow for some uncreated abstract objects, namely, those abstract objects that are part of God's nature, hence his quarrel is partly with us. Further, Craig thinks the bootstrapping worry an "insuperable obstacle" (115) for those who endorse the view (as we do) that God creates abstract objects (distinct from Himself). We agree with Craig that absolute creationism does fall prey to the bootstrapping worry, hence our MTA. Still, it is not up to God who He is, or whether He is divine, or what it is to be divine or Himself (Leftow 2012, 122). Hence, it is reasonable to think that God's nature, that is, God's essential properties, exist in God as uncreated abstract objects. There is no threat here to God's aseity. Further, as we mentioned in our chapter, the bootstrapping worry is not "insuperable." All that is required is some spadework on the metaphysics of substance-attribute possession. We find it curious that Craig continues to insist that the bootstrapping worry is insuperable without seriously engaging in the metaphysics of substance-attribute possession.

Co-eternal abstract objects

Craig insists that nothing can be co-eternal with God, "everything that exists, with the exception of God Himself, is the product of temporal becoming" (113). We agree with Craig that everything distinct from God is created by God. But we part ways in holding that God produces abstract objects eternally.

As far as we can tell, the biblical witness asserts only that *God* is eternal and is silent on whether there may be co-eternal abstracta. Craig cites the Church Fathers as a source for thinking nothing is co-eternal with God. The central worry of the Church Fathers, as Craig points out, is that nothing other than God (or God's attributes, parts, etc.) be uncreated. We agree. What we deny is that "x is eternal" entails "x is uncreated." Thus, we part ways with the Church Fathers on this point.

We now offer a reason for thinking abstracta are co-eternal with God. Recall, God's nature is not up to God. Further, if an attribute F is part of God's nature, it is no more up to Him what it is to be F than what His nature is (Leftow 2012, 122). Surely God's nature includes the property *being able to create a contingent universe*. Further, it is plausible to think that a necessary condition of being able to create the contingent universe is the existence and reality of platonic abstract objects—these structure-making properties that provide the character of any concrete world. If so, then God's creating abstract objects is not up to God, He creates them of necessity in virtue of His own nature, and they exist co-eternal with God.

The problem of universals

In the debate over the existence of abstract objects, Craig argues that the problem of universals is only of "marginal" (116) concern. Instead he focuses on the Indispensability Argument for platonism. If the latter argument can be shown faulty, then there are no compelling reasons, according to Craig, to think abstract objects exist. We think this is mistaken. Historically, the facts whose explanation posed the problem in the problem of universals were viewed as providing reason to think realism regarding universals true (i.e. multiply-instantiable objects exist). Recall that objects are either concrete or abstract. What would be involved then, in a concrete object being multiply-instantiable? Assume that a necessary and sufficient condition for a concrete object to be multiply-instantiable is that one and the same object would need to be multiply located (i.e. at different places at the same time). But this possibility is (to say the least) highly counterintuitive.[1] Hence, it is reasonable to conclude that concrete objects are not multiply-instantiable. But then, it follows that if an object is multiply-instantiable, it must be an abstract object.

So, what are the facts whose explanation motivates the problem of universals? We take it as a datum of our experience that there is a ready-made world and this world consists of natural groupings of objects. Things *resemble* each other, and these resemblance facts point to the *unity* of a class of objects. Plug these resemblance facts into a One Over Many Argument and we have good reason to think that the resemblance of "a is F" and "b is F" is grounded in the identity of Fness (i.e. Fness is a universal).

Craig (2011a) attempts to undercut this line of reasoning by arguing that (i) alleged resemblance facts supervene on qualitative facts (i.e. the "F" of "a is F"), and (ii) an account of qualitative facts, repeated *ad infinitum*, suffices to account for any alleged resemblance facts. An account of the qualitative facts are then provided—usually bottoming-out in bruteness—and the claim is made that the realist alternative is no better off in terms of explanatory power. In response, even if the nominalist account offered for qualitative facts is explanatorily on par with a realist account, this undercutting maneuver fails to explain resemblance facts. Rather, with a quick slight of hand, they have been swept under the rug. Even if each token of F can be explained, the natural groupings of qualitative facts—the various resemblance sets—lack an explanation. Hence, the problem of universals supplies us with good reasons to think abstract objects exist.[2]

The Indispensability Argument

Space prohibits a detailed discussion of Craig's analysis of the Indispensability Argument. Instead we offer a methodological point and a challenge. First, we think that Craig is approaching the question of abstract objects from the wrong starting point. He begins with linguistic/semantic considerations and reasons to an ontological conclusion. This approach puts the semantic cart before the metaphysical horse. Finally, however one understands ontological commitment, it is always the case that a truth has an ontology, and we challenge Craig to specify the ontology behind true divine ("God is good") and human ("Socrates is wise") predications.

Greg Welty

I commend Craig for his fine defense of divine aseity from scriptural, creedal, and patristic sources. There is indeed excellent precedent in the Church Fathers for "Christianizing the Forms." Yes, "it is not evident that abstract objects, if they exist, could not be things or individuals" (116). In my view, the "things" that are abstract objects (AOs) just are the divine ideas, and with Philo I hold that "the realm of Ideas does not exist independently of God but as the contents of His mind" (124n. 3). I too locate "the intelligible world in the Logos and, hence, in the mind of God" (124n. 6).

Craig states that conceptualism is the view that "abstract objects are replaced by some sort of mental or ideal objects" (115). I would not put it like that. Rather, AOs are *identified with* (not "replaced by") the divine ideas. Dualists and materialists about persons do not "replace" persons with something else. They both acknowledge persons and then give rival ontological accounts (van Inwagen 1986, 192–3).

Craig says that "lightweight platonism would not compromise divine aseity or universal creation because abstract objects do not really exist on such a view" (124n. 7). But *heavyweight platonism* would not compromise aseity or creation either, as long as the "heavyweight" objects in question are the divine ideas. (Presumably God isn't a lightweight, and theists aren't insouciant to think so.)

Craig distinguishes "two distinct philosophical debates": "the age-old dispute over universals," and "the philosophy of mathematics" (116). He thinks "the challenge of platonism to divine aseity concerns the second debate" (116). But the first debate is crucially about the ontological status of properties, and these *do* figure into the challenge of platonism to divine aseity. Morris and Menzel explicitly contextualize their position to both debates, since presumably necessarily existing properties are no less a threat to divine aseity than necessarily existing numbers.

Responding to the Indispensability Argument, Craig thinks he has reason to question either (I) the standard semantics for simple sentences, or (II) their truth value. Most of his objections to (I) can be alleviated if we put (I) into a more plausible form: (Ia) "If a simple sentence ... is literally true, then the objects that its singular terms denote exist, *unless we have a good reason for thinking otherwise.*" This makes clear the burden of proof, which seems to capture the intuitive basis for (I) anyway. Does *anyone* reject (Ia)? (Here I reverse the burden of proof Craig imposes on the platonist in Note 15.)

Craig says that if we accept (I), "then (II), which seems *prima facie* undeniably true, turns out to be far from obviously true and certainly one that the theist is at liberty to reject" (117). I may be missing something, but Craig seems to be saying that our acceptance of (I) can convert a "*prima facie* undeniably true" statement like (II) into something "far from obviously true." This seems like a *non sequitur*. Why would accepting (I) impact our acceptance of (II)? Yes, "the theist is at liberty to reject" (II). The question is whether this rejection is plausible, or is just special pleading because one does not like the conclusion inferred from it.

Craig wants to avoid platonist (read: (I)-style) understandings of "2+2=4," which would be "radical ontological assertions about the existence of mind-independent abstract objects ... Such a recondite metaphysical claim is not at all obviously true" (117). But if I understood correctly his earlier treatment of Scripture, the creeds, and the Church Fathers, these turn out to be "radical ontological assertions" about AOs, which we must take "to lie within the domain of their quantifiers"! Is Craig in two minds here? He allows simple scriptural claims to have "recondite metaphysical" implications, but disallows simple mathematical claims to have the same.

Craig bolsters his rejection of (II) by citing fictionalist Hartry Field, who defends his denial that "2+2=4" is true on the grounds that "analytic truths cannot have existential implications." Unfortunately, Field is committed to such truths having existential implications! After all, Field thinks that mathematics is *conservative*; it doesn't imply, all by itself, any contingent assertions about the world. And the consistency of mathematics follows from its conservativeness (Field 1980, vii, 13). Since mathematics is consistent, mathematical claims *could* all be true together. But since Field thinks that mathematical claims are false, then they must be *contingently* false. (They are false, but due to their consistency, they might have been true.) So it ought to be possible to describe the circumstances in which mathematical claims would be true. But that means the truth of mathematics *would*, all by itself, imply contingent assertions about the world. But if mathematics is conservative, then its truth *cannot*, all by itself, imply any contingent assertions about the world. It follows that Field's fictionalism "is a radically unstable position" (Hale 1987, 110).[3]

Craig bolsters his rejection of (I) by citing Jody Azzouni. Craig is right that "the quantifier of first-order logic" doesn't *automatically* "imply an ontology or carries ontological commitments" (119). But neither must we think the quantifier "is not ontologically committing until one so *stipulates*" (119, emphasis mine). For there may be a *good argument* that it does so commit, at least with respect to certain kinds of platonist objects. For instance, it is plausible to assume "that there is a speck of interstellar dust that is so small and so distant from us and any other language users there may be that no language user has any knowledge of it." If so, then it is equally obvious that "there are truths for which there is no linguistic expression." We cannot interpret the quantifier here substitutionally, for there is no linguistic expression that replaces *p* in "*p* and there is no linguistic expression for *p*" such that it comes out true. We must therefore quantify over objects rather than linguistic expressions. But that gets us language-independent entities which are the bearers of truth values: propositions (Welty, 2006, 41–4; cf. Loux 1986, 508; 1998, 148–51).

Scott A. Shalkowski

William Lane Craig's contribution begins by taking well-known biblical texts at what many would consider to be their face value. Citing creeds and Church Fathers, he demonstrates that he is not idiosyncratic in doing so. I wonder, though, whether we should treat the creeds and Fathers as authoritative on quite peculiar philosophical concerns. In the same way that Craig rightly observes that obvious workaday claims such as "2+2= 4" are no longer obvious when invested with platonistic meaning, so claims that God created all things seen and unseen is no longer theologically obvious when similarly invested. Agreed, biblical and early church writers no more had quarks in mind than universals or numbers, but theologically speaking quarks are just more detail to "the heavens and the earth" and are therefore contingent and within the scope of God's creation of the heavens and the earth. The unseen principalities and powers, whether personal or not, are similarly contingent and also come under the umbrella of God's creative act(s). We need not think that the Fathers were philosophically unsophisticated in order to think that on this count they had not weighed their options optimally. In the same way Roman Catholics maintain that the Pope is infallible only while Pope and only when speaking *ex cathedra*, so we need not take the creeds and the writings of the Fathers inspiring them as *ex cathedra* utterances about philosophical subtleties. We are entitled to wonder whether Augustine or Aquinas were correct on matters of neo-Platonic or Aristotelian metaphysics, so we may wonder whether the theological claims they or their predecessors made against the backgrounds of those metaphysics stand up to sustained scrutiny.

Craig is quite right to expect that philosophers put two and two together when constructing their theories and I agree with him that platonists have not done so adequately. It is not at all puzzling how two things and another two things are four things, but it is not evident what it even means to say that TWO (a specific platonic object) PLUS (another platonic object) TWO (the very same platonic object as before) EQUALS (a further platonic object) FOUR (yet another platonic object). From the platonist's mouth, it seems like we have merely named four distinct objects and not asserted anything. I, for one, do not know what this means and attempts to clarify it tend to slide into what is quite concrete and nominalistically-friendly (as above) or else into more mathematics, which is no help in interpreting the original mathematical claim.

I would like just a bit more discussion of how Walton's pretense theory helps mathematical fictionalists. If we ask an author of fiction about an ontological commitment to her leading character, the question is easily waved aside as exhibiting a failure to grasp that the work is fiction, in the standard case. Mathematicians could have resolved the platonist/nominalist dispute quite easily long ago, if pretense were prominent in their thinking. Walton-style fictionalism runs the risk of literally being our pretense about the pretenses of the users of mathematics. If one is in the game of saying what mathematics is all about, that seems doubly wrong. If the game is to give the proper semantics for mathematical sentences or assertions, it still seems wrong. Furthermore, it is not obvious why the mathematicians' pretenses could be relevant to real-world applications. If pretending helps us do better mathematics, the philosopher should ask what it is all, really, about that makes application possible. Noting only that there is pretense stops too soon. Fictionalism makes applied mathematics no less puzzling than does platonism, perhaps more so, since pretending is not usually a good way to better make one's way in the world.

I think I share Craig's inclination to let quantifying expressions sometimes signal ontological commitments and sometimes not. I would, though, not frame things in terms of sometimes "quantifying over" things that do not exist, there being none of those things to/with which to do anything. We have talk and in specific cases, the question is how to interpret it. I concur that uses of "there is/are" are not ontologically committing and that appeals to formal languages are misguided for the reasons he gives. I would prefer, though, not to avail myself of any reference to "thin" existence. Let us stick with "there is/are" constructions and embrace that "there is a chance he will attend" does not commit one to chances as objects, since this is merely one way to express something like "he might attend" or that "he probably won't attend." The question is which wears the trousers and nominalists can hold out for "paraphrases" that are quite obviously not ontologically committing.[4]

Graham Oppy

Craig argues: (1) That Scripture requires rejection of uncreated abstract objects; (2) that the central objection to anti-platonism about abstract objects is the Indispensability Argument; (3) that Quine's treatment of ontological commitment is bankrupt; (4) that there are good reasons to deny that there are some literally true simple sentences that refer to abstract objects; and (5) that we are free to quantify over whatever we wish quite independent of whether those things actually exist.

Ad (1): Craig admits that it is unlikely that Paul and John had abstract objects in mind when they claim that *all things* are from God (1 Cor. 8.6, 1 Cor. 11.12; Rom. 11.36; Jn 1.1–3). However, he insists that it is very likely that they intended their quantifiers to be "unrestricted once God is exempted." On its own, this seems pretty weak: Why couldn't it be that Paul and John just had causal objects in mind? Perhaps, as Craig suggests, John—following Philo—thought that "the intelligible realm of what we would today call 'abstract objects' is contained ... in the divine Logos"; but, in that case, surely John did have abstract objects in mind! It is probably also worth noting here that Plato and Pythagoras did *not* hold views about what we would today call "abstract objects;" rather, they held contentious views about *some* of the things that we might be inclined to class as "abstract objects." Even if it seemed acceptable to John to locate "the Forms" in the mind of God, it might not have seemed acceptable to him to place propositions, or states of affairs, or some other class of abstract objects in the mind of God.

Re (2): Craig—"following Balaguer"—formulates "the Indispensability Argument" as follows: *(A) If a simple sentence is literally true, then the objects that its singular terms denote exist. (B) There are literally true simple sentences containing simple terms that refer to things that could only be abstract objects. Therefore (C) Abstract objects exist.* It is probably worth observing that there are many other Indispensability Arguments, and that the discussion of those other arguments brings up very different considerations. (See, for example, Colyvan (2001).)

Ad (3): I think that Craig is not entirely fair to Quine. Quine thought that, when engaged in the project of systematically limning reality, one's use of quantification would reveal one's ontological commitments. It is not essential to this thought that one use first-order language (though Quine himself abhorred the use of any other language for this purpose); nor is it essential to this thought that the sentences of ordinary language can be paraphrased into canonical form (Quine was quite happy to dismiss attitude ascriptions as "second class" discourse *from the standpoint* of the project of limning reality). What seems to me to be the centrally contentious Quinean thought is the idea that, when engaged in the project of limning reality, one has no need to engage in certain kinds of pretense or to use pieces of vocabulary that are best given a fictionalist reading. Quine is a platonist because he thinks that, when one is engaged in the project of limning reality, one cannot avoid quantifying over numbers *and* because he thinks that this quantification over numbers cannot be explained away in fictionalist terms.

Ad (4): Craig offers three reasons for favoring fictionalist interpretations of simple mathematical sentences such as "1+1=2": (a) axiomatization naturally invites a fictionalist interpretation; (b) creative freedom makes set theory particularly apt for fictionalist interpretation; and (c) the "incompleteness of mathematical entities" makes set theory especially amenable to fictionalist interpretation. These reasons seem pretty weak to me. In particular, it is worth noting that there are platonists who suppose that, for each consistent mathematical theory, there are objects that serve as truthmakers for all of the claims of that mathematical theory. If those platonists are right, then all of Craig's reasons have no force. Moreover, of course, there are plenty of mathematicians who suppose that mathematicians do not have as much freedom as Craig supposes: The results of mathematics are there to be discovered; we are not just free to make them up (see, e.g. Woodin (2011)). Despite all of this, I am skeptical that there are literally true simple sentences in which the singular terms refer to abstract objects, at least granted the further assumption that a literally true simple sentence cannot, at the same time, be nothing more than a piece of fiction. If you think that "Santa has a white beard" is literally true—because that's what the fiction says—then, of course, you're going to think that there can be literally true simple sentences in which the singular terms do not refer to objects that belong to Causal Reality.

Ad (5): As already noted, the key question is not whether we are free to quantify over whatever we wish quite independent of whether those things actually exist, but rather whether we are free to do this when we are engaged in the project of limning reality. Perhaps Craig might claim that, in this case, we have just *stipulated* that the quantifiers are ontologically committing. If so, fine: that's what Quine himself did! If you are giving an ontological inventory, for the purposes of philosophical theorizing, then no doubt you should eschew the kinds of things that we ordinarily say (exemplified by the lists in Craig's paper)!

A final thought. Craig is very quick to dismiss platonism about properties, on the grounds that we would explain John's being fleet by adverting to other properties that he possesses: his being muscular, well fed, consistently trained, and so forth. But, if we explain properties in terms of other properties, there are only three possibilities: explanation eventually runs in a circle; explanation regresses infinitely; explanation terminates in properties that cannot be explained in terms of other properties. I guess that Craig would take the third option; but, if so, he hasn't *completed* his anti-platonistic account of properties.

Notes

1   For more see Grossmann (1992, 11–13).
2   For more see Gould (2012).
3   Craig finds the "pretense theoretical approach to mathematical statements" to be "extremely plausible" (118). But Jerrold Katz's reference to the Sherlock Holmes corpus gives me pause: "There is a basic difference between mathematics and literature: consistency is an absolute constraint in mathematics but not in fiction.

The explanation is obviously that fiction is fiction and mathematics is fact" (1998,
Ꮮ   13–14).
4   I use the scare quotes merely to make clear that nominalists need not maintain
    that the paraphrase is semantically equivalent to what is paraphrased. Even if the
    paraphrase loses some features such as the fit with scaling that permit us to speak
    of greater and lesser chances, it may still express what the original is really about. It
    is not as though there are tiny chances more of which yield large ones and it is not
    as if chances come in different sizes, even for one prone to take quantification over
    chances seriously. If there are tiny chances how do they aggregate? If they come in
    different sizes, how does a chance of the relevant size attach to the relevant claim one
    makes, whether the claim is construed as an abstract proposition or as a concrete
    utterance or inscription? One thinking these are silly questions does not really take
    the relevant ontological project seriously, either.

Response to Critics

William Lane Craig

Theological considerations

The crucial question concerning a biblically adequate doctrine of divine aseity is whether the biblical authors intended the domain of their quantifiers to be so restricted as to permit *abstracta* to escape God's creation.[1] Yandell commits a hermeneutical *faux pas* when he intimates that nonscriptural reasons could motivate our so interpreting them. No, we must be guided by authorial intent. We need reasons taken from the writings of Paul and John themselves for restricting the domain of their quantifiers. But there is none; quite the contrary. As monotheistic Jews they held that everything apart from God has been created by God. Were they challenged with alleged counterexamples, like sin, temptation, and the items on Hofweber's list (my lead essay, p. 120), they would not have conceded that there are, after all, uncreated things but could plausibly reply that these are not really things, i.e. beings, and so no revision of their doctrine is required.

Contrary to Gould/Davis the biblical witness asserts more than that God is eternal; John says that everything other than God and His Logos belongs to the realm of things that have come into being (*egeneto*, Jn 1.3). That is why the Church Fathers recognized that there could be but one *agenetos*. I agree with Shalkowski that we should not treat the creeds and Fathers as authoritative; but I claim that they have correctly drawn out the implications of Scripture regarding divine aseity and *creatio ex nihilo*.

It is disappointing to realize that ultimately Gould/Davis's view is no better than Yandell's. For, as their replies make clear, when it comes to the bootstrapping problem, their "solution" is to abandon absolute creationism and revert to platonism. For they hold that there are uncreated abstract objects, namely, various properties which God has essentially, like *omnipotence*. They try to soften the blow by insisting that these abstract objects are "in" God and part of God. But if they agree with the overwhelming majority of realists that properties are constituents of things or in things only by way of exemplification,[2] properties remain objects distinct from God. Worse, given the platonist's ontological assay of things, God is divine only in virtue of His standing in relation to such objects, so that God's deity depends upon these beings. This is an outright denial of divine self-existence.

Finally, we also have the philosophico-theological grounds for anti-platonism mentioned in my reply to Shalkowski.

The Indispensability Argument

The modest aim of my essay is to defend the tenability of anti-realism with respect to abstract objects in the face of the Indispensability Argument, the most important argument for platonism. Contra Gould/Davis it is not I but the platonist who, in offering this argument, puts the semantic cart before the metaphysical horse, and I agree with them in rejecting this approach.[3] Recall the argument:

(I) If a simple sentence is literally true, then the objects that its singular terms denote exist. (Likewise, if an existential sentence is literally true, then there exist objects of the relevant kinds.)

(II) There are literally true simple sentences containing singular terms that refer to things that could only be abstract objects. (Likewise, there are literally true existential statements whose existential quantifiers range over things that could only be abstract objects.)

(III) Therefore, abstract objects exist.

Against (II) I defend the viability of fictionalism. Yandell reminds us that Balaguer is in the end, not a fictionalist, but an arealist (see Figure 1, p. 40). But I carry no brief for arealism; it is anti-realism that I defend. Indeed, since it is impossible that objects uncreated by God exist, there must be a fact of the matter here, and therefore arealism is necessarily false.

So I agree with Welty in rejecting Field's strange view that mathematical objects only contingently fail to exist. It is metaphysically impossible that such uncreated objects exist. Does that imply that mathematics is therefore inconsistent? Not at all, since the metaphysical modality of which we here speak is a broader sort of modality that does not preclude mathematics' possibility in a stricter sense.

Even though Welty himself rejects (II) because he thinks that the referents of mathematical singular terms are not abstract objects but divine ideas, he is not sympathetic to fictionalism. He points out that mathematics differs from fiction in its demand for consistency, which he takes to be indicative of a concern for truth. But, despite its name, fictionalism does not hold that mathematics is of the genre of fiction, but merely that mathematical statements are not true. Mathematicians are concerned with consistency because they are in the business of deriving theorems from axioms, and if the axioms are inconsistent, then anything and everything follows, making the enterprise pointless.

Yandell asks about the status of logical truths like "Metaphysical identity is necessary" from a fictionalist perspective. Insofar as these involve quantification over abstract objects or singular terms for such objects, given the customary criterion of ontological commitment, such statements are not true.[4] That does not, however, prevent our truly asserting, for example, that necessarily, Yandell = Yandell.

Shalkowski thinks that Walton-style fictionalism runs the risk of misrepresenting what the practitioners of mathematics are really doing. But here recall the distinction drawn in my reply to Oppy between hermeneutic and revolutionary nominalism (188–9). There has not been to date any sociological survey of professional mathematicians to determine what they mean by their mathematical statements. So I am not defending hermeneutical nominalism but arguing that a pretense theoretical approach is one tenable interpretation of such discourse.

Oppy is unpersuaded by my three analogies between fictional and mathematical discourse. But to subvert these he is forced to recur to full-blooded platonism (*cf.* 135), a dubiously coherent position espoused by a very few philosophers, according to which even mutually inconsistent mathematical theories have, as Oppy notes, truthmakers. Yes, there are mathematicians who are platonists and so deny the freedom of which I speak. But—not to mention the variety of set theories on offer today—unless we add to ZFC set theory an Axiom of Constructibility so as to ensure that the universe of constructible sets L which is a model of ZFC is identical to the entire universe of sets V (L =V), the mathematician's imagination may ascend boundlessly through inaccessible cardinals, Mahlo cardinals, indescribable cardinals, to partition cardinals, measurable cardinals, and so on. Pretense theory makes far better sense of this remarkable freedom than does platonism. Within the bounds of logical consistency, we are free to make believe that there are mathematical entities of every imaginable sort and to explore the consequences without concern that we are thereby misdescribing reality.

Finally, I second Shalkowski's claim that fictionalism does no better than platonism in explaining the applicability of mathematics to the physical world. My take on the so-called "unreasonable effectiveness of mathematics" is that applicability, *for the fictionalist and platonist alike*, requires theism.[5] God has constructed the physical world on the mathematical structure that He had in mind, and therefore mathematics is applicable to the world.

All this has been said with respect to premise (II), when, in fact, it is premise (I) that I most vigorously protest. Why adopt the metaontological criterion of ontological commitment that (I) expresses?

What is wrong, first, with a neutralist perspective on quantification? Notice that neutralism is not the same as quantifier variance, the view that there are two senses of "existence" expressed by the first-order existential quantifier. I agree with Shalkowski that we should shun appeal to a "thin" versus "thick" sense of "existence."[6] Rather the view is that "there is/are" and the formal quantifier which symbolizes such expressions is just neutral, rather than commissive.

Welty presents an argument for taking the first-order existential quantifier to be ontologically committing. But what he gives is an objection to *substitutional* quantification. This betrays misunderstanding, for Azzouni's neutralism concerns objectual, not substitutional quantification.[7] Wholly apart from its merits, therefore, the objection is irrelevant to neutralism.

Oppy insists that we can just stipulate that we are using the first-order existential quantifier to make ontological commitments. Fine; then in the stipulated sense I deny that there are abstract objects, just as I deny that there are holes, Wednesdays, and prospects for success. So long as we are clear that we are speaking in a metaphysically heavy sense, the anti-realist can make his commitments clear. Thus, it appears that none of my collaborators has any substantive objection to neutralism.

So, second, what is wrong with a deflationary theory of reference?

Yandell, in saying that according to nominalism mathematical statements "involve no reference to abstract objects," shows that he has not grasped Båve's theory, for it allows a person successfully to refer to, say, 2, even though 2 does not exist.

Welty wants to revise (I) such that objects denoted by singular terms in true sentences must exist, *unless we have a good reason for thinking otherwise.* I am dubious that there should be such a presumption; but in any case we surely do have excellent reason for thinking that uncreated abstract objects do not exist, namely, the theological considerations surveyed above. It must be remembered that Welty himself agrees that such objects do not exist. When he identifies abstract objects with God's ideas, he is speaking merely functionally. So, again, I see no substantive objection to a deflationary theory of singular terms which allows us to talk about abstract objects without ontological commitment.

Hence, I think that the principal argument for platonism is a failure, *QED.*

The problem of universals

Gould/Davis think that facts of resemblance require platonic properties. Unfortunately, in our limited space I can hardly reply in detail to Gould/Davis and Oppy's objections to what I have said *elsewhere* on this head.[8] I can but state my opinion that Gould/Davis basically just reiterate the demand for an explanation of resemblance without responding to my reasons for thinking that no explanation is required besides an account of why a thing is as described. *Pace* Oppy, I did not mean that the having of a property is to be explained in terms of the having of another property, since there are, in a metaphysically heavy sense, no such things as properties; rather we can rest content with a scientific explanation of why, for example, the dog is brown without adverting to suspicious metaphysical entities like properties.

Notes

1   Contra Oppy, the issue is, to repeat, *not* what John and Paul had in mind, but the unrestrictedness of their quantifiers. Still, given the Johannine Prologue's affinities to Middle Platonism, I think it not at all unlikely that its author took the platonic realm of being to reside in the Logos and the realm of becoming to comprise only causal objects.
2   So Moreland (2001, 126).
3   They insist that truth must have an ontology; but I reject this claim (see Merricks 2007). Besides, an ontologically neutral, deflationary theory of truth is defensible (see Båve 2006). In any case, the question remains whether *abstracta* must be part of that ontology.
4   This is why, to answer Welty's question, accepting (I) impacts accepting (II). Given the criterion of ontological commitment, (II) is seen to be both implausible and theologically unacceptable. Welty himself rejects (II), since divine thoughts are not abstract but concrete objects. I agree that the scriptural passages I cite have radical metaphysical implications; but the difference between them and elementary arithmetic sentences is that as Christians we are committed to the truth of scriptural

teaching, whereas the sentences of elementary arithmetic are not obviously true given the customary criterion of ontological commitment. Indeed, as Christians we must advert to either anti-realism, as I do, or nonplatonistic realism, as Welty does, regarding such statements.

5   See my discussion in Craig (forthcoming).

6   Note that in so doing we obviate any need to "hold out for paraphrases" of abstract discourse. Resort to paraphrase is the procedure of those who *accept* the customary criterion of ontological commitment but want to avoid the fantastic commitments it would foist upon us.

7   Philosophers typically distinguish two interpretations of the first-order logical quantifiers: the objectual (or referential) and the substitutional. The objectual interpretation of the existential quantifier conceives it as ranging over a domain of objects and picking out some of those objects as values of the variable bound by it. The substitutional interpretation takes the variable to be a sort of place-holder for linguistic expressions which can be substituted for it to form sentences. The substitutional interpretation is generally recognized not to be ontologically committing. But Azzouni maintains that even the objectual interpretation of the quantifier is not ontologically committing until one so stipulates (Azzouni 2004, 54).

8   Craig (2011a).

5

God with or without Abstract Objects

Scott A. Shalkowski

The magnificence of God, if God is any decent kind of monotheistic deity, is to be not only unsurpass*ed* (too easily done), but also unsurpass*able*. Let us stipulate that all parties agree. Let us also stipulate that all agree that God is sovereign, so that things turn out as God wants them to be, at least at some level of generality. Finally, stipulate that as there is asymmetry regarding who gets to boss whom, there is asymmetry regarding who is dependent upon whom. For theists maintaining that God is (at least) so characterized, we have the makings of a theological problem.

Abstract objects, at least as conceived by platonists, exist necessarily. Furthermore, they limn the ultimate structure of reality. Platonic universals are to give concrete reality its structure, they are to be singular in themselves, but multiply instantiable, thus permitting us to speak literally and truly when we speak of distinct objects having or possessing *the very same* property, attribute, or characteristic no more and no less than when we speak of one group of objects as standing in the very same relation as do the objects of a distinct group.

Mathematical objects are supposed to be the distinctive subject of study of mathematicians. Those who distinguish between pure and applied mathematics think that the pure mathematicians are those concerned solely with abstract objects in their characteristic intellectual endeavors. Numbers, functions, and, perhaps most basically, sets are supposed by mathematical platonists to be like platonic universals. They exist necessarily.

The theological problem arises for those who think that God created all that there is and also that both God's existence and God's characteristics are independent of anyone and anything else. The creation doctrine is threatened, if abstract objects are uncreated. The independence doctrine is threatened, if existing or having distinctively divine attributes requires that there be abstract objects.

In this contribution, I defend two claims. First, the theological problems do not arise, because there are insufficient grounds for thinking that there are abstract objects. Second, the theological problems do not arise because even if abstract objects do exist as platonists think they do, they pose no problem for God's sovereignty or aseity. The argument for the second has two components. First, there are limits and then there are limits. The so-called limits platonism would place upon God are merely notional and none any should care about. Second, it is not mandatory for at least Christian theists to think that the doctrine of creation requires that abstract object are created and it is not mandatory to think that the kind of sovereignty or aseity that a theologian should care about is impugned by the existence of abstracta.

I set aside one not uncommon view about universals which, if true, immediately reduces the apparent theological problem. I ignore for the remainder of this discussion the thesis that universals (and its analogues for other abstracta) are Aristotelian in nature, i.e. that they exist contingently and that they exist only when instantiated. I note in passing that as stated the Aristotelian thesis about universals is imprecise about whether the "only when" is not only modally but also temporally sensitive. One thesis is that universals exist, to use the popular metaphor, in any possible world in which there are particulars that instantiate it. It is a further refinement of the thesis to determine whether universals exist in those worlds only *when* they are instantiated. I ignore this view, since even though the metaphysics of the matters is not perfectly obvious, it is at least plausible to suppose that one viable theistic option is that unlike Plato's platonic option, Aristotelian universals are dependent upon God. All universals pertaining to God's intrinsic characteristics exist only if God exists and so God is the necessary condition for their existence. Those universals dependent upon other things for their existence still depend upon God, since all of those other things depend upon God as creator, according to standard theologies.

The cases for abstracta

At the root of much metaphysical thinking is some variation of a truthmaker principle. In its most general form the truthmaker principle is that Truth supervenes upon Being; truths do not just "hang" "ungrounded." The basic idea is that necessarily, a truthbearer is true, only if something makes it true. Perhaps one begins with a common sense ontology of, to use a technical term, *individuals* such as Aristotle and Peggy Sue, but familiar arguments lead many to think that a philosophically-suitable ontology will require expanding our ontological horizons to include universals, propositions, and numbers. "Aristotle" and "Peggy Sue" function as names in truths, lending credence to the claim that those expressions successfully refer. Similarly, "justice," "red," "7," and "the set of primes less than 100" appear in truths ("Justice is a virtue," "Red is a color," "7 is prime," and "The set of primes less than 100 is countable"), lending credence to the claim that those expressions successfully refer. Perhaps 7 can be thought to be an individual, just not an individual as concrete as Aristotle, but the referent of "red" is not plausibly thought to be an individual. Hence, "object" is broader than "individual," so that universals would count as countable objects in our ontology alongside more familiar individuals. One of the more prominent proponents of both a truthmaker principle and this commitment to universals was D. M. Armstrong (Armstrong 1978, 1997). Among many others regarding universals are Michael Loux (1978) and Roderick Chisholm (1989).

Lest one think that individuals suffice to make true claims that appear to be about abstract objects, even common sense will lead us to think otherwise. Individuals exist in great number and variety, but in the absence of good reason to think that their variety is maximal, i.e. the greatest possible, then it seems that there are unexemplified characteristics (Chisholm 1989, 141–2).[1]

Chisholm claims that there is no way to paraphrase such truths into truths about individuals. If a paraphrase is to preserve the meaning of the paraphrased, then he is right; the original is about characteristics while a paraphrase will be about individuals. If a paraphrase is merely to exhibit the truth-conditions of the paraphrased, then whether he is right depends upon what else one countenances. Embrace sufficiently many individuals suitably unlocated relative to us and you might think that a suitable paraphrase is available (Lewis 1986).[2] There may be no individuals here in the actual world with said characteristics, but there are in other, merely possible concrete worlds. Either way, limiting ourselves to the existence and characteristics of actual concrete individuals will not suffice for a paraphrase, leaving the initial plausibility of platonism about universals intact for most.[3] Cutting off the prospect that unexemplified characteristics can be accommodated by an irreducibly modal truth because it is *possible* that objects exhibit characteristics that no object happen to exhibit and thus cutting off the move to platonism, Peter van Inwagen argues for platonism about universals from the observation that actual objects share characteristics (van Inwagen 2004, 113–24). Such are the broad contours of grounds for embracing universals.

Another route to abstract objects is through truths themselves. Not all of history has been human history. It is true that before there were humans there were the Sun, Moon, and stars. It might be natural to think that if there are things that bear truth value, those things are beliefs, assertions, or sentences, each of which are concrete items perfectly acceptable to nominalists. What to do about truths that antedate humans, though? If before the advent of humans there were truths about the Sun, Moon, and stars, then there were truthbearers before humans. So beliefs, assertions, or sentences were not eligible to be the bearers of truth. Hence, abstract propositions are required as those truthbearers.[4]

Finally, mathematical objects are embraced for reasons similar to those provided on behalf of universals and propositions. Like abstract nouns such as "justice" and "red" that seem to refer in the context of truths, so too numerical expressions like "7" and "the set of primes less than 100" appear in the context of truths and, so, seem to refer no less (Hale and Wright 2001). For others, the argument is slightly different. As Chisholm and van Inwagen think that quantification over properties and relations signals a commitment to properties and relations and the *unavoidable* quantification provides epistemic grounds for that commitment, so the unavoidable use of quantified mathematical discourse in the context of our best theories of the world provide grounds for thinking that there are mathematical objects (Quine, Ontic Decision 1960; Putnam 1971; Colyvan 2001).[5]

Dissolving the problem: Part 1

The most comprehensive strategy for avoiding platonism is to reject the most general form of the truthmaker principle. Truth does not supervene upon Being. Perhaps there is no fair dinkum object designated by expressions like "the world" to "make true" some truths, so not only are there no individuals or groups of individuals to render true some truths, there isn't even "the world" to render them true. Or, perhaps, there is such an all-encompassing object, but there is no meaningful sense in which it renders some truths true; they just are true. One who thinks that at least some basic truths of necessity and possibility are true but not in virtue of how things are categorically or one who thinks that there are irreducible counterfactuals of incompatibilist freedom might think that these are just foundational truths and that adding "about the world" adds nothing of substance beyond expressing that they are true. Irreducible possibility claims just amount to claims that things could have been this way or that and irreducible necessity claims just amount to claims that things must be this way or that. Pick your favorite examples. Euclidean triangles must have internal angles that sum to 180 degrees. Mammals must give birth to live young and not by way of laid eggs. Water is essentially H_2O. It is possible to checkmate an opponent in fewer than 50 moves. I could have chosen engineering over philosophy. Wherever the irreducible modal claims lie, they are not about an over-arching reality—the world—but about things that are or could be part of the world: triangles, mammals, water, endings to chess matches, or life choices of individual people. There are useful options that are too little explored in this connection, but there are other avenues that will seem less disorienting to those still wishing to retain the general truthmaker idea.

All of the platonist strategies surveyed share the feature that the way we currently express ourselves is the place to begin our investigation and that no part of the investigation should involve asking how we came to express ourselves this way. There is no question that we express ourselves—and do so reasonably well—when we say things like "Justice is a virtue" and "Red is a color." Such sentences are grammatically similar to "Leeds is in Yorkshire" and "The United Kingdom is an island nation." "There are some napkins on the table" is similar to "There are some anatomical features that insects have and spiders also have," to use one of van Inwagen's examples (van Inwagen 2004, 114). If we express truth with all of these, as I think we do, and if we have apparently referring expressions in some that actually do refer or quantificational expressions that sometimes do range over existents, then what besides nominalist prejudices prevent recognizing existents as referents or members of the relevant domains for the others?

Before wandering into the philosophy or theology seminar rooms, what were we trying to express when we made claims that appear to commit us to abstract objects? Were we groping for ways to express something about the contents of Plato's heaven with all of the wonders and horrors of the abstract? Or, were we instead trying to express something about the concrete but with a modicum of efficiency that required a greater degree of generality in our articulation? In short, is it plausible to think that we get to the sensible use of "There are some anatomical features that insects have and spiders also have," "Before there were humans, it was true that the Sun, Moon, and stars were doing their things," and "7 is prime" because we struggle to articulate insights into *abstracta* or because we struggle to articulate insights into the concrete by way of acts of *abstraction*? I make a case for the latter, based on the principle that "we" begin with warranted beliefs about the concrete and that if all moves to abstraction are those that a nominalist can happily countenance, then there are insufficient grounds for the move to platonism in the first place.[6]

I begin with the case for propositions. That is the most straightforward. The construction "it is true that" and its cognates serve many different purposes. Sometimes it is nothing more than a way of making explicit one's agreement with or concession to the claim of another, as when that expression appears before a repetition of what another has already said. "Is true" also permits us to make indirect reference to the content of what has been said without repeating it, as in "What John just said is true." Now it may be that John has said a lot and perhaps because he is an expert and I am a rank amateur, much of what he said was rather inscrutable to me. Claims regarding the truth of John's assertions permits me a very efficient means of effectively repeating them for the sake of the conversation but without the tedium of actually doing so.

Now John in all likelihood did not speak explicitly about truthbearers and their truth values. He spoke of whom he voted for in the last election and why, of his views on the current political landscape, or of what he wants to be when he finally grows up. In explicitly linguistic terms, the claims of John's that I say are true were claims made in the object language, not in the metalanguage. He was not concerned at all with truthbearers and their truth values, he was concerned with reality, with how things are.

Like John, our primary concern about the Sun, Moon, and stars in the past is a concern about those celestial objects. When we *say* that before any of us were around to care about them, it was true that they were doing their things, in the first instance our concern is not with whether there really were truth bearers that really were true while the rocks were still hot. We are not concerned with:

(T) Millions of years before the advent of humans, "The Sun is burning" was true.

We are concerned with:

(S) Millions of years before the advent of humans, the Sun was burning.

We did not create or invent the Sun and we did not determine its history. In no interesting way is the Sun's existence and character a matter of our creation or determination. In this sense, the Sun's existence and character is objective. Those drawn to (T) frame issues about objectivity in metalinguistic terms, but those terms are unnecessary. If we remain in the object language, which is after all our primary means of speaking about reality, we see that truth is neither here nor there. Concerns about the objective nature of the Sun are only obliquely expressed in (T). (S) gives us all that we need, yet it has nothing to do with truthbearers and truth values. It concerns the Sun. So, we should not grant the initial assumption of the platonistic reasoning for propositions. There is no good reason to think that it was true millions of years before the advent of humans that the Sun was burning, even though there is overwhelmingly good reason to think that millions of years before the advent of humans, the Sun was burning. The preceding sentence implicitly shows the slipperiness of that reasoning; it often involves insufficient attention to issues of object language and metalanguage. Once those are separated cleanly, we can do with the object language and see that the introduction of truth-predicates into a metalanguage is merely a tool of convenience and of no metaphysical significance.

Properties as abstract objects can be treated similarly. Consider an earlier example:

(A) There are some anatomical features that insects have and spiders also have.

The convenience here is that I'd like a means of expressing similarity, but a means sufficiently abstract that I will have a tool to use in many different circumstances. It turns out that insects and spiders have legs, brains, eyes, hearts, exoskeletons, and much more in common. Similarly for other individuals and kinds of individuals. I'd like to be able to say that Charlotte and her baby spiders are similar, I'd like to be able to say that Charlotte and Jiminy Cricket are similar, and I'd like to be able to say that what is so for Charlotte and Jiminy will remain so when I have in mind other individual spiders and insects.

Once again, my interest is not in abstract objects, but it is in the abstract treatment of concrete objects. Sometimes I just am not that interested in Charlotte and Jiminy. I am interested in other animals extraordinarily like Charlotte, so I introduce "spider" and similarly for Jiminy "insect." Sometimes I am interested in having legs, sometimes in having brains, eyes, hearts, or exoskeletons and when I am, I'll say so. Sometimes, though, I am not that concerned with whether we focus on hearts or skeletons or any of the others, so it is a convenience to introduce "anatomical features."

Now is (A) accurate because there is an abstract reality and "in" that reality there are the abstract kinds of spiders and insects and abstract anatomical features, the specifics of which are other abstract objects such as being brainy, being sighted, being a cordate, etc. suitably related to make (A) accurate? Or, is it rather that we begin with, perhaps, concerns about Charlotte and Jiminy and about whether they each have eyes and exoskeletons, but then as our thinking and conversations advance we care less and less about the individuals and less and less about legs and skeletons so that (A) is now a useful tool for expressing what I want to express about Charlotte and her kin as well as about Jiminy and his kin and about how well or poorly they and their respective kin compare to each other? It is not difficult to maintain that the concern was and is about concreta and not about abstracta. The more the platonist is compelled to spell out the details of the platonist metaphysics, the less plausible it is to think that the duty of (A) is to express specific information about abstract objects and the more plausible it is to think that its duty is to express abstract information about concrete objects. Lest one think that this is a distinction without a difference it is not hard at all to construct a train of human interests and linguistic behavior that takes us from "Charlotte has a brain" and "Jiminy has a brain" to (A), while it is quite difficult—probably requiring a fair amount of time in the philosophy seminar room—to construct similar sense in the use of (A) to articulate a primary interest in abstracta.[7]

The nominalist's tack regarding mathematical objects is now sketched. Early mathematical discourse was quite firmly rooted in the concrete, for record keeping and for business transactions (Robson 2008). Numerical constructions with which we are so familiar (e.g. "7+5 =12") can be seen as instances of degenerate predication. So long as we are summing the sheep we have, we can use pastoral predicates:

(P) 7 sheep + 5 sheep = 12 sheep.

As soon as I wish to sum other farming commodities, such as adding the sheep in the field to the sheaves of grain in the barn, (P) will not do. The predicates don't work. 7 sheep and 5 sheaves yield 12, but neither sheep nor sheaves. One option is to find a more general predicate so that some addition and farm-related predication makes sense:

(F) 7 farm products + 5 farm product = 12 farm products

thus, showing that I don't really care at the moment whether I'm summing sheep, sheaves, sheep or sheaves, or even shears or scythes. Such acts of abstracting away from the details of the individuals that are the subject of our summings can continue, but not forever. At some point—whether for deep metaphysical reasons or for somewhat superficial reasons of inattention to detail—the predicates become otiose. It is informative to tell me that I am adding together the sheep in two portions of a field. It is not informative to tell me that I am adding 7 objects of some kind or other to 5 objects of some kind or other. The predication being useless, it is quite reasonably discarded. Once it is discarded, we just have the familiar arithmetic equation.

The equation arrives on the scene, though, with no required deep insight into a realm of peculiar objects. They are peculiar, but not because the nominalist finds them so. The nominalist's preferences are not especially interesting to platonists. Rather they are peculiar because of what the platonist says about them. We have distinct objects that when added together "form" a new one (many equivalent new ones, actually), but they are not typically *composed* of one another. They are distinct objects, but their only real intrinsic features are how they stand relative to each other in some sequence or hierarchy. They are abstract, yet sometimes perfectly concrete objects are their proper members.

What has been said of the mathematical discourse relevant to arithmetic can be extended to other portions, including the discourse of sets. Our set-theoretic discourse is what we use when our concerns are so abstract that we care only about the distinct identity of individuals. Nothing else comes into play. If we take seriously the claim that all of mathematics can be reduced to or at least translated into set theory, then no more need be done to show that as with propositions and properties, the nominalist is justified in thinking that there is no warrant for the metaphysical step to platonism.[8] If there is sense in the use of abstract nouns and the quantification over truths, properties, or numbers or any other use of such discourse, we can account for our use of that discourse—even to speak seriously and truly—as serving our purposes to speak indirectly or abstractly about the concrete rather than to speak directly about the abstract. From the metaphysical side of things, our apparent theological problem dissolves.

Dissolving the problem: Part 2

Suppose, *pace* Section 3, theists are stuck with abstract objects. What's the theologian to do? The problem divides. How to deal with the prospect of abstracta, if one adheres to some form of perfect being theology and how to so deal, if one does not so adhere. I take up the former in this section and the latter in the next.

Perfect being theologians give no quarter to those who wish to rethink God's attributes or the philosophically-inspired glosses put upon them. God is the greatest being possible. Standard platonism about abstract objects is that those objects are uncreated, so not subject to God's sovereignty. They are what they are and necessarily so. Being a concrete individual, God possesses attributes but only by virtue of being appropriately related to the relevant platonic objects. Furthermore, those objects bind God. The universal *being a spider* prohibits God from creating the spider Charlotte just any way God likes. No exoskeleton, no Charlotte. Mathematical objects make God unable to generate 13 from 7 and 5 and logical objects, if such there be, prevent God from rendering *modus ponens* invalid. Even God cannot produce invalidators for standard mathematical and logical deductions.

Remaining neutral regarding the scope of necessity, let us simply stipulate that abstract objects place boundaries on possibility. Not only are those objects immutable, they couldn't have been otherwise. They do not change, they could not change, and they could not have (begun to be) otherwise. No such necessity places a theologically troublesome restriction on God.

The theistic apologist has a theoretical motive for thinking this. When doing big-picture religious apologetics, one of the key questions is: How do we know when we should stop asking "Why?" questions? Many things, both theological and empirical, are subject to further explanation. Things are this way, but they are not *just* this way. Things are this way *because* of the way(s) some other things are, and so on for those other things. At some stage, theist and atheist confront the issue of under what conditions this process should stop.

It is sometimes alleged that a simple child's question undermines cosmological arguments. The argument charges that the world requires a Cause. Not so, implies the child-inspired objector. One can always ask a version of the child's "But, Daddy, who made God?" thus stumping the religious apologist with self-contradiction. God cannot be the Ultimate Cause, the Stopping Point for All Explanation, if everything must have a cause or a further explanation.

Set aside that no respectable cosmological argument begins with the troublesome premise that everything must have a cause (distinct from itself), showing that the child-inspired objector is childish at that level of objection. Note only that on some of the more important versions of that particular argument, a particular modal fact about the cosmos—that it is contingent—is noted. From there it is inferred, however justly, that there is a Necessary Being that explains this big contingency.

At this point, those resisting the argument will in one way or another suggest that we should just make our peace with this big contingency. That's all there is; get over it.

At one point in the development of the cosmology, this much seemed to be implied by Big Bang physics. Given the nature of that event, the intimate intertwining of space and time, the basic theoretical framework might have been taken to imply that on the basis of well-confirmed theory, asking "But, Daddy, who caused the Big Bang?" exhibited the failure to grasp that the question is ill-conceived. All theories have their fundamentals and with those fundamentals there are questions that the theory must treat as unaskable. When the theory is supposed to be one's most fundamental theory of the subject matter, the unaskability of those questions is absolute. On this most structural level, all fundamental theories are on a par.

Not all important features of theories are structural, however. There will be differences regarding the things treated as fundamental by a theory. God is supposed to exist necessarily, if at all, while the cosmos is supposed to be the contingent. For a contingency, there is nothing ill-conceived in asking after its cause or explanation. Indeed, that is effectively what Super String theorists and Quantum Gravity theorists have done. They resist the thought that the Big Bang was the Ultimate Contingency and they treated seriously the child-inspired question. This was perfectly sensible, given that the explosion and its character was most plausibly thought to be contingent. That those allegedly more fundamental theories might show no advantage over Big Bang cosmology does not show that the question that inspired them is ill-conceived, only that attempts to answer it yielded no advance in physical theory.

God, like other necessities, is quite different. When it is recognized that something exists necessarily or is necessarily thus-and-so, it is not a deeply insightful question to ask about its cause or explanation. It is to invite properly the return question, "What part of 'necessary' don't you understand?" Necessity really is the ultimate stopping place. God, in the dialectical context of some cosmological arguments, is that necessity that takes some theoretical options off of the table, options that properly remain when thinking about contingencies.

The moral is that it is a mistake to think that there are deeper explanations for necessities. It is similarly mistaken to think that the limits of possibility are akin to chains that bind anyone, even God. If it is not possible for things to be or have been otherwise; there is no*thing* God could have done otherwise. If there was no thing God could have done otherwise because no-one could have done otherwise, how is it any failing of any divine attribute that God is unable to do it? If there is no other way for God to be, how is it a failing of any divine attribute that God possesses it and not another? Believers in incompatibilist freedom already make their perfectly proper peace with the fact that there are some possibilities that even God cannot insure, such as my freely performing some action. That is no troublesome limit on divine sovereignty precisely because it's just what freedom *is* that excludes God's insurance from free creaturely action. Any limits imposed by abstracta are no different. That the platonist thinks of these limits as a matter of the existence and character of objects is neither here nor there. It's the modal character that matters and dissolves the problem.

What of God's independence? Similar remarks apply. Suppose that dependence is in the neighbourhood of a condition such as: If those objects did not exist or were different, God would not exist or would be different. This is just in objectual garb the idea that God is and couldn't be otherwise, at least regarding God's distinctively divine attributes. That is just what it is to be God. It makes sense to worry that God might be inappropriately limited by the existence and character of abstracta, if there were something on the other side of the limit, but there is nothing metaphysical that is like a fence that prohibits God from exploring some territory. There is nothing on the other side of the fence. That's what it is for the limits to be absolute and not relative limits. The metaphors of "limit," "fence," and "binding" obscure the fact that once something is recognized to be necessary, it is ill-conceived to ask why God does not or could not have done/made things differently, just as any child who asks who made God simply fails to grasp God's necessity and has not discovered deep failings of typical cosmo-logical arguments. In a second way, our theological problem dissolves.

Dissolving the problem: Part 3

The theological problem arises, in part, by way of biblical assertion. Colossians 1:16: "For in him all things were created in heaven and on earth, visible and invisible, whether thrones or powers or rulers or authorities; all things have been created through him and for him." Revelation 4:11: "… for you created all things, and by your will they were created and have their being." [9]

Those of us who have spent much time in the philosophy seminar room, however, should be quite cautious about importing philosophical theories into biblically-motivated theology. However insightful Plato, Aristotle and many others have been, only with great care should we permit their concerns to inform theology. For instance, change and corruption were seen to be part of the (obviously) imperfect world of concreta. Perfection would permit no change, since change could only take something from perfection to imperfection. Such arguments assume, dubiously, that perfection is a unique state or character. Christian theologians who think that God sometimes acts graciously implicitly concede that God is under no moral obligation to act in some particular way that is gracious and also that the gracious act does nothing to impugn God's perfection. Hence, God's perfection fails to delineate all of the specifics of God's attitudes and actions. Whether all arguments for very strong understandings of God's immutability can be dispatched in this way or not, the lesson is that the ideas about God that biblical writers tried to convey may not be best understood in terms of the tools bequeathed to us by Western philosophy. Only if the writers of Colossians and Revelation are plausibly thought to have had all of the objects in Plato's heaven in the scope of their use of "all things" do these or similar passages even give us reason to think that self-existent abstract objects would be counterexamples to the claims that God created all things.

Furthermore, even Biblical writers seem to have no thought that they would be counterexamples. John 1.3: "Through him all things were made; without him nothing was made that has been made." Even if the abstract objects exist, they were not the subject of early declarations about God's creative act, if they were not the kind of thing that was or could be created. The burden of these writers was only to declare the God of Abraham, Isaac, and Jacob to be the creator of the heavens and the earth, as normally understood, remaining silent on how things are philosophically understood.

Suppose, *pace* the previous two sections, that no escape is available and we have clear proof that a perfect being is precluded from existing by the existence of the abstract objects, the existence of which we have further clear proof. This is a victory of sorts for those rejecting God's existence, but it is not much of a victory. At the very most we have a proof that one, quite specific and philosophically-loaded theory of the divine fails. But, given that specificity and loading, for all that proof shows, reality might still be very far from what typical atheists maintain. For all that imagined proof shows, there may well still be a creator of the world who has miraculously intervened in human affairs, who is triune, one of whose persons secured the means of salvation by way of incarnation and resurrection. The moral and religious demands upon us may be no less than they were thought to be prior to the production of this proof. In the most important respects, Christian theology would be left intact. Any threat to religious belief and practice is minimal, even if there are abstract objects and even if no perfect being could exist alongside them. In a third way, then, the problem of abstract objects dissolves.[10]

Conclusion

The problem of abstract objects in theological contexts is not much of a problem. The grounds for thinking there are abstract objects is weak. My judgment on that matter is on philosophical grounds alone and not due to any perceived conflict with theism. Deflationary options are available and their availability undercuts the warrant for thinking that there are any objects beyond "ordinary" individuals. Adding more objects to our ontology does nothing to help us understand those individuals.

Even if I am wrong in my defense of nominalism, perfect being theology is not threatened by the existence and character of abstract objects. Necessities are the end point for explanations and absolute necessities are the absolute end points for explanations. If there are abstract objects and if they are the necessary existents that ground necessities, then it not only makes no sense to suggest that God somehow explains them, it is also unnecessary to think that any "limits" they impose upon God threaten divine supremacy and majesty. There is nothing beyond those limits that God is unable to do, since there is nothing beyond those limits. Sentences that seem to state what is beyond those limits are just expressing what is impossible and being unable to bring about the absolutely impossible is a problem how, exactly?

Even if I am wrong about whether perfect being theology is threatened by the existence of abstract objects, perfect being theology extends beyond the most central core of theological fundamentals and its passing would not do irreparable damage to lived religious traditions. Investing too much in perfect being theology forces us to miss how much is left if that stock crashes. Religiously speaking, nearly everything is left. So, from an apologetic standpoint, the existence of abstract objects need not be resisted.

Notes

1 As quoted in Leftow (2006, 327).
2 Lewis never embraced the specification of truth-conditions as the substance of a *paraphrase*, however. His ontological program was in service of the reduction of modality.
3 Lewis's plurality of worlds permits a place for God (not *in* any world but existing *from the standpoint of* all). Some adjustment is required for theists prepared to embrace the plurality thesis to dispense with abstracta. (1) God exists in no spacetime. Theists will need to differentiate God from other necessary existents, which also exist merely from the standpoint of all worlds. (2) The worlds just are, for Lewis, and not the product of divine creativity. (3) Worlds impermissible for God to create or actions impermissible for God to permit are (presumably) possible in the standard Lewis system. Theists adopting the broad contours of the plurality thesis must deem such *merely apparent* possibilities. (4) Lastly, God must not only be able to create the worlds but also intervene in at least some of their causal structures or else miracles must be deemed not only nonexistent, but impossible.
4 Both of these arguments are hasty from the perspective of those who embrace the general truthmaker principle but expand their ontology to neither abstract objects, as do the platonists, nor to possibilia, as does Lewis, but to God instead. Brian Leftow (2006, 2012) presses God's mind into service in place of both abstracta and possibilia.
5 Of course, I have inverted the order of inspiration, since Quine's and Putnam's versions of indispensability considerations antedated the explicit appeal to parallel considerations by Chisholm and van Inwagen.
6 Note that the emphasis is on warrant and not on what forms of expression are unavoidable, strictly speaking, or indispensable for some purpose or other. The latter must be proxies for the former, if they are to tell us anything about how we should (epistemically speaking) think the world is anyway. I propose to go to the epistemic issue directly to make the case that indispensability is not a good proxy for warrant.
7 This way of handling the apparent commitment to abstract properties is similar to, and indeed inspired in part by, that of Joseph Melia's (2005) sensible nominalism.
8 This way of undermining mathematical platonism is developed much more fully in an unpublished manuscript.
9 New International Version.
10 For a fuller treatment of related issues, see Shalkowski (1997).

Response to Scott A. Shalkowski

Keith Yandell

Professor Shalkowski tells us the there is no problem concerning God and abstract
objects. First, there is scant reason to think that there are any abstract objects. Second,
were there such things, it would be impossible that they be created, and since God's
omnipotence does not include doing absolutely impossible things, it would not be
threatened by God not having done so. There is no such thing as doing the logically
impossible, and hence no such sort of thing for God to be unable to do. The second
point seems to be entirely sound. As he nicely put it, the supposed fence that limits
God's power to doing the possible is a structure with nothing whatever on the other
side. The first point is less secure.

The focus of the argument that the friend of abstracta walks on thin evidential ice
focuses on discussion of the view that there are sentences that express true propositions that contain referential terms that have two properties: (a) the propositions
expressed are true only if there actually is something to which at least one of those
terms refers, and (b) that reference cannot be to something concrete. Then, assuming
that everything is either concrete or abstract, it follows that some abstract items exist.
The concrete-abstract distinction is easier to illustrate by example than it is to state in
clear terms. I suggested that an abstract object is aspatial, atemporal or everlasting,
causally impotent, mindless, and necessarily existing.

A simple argument starts with the claim that (1) *It is (broadly and narrowly)
logically possible that there be necessarily existing items.* Then one remembers that a
proposition that is necessarily true if true is also necessarily false if false. The second
premise is (2) *If it is (broadly and narrowly) logically possible that there are necessarily
existing items, then it is (necessarily) true that there are necessarily existing items.* The
conclusion follows that (3) *It is (necessarily) true that there are necessarily existing
items.* Given at least a defensible perspective on modal logic—one on which what is
necessary is necessarily necessary, what is contingent is necessarily contingent, and
what is possible is necessarily possible, and seeing that the idea that existential statements cannot be necessarily true is mistaken—this gives us a powerful argument for
there being something that has necessary existence. This argument does not depend
on philosophy of language, on general terms having reference to universals, or the like.
It is analogous to the best version of the ontological argument (Plantinga's version) in
that it relies on one being justified in believing that (1) is true. The counter to this is
an argument that runs: (1*) *It is (broadly and narrowly) logically possible that there be
no necessarily existing items.* Then (2*) *If it is (narrowly and broadly) logically possible
that there are no necessarily existing items, then it is necessarily true that there are no
necessarily existing items*, and one can infer to (3*) *It is necessarily true that there are
no necessarily existing items.*

The basic idea of the arguments is that if a proposition P is either necessarily true or necessarily false—that is, either Necessarily, P or Necessarily, not-P—then whichever of P and not-P is possibly true is a necessary truth and whichever is not possibly true is a necessary falsehood. Then things rest on which of (1) and (1*) is true. If it seems to one at least highly plausible that (1) is true, and since (2) seems clearly true, then one will infer that (3) is true. It seems to me reasonable to believe that (3) is true, though perhaps not unreasonable to believe otherwise. The argument seems at least as good as many others in philosophy whose conclusions are widely thought to be reasonably, even correctly, believed. If this is right, and the (1)–(3) argument is at least as good as the (1*)–(3*) argument, then accepting (1) is not something for which the reasons are disappearingly faint. As I have suggested, the obvious candidates for being a necessarily existing item are God and abstracta (or both), this puts belief in abstracta in better shape than Professor Shalkowski suggests.

It is true that when an ancient shepherd counted his 13 sheep he was not intending to say that the number 13 exists as an abstract object, much less talking about whether numbers could or could not be analyzed into sets. But then he probably also was not intending to say anything about God as the creator of a sheep-containing world, and it is frequently held by Christians that, without God's creating, there would be no sheep. The claim that his words commit him to only what he intends them to refer to seems to me incorrect. Once one seriously uses a sentence—is not just reciting for voice exercise or acting in a play—the truth-conditions of the sentence are whatever the agreed upon sense of that sentence requires. He does not decide what the truth-conditions of what he says will be.

If Mary and her daughter Martha sound just the same when they speak, and hearing Mary speak from the next room as Tom asks Martha's father for her hand saying "Sir, I want to marry the woman whose voice we just heard," he intends to refer to Martha, but actually refers to Mary (who after all is the woman whose voice was just heard). If what he says is true, he requests bigamy. He did not say what he intended, but what he said has truth value involving his intentions and Mary. That it is persons who use words to refer does not entail that it is sufficient to make what they say to be true if what they intended to say is true. If I say that the car needs gas, what I say is false if what it needs is not gas but oil, even if I intended to say it needs oil.

I take propositional necessity to be primitive—not reducible to something else. That seems to require either God or abstract objects. If the line of reasoning from which these brief remarks are taken is right, then God, conceived as necessarily existing or abstracta (or both) exist. This metaphysical argument for propositions is not from philosophy of language. I think it is all the better for that. So the case for abstracta seems to me not as bleak as Professor Shalkowski suggests.

Paul M. Gould and Richard Brian Davis

Scott A. Shalkowski's genial essay is divided into two parts, the first arguing that there is little warrant for believing in abstracta, and the second that even if there were, abstract (platonic) objects threaten neither God's sovereignty nor his aseity. His conclusion is this: "The problem of abstract objects in theological contexts is not much of a problem" (153). Since we are in substantial agreement with the second part of Shalkowski's essay, we shall focus our attention on the first.

One of the theoretical advantages of MTA is that it sidesteps the many thorny problems laid at the door of platonism by nominalists. Nowhere is this more evident than in Shalkowski's attempt to "deflate" the truth–predicate with a view to under-cutting the basic rationale for positing abstract truthbearers (propositions). Consider a time before there were any human beings (say, the Jurassic Period). Surely, if we are realists, we shall want to affirm

(1) It is true that the Sun was burning in the Jurassic Period.

Now if that's right, we might go on to argue for propositions as follows:

(2) If (1), then the proposition *the Sun is burning* was true in the Jurassic Period.

(3) Necessarily, if *the Sun is burning* had been true in the Jurassic Period, then *the Sun is burning* would have existed in the Jurassic Period.

And then from (1)–(3) we neatly infer

(4) The proposition *the Sun is burning* existed in the Jurassic Period.

Now what about that proposition? What sort of thing is it? Well, it can't be a *concrete* truthbearer (e.g. a sentence inscription, belief, or assertion); after all, at the time in question we human beings hadn't yet put in our glorious appearance. The proposition in question must therefore be an *abstract* platonic object.

Shalkowski's aim is to undercut this motivation for platonism. He has no quarrel with (1); that isn't the problem. What Shalkowski denies, rather, is (2)—namely, that (1) has any truth bearing implications. We think this is a mistake: (1) *does* have such implications, though not of the platonic sort. Why then does Shalkowski reject (2)? Well, for one thing, the construction "it is true that" in (1) can serve "many different purposes" without invoking a propositional truthbearer—for example, "making explicit one's agreement with or concession to the claim of another" (147). Moreover, if our present concern is with the Sun's objective existence in the past,

(1*) The Sun was burning in the Jurassic Period

"gives us all that we need." Its content is equivalent to that of (1). But notice: (1*) "has nothing to do with truthbearers and truth values. It concerns the Sun" (147). Hence, we can dispense with truthbearers.

But isn't this conclusion hasty? No doubt (1*) isn't itself about a proposition. And yet surely it is a truthbearer. Note first that it *concerns* the Sun; it is *of* or *about* it. More than that, it *represents* the Sun as having been a certain way at a certain time. But then just as surely, since (1*) and the things it represents aren't identical, anyone who wants to know about the status of the Sun in the Jurassic Period wants to know whether (1*) gets things right. She wants to know whether things *are* the way (1*) represents them as being. She wants to know, in other words, whether (1*) is *true*. Here we are not simply asking whether (1*) is true in some vacuous, deflationary sense, as in this substitution instance of Tarski's T schema:

(SI) "(1*)" is true (or corresponds to reality) if and only if (1*).

As Craig (2012) notes, every statement, if true, is true in this sense, just as every true statement has the property *being known by God*. But such properties, he says, are trivial and insubstantial; they don't do any explanatory work.

Of course, the savvy realist will insist that there is more to truth here than meets the eye. The anti-nominalist's truth property is explanatory and thus substantial. The biconditional in (SI) is subtly misleading; it suggests that the sole relation obtaining between left and right biconds is one of trivial mutual entailment. But the fact is, it isn't. There is also an explanatory asymmetry running from right-to-left: (1*) explains *why* "(1*)" is true. But the explanation doesn't go in the other direction.

Someone might object that our take on truth entangles us in the futile project of seeking "correlates in reality for all of the singular terms" in (1*) (Craig 2012). Well, if truthbearers were sentences with parts, perhaps it would. But as we say in our lead essay, no concrete object comes within a country mile of being intentional or object directed. Not so, of course, if (1*) *qua truth bearer* is a divine thought (as it is on MTA). That some of God's thoughts during the Jurassic Period would be directed upon (and made true by) the Sun and its features is just what we would expect.

For his part, Shalkowski seems open to the possibility that (1*) might not be made true at all. "Perhaps," he says,

> not only are there no individuals or groups of individuals to render true some truths, there isn't even "the world" to render them true. Or, perhaps, there is such an all-encompassing object, but there is no meaningful sense in which it renders some truths true; they just are true. (146)

Here you don't have to embrace truthmaker maximalism—that every truth has a truthmaker—to recognize that something is definitely askew if (1*) comes out as a brute, unexplained fact. Perhaps some truths are like this; surely (1*) is not among them.

The upshot is this. There neither are nor can be any concrete or platonic truthbearers—either now or in the Jurassic Period. It doesn't follow, however, that the proposition *the Sun is burning* wasn't then true; for this is simply the thought God had about the Sun long before any of us arrived on the scene.

Greg Welty

According to Shalkowski, platonist arguments for universals or propositions "are hasty from the perspective of those who embrace the general truthmaker principle but expand their ontology ... to God instead" (154n. 4). Actually, as one of those who expands his ontology to theism, I find many of the platonist arguments to be quite persuasive rather than hasty. What I find hasty is the immediate assumption on the part of many platonists that it is *causally inert entities made out of abstract stuff*, rather than mental items like ideas, that are best suited to satisfy the relevant ontological conditions that emerge from the best platonist arguments. It is however "hasty" to multiply ontological kinds beyond explanatory necessity. So I feel the force of the platonist arguments, but I think such arguments point in the direction of theism.

Shalkowski seems to think that if we don't "intend" to speak of abstracta, or if our "concern" is not with abstracta, that therefore our ordinary talk need not commit us to such. I think this is a false dilemma. When we say "Spiders share some of the anatomical features of insects," why think we are trying to express something about abstracta *or* concreta? Rather, we are trying to express something about *reality*. Further reflection then helps us see how that reality is best characterized (van Inwagen 2004). So Shalkowski is either overspecifying our intentions or overreading their absence. He thinks we must be intending *either* the abstract or the concrete, and since it's not clearly the first it must be the second. But can't I talk about something and then later come to see better the kind of thing I was talking about? I make some claims about Goldbach's Conjecture (GC). Someone points out that given those claims, it turns out that GC must be necessarily true if true at all. So I was talking about a necessary thesis all along. I wasn't *intending* to talk about necessary truth—that wasn't on my mind at all. But when faced with a good argument that my claims (if true) would commit me to this additional fact about GC, I reasonably say, "Yes, you're right. GC must be true." Surely I can't turn back the argument by saying, "But I never had necessity in mind. I wasn't 'struggling' to articulate *that!*"

We must be wary of committing an intentionalist fallacy: If in speaking X we are not concerned with Y, then in speaking X we could not be committed to Y or engaging in reference to Y. But I could be committed to many things I don't intend to be committed to. I don't intend to give insult, or confuse two people, or contradict myself, but I can pretty clearly end up doing those things with my speech. Someone could sort us out here by giving an argument of some kind in each case: "When you really think about it, you were saying ..." A witness can be convicted for making unintentionally self-incriminating statements. I can later learn that my claim about water was making reference to a compound of hydrogen and oxygen, that my claim about phlogiston was referring to (the absence of) oxygen, that my claim about Clark Kent was referring to Superman, that my claim about the Morning Star was referring to Venus. It's not clear what my intentions or concerns have to do with it, *if* we have a good argument that the implication follows.

I agree with Shalkowski that speaking "abstractly about the concrete" might be a means of efficiency, "a convenience," a linguistic shortcut to save time (149). But in that case it should be possible to give a nominalistic paraphrase, the only fault of which is its lacking efficiency. Platonists (like van Inwagen, in the article cited) challenge the adequacy of such paraphrases. So that's where the argument takes us. We can't prematurely close it off by citing our aims and intentions. Shalkowski's principle is "that 'we' begin with warranted beliefs about the concrete and that if all moves to abstraction are those that a nominalist can happily countenance, then there are insufficient grounds for the move to platonism in the first place" (147). But that's a pretty big "if"! Can the paraphrases be supplied?

On the theological side of the ledger, I agree that "it is a mistake to think that there are deeper explanations for necessities" (151). But if this *is* a mistake, then this is a reason for theists to *reject* platonism. For theism posits God as necessary, while platonism seems to indicate that God's necessity is explained by something deeper, something distinct from and independent of God himself. Shalkowski's (true) observation generates the conflict, rather than dissolves it. "That the platonist thinks of these limits as a matter of the existence and character of objects is neither here nor there" (151). No, it *does* matter. What are these "objects"? Platonic entities distinct from God? If so, then if these limits are "a matter of the existence and character of objects" *that are distinct from God and are independent of God*, then God's limits are imposed by something distinct from Him. If platonism is true, then the platonic objects (*and not God*) are the truthmakers for necessary truths. Yes, if the platonic objects are necessary then there is not "something on the other side of the limit." No one is supposing there is. Rather, the platonist perspective proposes a view of what constitutes this limit: these objects *and not God*. That unacceptably compromises His aseity.

There are two questions here:

(i) What constitutes the limits?
(ii) Are the limits necessary?

Shalkowski seems to think that theists/platonists giving a common "yes" answer to (ii) deflects any threats to divine aseity generated by a distinctively platonist answer to (i) ("the abstract objects, and not God"). But a platonist answer to (i) means that the divine limits specified in (ii) are constituted by something *other* than God. This wouldn't be the case if platonism were false. Thus the platonist/theist conflict.

William Lane Craig

Scott Shalkowski's paper is divided into two halves, the first of which I applaud enthusiastically and the second of which I find unfortunately wanting. In the first part of his paper he contends that the arguments for the existence of abstract objects are weak; in the second part he maintains that the existence of uncreated objects is of little theological importance. I shall make a few observations in passing about the first part of the paper before moving to the question of the theological significance of platonism.

The first part of Shalkowski's essay is an interesting illustration of how the two debates over nominalism alluded to in my lead essay (116) merge. Universals might be platonistically construed as abstract objects, in which case they become examples of uncreated objects. Thus the centuries-old debate over the existence of universals spills over into the recent debate over the existence of abstract objects. A nominalist in the second debate need not be a nominalist in the first debate, as Aristotelianism illustrates.

It is also worth observing that all of the arguments for platonism surveyed by Shalkowski are instances of the Indispensability Argument. They all presuppose the customary criterion of ontological commitment. Shalkowski's key claim in response to the Indispensability Argument is that if there is sense in the use of abstract nouns and the quantification over truths, properties, numbers, or any other use of such discourse, we can account for our use of that discourse—even to speak seriously and truly—as serving our purposes to speak indirectly or abstractly about the concrete rather than to speak directly about the abstract.

This seems to be an expression of a view called figuralism, which has been ably articulated and defended by Stephen Yablo. According to this view abstract discourse is misunderstood if it is taken literally. Rather it is a species of figurative language. Figurative speech, properly interpreted, may be true even if, taken literally, it is false. The distinctive contribution of figuralism to the current debate is its contention that talk of abstract objects ought to be understood figuratively, not literally, and may therefore, *pace* the fictionalists, be taken to be true without ontological commitment to abstract objects.

Yablo thinks that talk of abstract objects involves the use of "existential metaphors," that is to say, metaphors "making play with a special sort of object to which the speaker is not [ontologically] committed" (2000b, 293). Numerical terms, for instance, are existential metaphors, useful, and sometimes indispensable, for expressing truths about the real world. "It is only by making *as if* to countenance numbers, that one can give expression in English to a fact having nothing to do with numbers, [e.g.] a fact about stars and planets and how they are numerically proportioned" (Ibid., 295).

I think that Shalkowski's view is a sort of figuralism, a stance I find both plausible and attractive. Still, Shalkowski is not as clear as he could be, and so I should like to hear more from him in his final response as to whether he thinks that the anti-platonist should go the figuralist route.

Turning to the second part of his essay, I want to urge Shalkowski to reconsider his position concerning the compatibility of platonism with biblical theism. I agree that the necessity of abstract objects poses no threat to divine sovereignty; the doctrine of divine sovereignty is a red herring in this debate and ought to be left aside. Rather the issue is divine aseity and *creatio ex nihilo*.

I understand the motivation "from an apologetic standpoint" (154), as Shalkowski puts it, to minimize the incompatibility of platonism and biblical theism. But given the weakness of the arguments for platonism, such a motivation is misplaced. For it involves terrible theological compromise. A theism according to which God is not the creator of all reality apart from Himself but is just one uncreated being amidst an incomprehensible multitude of uncreated, independently existing beings is both unbiblical and far too weak to be a plausible conception of maximal greatness.

Shalkowski makes no serious attempt to engage exegetically with the relevant biblical data. He says, "Only if the writers of Colossians and Revelation are plausibly thought to have had all of the objects in Plato's heaven in the scope of their use of 'all things' do these or similar passages even give us reason to think that self-existent abstract objects would be counterexamples to the claims that God created all things" (161). If Shalkowski means that the biblical writers must have had abstract objects *consciously* in mind, then his claim is plainly false. For neither did they have fermions and bosons in mind, yet these would fall within the range of their quantifiers. But if he means merely that abstract objects must also be within the range of the quantifiers, then his claim is trivially true. The real issue is whether the biblical writers intended to make a truly universal statement. As I explain in my lead essay, they surely did intend to speak of everything apart from God Himself. Shalkowski's handling of Jn 1:3 in particular is, I must say, superficial, ignoring the prologue's affinities with Middle Platonism and Philo of Alexandria's Logos doctrine.

Moreover, as the ante-Nicene Fathers clearly saw, the postulation of a multiplicity of *ageneta* yields a metaphysical pluralism which is theologically unacceptable. God becomes just one being among many, a literally infinitesimal part of reality, most of which exists entirely independently of Him. Such a God is not maximally great, for a maximally great being would be the sufficient reason or ground of being for every thing apart from Himself, not just for a relatively few things. Worse, if platonism's ontological assay of things implies that God exists because He exemplifies certain independently existing properties, then God does not exist *a se*. A robust theism therefore rules out platonism.

What is called for, then, is not theological compromise but a repudiation of the arguments for platonism. Fortunately, as Shalkowski indicates, the case for platonism is far from compelling.

Graham Oppy

I agree with almost everything that Shalkowski says. *First*, it is not clear to me that there are good grounds for thinking that there are abstract objects. Perhaps I am *less* firmly persuaded than Shalkowski that there are insufficient grounds for thinking that there are abstract objects, but I am broadly sympathetic to the kind of explanatory project that he sketches. Shalkowski's views seem to me to be very close cousins to Yablo's figuralism. *Second*, it seems to me that, if there are *pure* abstract objects, then, because the nature and existence of those abstract objects is absolutely necessary, the nature and existence of those objects could do nothing to impugn God's perfection, or majesty, or whatever. And, if there are *impure* abstract objects, then it is straight-forwardly evident that those objects could do nothing to impugn God's perfection, or majesty, or whatever. *Third*, there is no good argument from Scripture to the conclusion that God must be the creator of whatever pure abstract objects there may be. As I noted earlier, in agreeing with Yandell, it is hard to find any reason to suppose that, when the biblical authors referred to "all things," they were referring to more than the denizens of heaven and earth, and there are pretty good reasons for suspecting that, when the biblical authors referred to "all things," they had only the denizens of heaven and earth in mind. Moreover, I agree with Shalkowski that Christian belief and practice does not depend upon there being a perfect being that conforms to the conceptions of contemporary "perfect being" philosophers (and I would add that, when those philosophers call themselves "traditional" theists, the self-application of that label does not add any weight to the claim that their views have a particularly central place in the intellectual history of Christianity).

I do disagree with some things that Shalkowski says about cosmological arguments. Since it is more fun to discuss things about which there is disagreement, let me turn to that topic. Shalkowski says that, in response to cosmological arguments that appeal to the contingency of the cosmos, those who resist the argument all end up suggesting that we should just make our peace with this big contingency. I demur. If you think that God made the cosmos, and if you think that God's making the cosmos was the result of a free decision on His part, then, of course, you will think that the cosmos is contingent: God might have refrained from making a cosmos; or He might have made a very different cosmos. However, if you think that the cosmos is all that there is, then, at the very least, you might reasonably be undecided whether the existence of the cosmos is absolutely necessary. Suppose, for example, that the cosmos has a finite past, and that we can talk sensibly about the first moment of that past. I say that it is a reasonable speculation that the cosmos of that first moment is absolutely necessary: It could not have failed to exist, and it could not have been other than it was. Every complete way that things might have gone begins with the cosmos as it was at that first moment. Of course, if there are no chance events—because determinism rules—then there are no other ways that things might have gone. But, if the historical evolution of the cosmos is chancy, then there are other ways that things could go. I add to this that, if we suppose that the historical evolution of the cosmos is governed by laws, then the laws are absolutely necessary (but also observe that we might prefer a metaphysics on which laws are traded in for powers that belong to the cosmos and its constituents). If you are a theist, you may insist that intuition supports the view that the cosmos is contingent. I don't accept this. Sure, if you are a theist, you'll have this intuition. And, because theism has been dominant in the West for a couple of millennia, the intuition that the cosmos is contingent has become pretty deeply entrenched. But, without theism, there isn't anything that tells in favor of the intuition. Certainly, I don't have it. (That's not to say that I have a strong intuition that the cosmos is necessary. I guess if asked to choose, that's the view that I'd support. But there are lots of competing views that I see no way to rule out. Perhaps, for example, the properties of the cosmos at the first moment might have been other than they actually were—in that case, the properties that the cosmos had at its first moment would be brute and inexplicable. Perhaps, to take another example, it might be that it is contingent that there was a first moment at which the cosmos existed: perhaps there could have been no cosmos.)

These kinds of considerations matter for the arguments for theism that Welty (and Leftow, and others) try to develop. They claim that theistic conceptualism is more theoretically virtuous than competing positions (including competing naturalist positions): It offers the best combination of ontological and ideological simplicity, fit with data, explanatory power, fit with other well-established theory, and so forth. But I say that theism does no better than break even with naturalism on fit with data, explanatory power, fit with other well-established theory, and so forth, and does clearly worse on ontological and ideological simplicity (essentially because it adds God to the natural world, and doesn't take anything away). By my lights, naturalism, with or without abstract objects, beats theism, with or without abstract objects. (Of course, I haven't offered an *argument* for this last claim here; I'm merely recording how I see things. I have, however, tried to argue that evaluation of the merits of theism and naturalism reaches the same conclusion with or without abstract objects.)

Response to Critics

Scott A. Shalkowski

I am grateful to the other contributors for their thoughtful replies to my lead article. For the most part, I am inclined to retain my original positions. Both Yandell and Gould/Davis use arguments against nominalism that strike me as question-begging. Of course, if platonism or MTA about truthbearers is correct, then Yandell's (2)/(2*) and Gould/Davis's (2) are true. Indeed, they are true only if platonism or MTA is true. As key premises in an argument *for* platonism or MTA about propositions, however, they are unavailable because question-begging. I have kept my own discussion in the object language as much as possible, in part, so that no claim I use has the illicit air of triviality that surrounds those premises.

That air of triviality arises, at least in part, because pragmatic factors produce an illegitimate bias. Of course, for any specific example we care to examine, there will be truthbearers available to plug into claims of the form: If p, then "p" is true, even by nominalist lights. Platonists, though, require more than that every time we actually examine cases, there are truthbearers; they need them even for states we never contemplate.

Whether activists are entitled to their premise depends on the larger function of the argument in which it figures. If they first argue that platonists are right that there is a duty to be done but wrong about what serves that duty, then they are not entitled to it. If they finesse that duty into an argument for theism, perhaps by way of an inference to the best/most economical explanation, then they are not entitled to it. If traditional theism is already established, *then* they are entitled to claims of that form, but in ways with which nominalists can be content. Consequently, I still find no metaphysical grounds to embrace platonism or MTA, on the basis of arguments relying upon versions of (2).

It's no part of my anti-platonist argument that the T-schema exhausts a theory of truth. Any explanatory asymmetry regarding the portions of the schema is a separate matter. I agree with Gould/Davis that it doesn't follow from anything I wrote that there were no truths during the Jurassic Period. They, like other theists, are free to maintain that there are concrete truthbearers: God's thoughts. Their argument that intentionality is required for truth remains intact.

In reply to Welty, I see no problematic intentionalist fallacy. I concede that plumbing the depths of my intentions and commitments might not be straightforward, but determining my commitments is one thing; determining how things are regarding that to which I'm committed is another. Children are committed, in more ways than one, to their favorite toys; they are not, however, committed to the bosons that give them mass. How can they be committed to what they have no acquaintance or comprehension? It may well be that Ratty's limbs contain bosons that make them massive, but my granddaughter, Millie, has no commitment to *them*, even if the limbs would not exist without them.

Welty is also concerned about the availability of nominalist paraphrases of platonist-looking claims. I can see no reason for thinking either that there are—or that nominalists need think there are—paraphrases equivalent to the item paraphrased. If the broad outlines of my account of why we find useful what we are told are platonistic-looking sentences, there will be none. Nominalism is none the worse for that. Sometimes my concern is with Charlotte, Jiminy, and exoskeletons, sometimes with Jeter, A-Rod, and their injuries. Only what makes the relevant sentences true in a nominalistically-friendly fashion is needed in each case, while the typical demand for paraphrase requires that the very same nominalistically-friendly thing apply to both cases. While interesting if so, it is no part of the anti-platonist project that there be single, all-purpose paraphrases even of a given platonist-looking sentence.

Craig and Oppy liken my view to Yablo's figuralism. I do not take my view to be an instance of fictionalism because I do not cede that the appearances are platonist appearances and that the appearances warrant a "standard" platonist-friendly interpretation of those expressions which, thus, force nominalists to put those expressions to some "nonstandard" use. There is the tendency to overgeneralize Quine's criterion of ontological commitment, which was limited to the domain of quantification in our best scientific theories. Even those who think that our best theories need not be scientific should recognize that many ordinary instances of quantification and apparently singular terms do not carry commitments. I do some things for Judith's sake, others for Jeanna's, and yet others for Elana's. No one should do existential generalization, wonder if the sakes of distinct people are themselves distinct and then conclude that I am committed to at least three sakes! Since there are plenty of examples like this, we should think that platonists illicitly arrogate to themselves claims to standard usage. I maintain that even in the strongest case for platonism about abstracta—mathematics—it is not hard to see how the very appearances platonists claim for their own can be innocent of platonistic pretensions. I see no grounds for seeing any figures of speech being deployed by those who use the language of mathematics, propositions, or properties, so they play no role in my rejection of abstract objects. As I said in my reply to Craig, I think figuralism is doubly wrong. It is wrong about the presumptions of the appearances and it is wrong about the semantic intentions of users of mathematical language.

I am unable to see in Craig's reply sufficient grounds for thinking that biblical writers had completely unrestricted quantifiers in mind when declaring the scope of God's creative acts. Indeed, John "hedges" on exactly this point. My remarks on Welty's comments apply here as well. Regarding the works of the Church Fathers, I do not yet see that other contributors have given me grounds to rethink the idea that our freedom to assess the thought of Plato and Aristotle is curtailed when the Fathers formulate their ideas in terms of faulty Platonism or Aristotelianism (or any other philosophical–ism).

Graham Oppy's comment regarding necessary/contingent being requires more extended comment. So far as I can tell, he posed no challenge to my "What part of 'necessary' did you not understand?" as having show-stopping force. His challenge is that it is no more appropriate for theists to use it than it is for naturalists. My initial remark took for granted that the cosmos is contingent and if there is no Creator, it is brutely contingent. It likewise took for granted that if God exists, then God exists necessarily. Now it may be that my remarks in the paragraph above can be wielded against me at this juncture. Aquinas, building upon Aristotle, had ideas about causation, explanation, necessity, and contingency that make better sense of moving from the contingent—because changeable—cosmos to the necessary—because Unmoved—Mover than we can make using rather different ideas. I take Oppy's challenge to be to identify why, when God and the cosmos are each proposed as the ultimate stopping point for explanations, one should be deemed necessary and the other not.

I take for granted that being the ultimate end point of explanation is insufficient for necessity. We think that there is plenty of contingency about in the cosmos, at a minimum the "initial conditions" and the laws of nature. Cosmologists seem content to think of these as contingent; they flirt with how universes would have been had conditions of, say, the relative proportions of matter and anti-matter been different or had the laws been different. Those who think God acts freely, think parallel things. God created, but might not have. God created this, but might have created that instead.

I find it natural to think of God's contingencies as not implicating what it is to be God. Creating that rather than this would not have required a different person, but only different actions from that very person. That is no more troubling than our ordinary counterfactual reasoning about ourselves. Similarly, the contingencies of the initial conditions (perhaps constrained by the types of objects our cosmos comprises) seem to be alternatives for this very cosmos and not another. The laws and/or the relevant physical constants go deeper and perhaps to what is essential to this particular cosmos.

Cosmologists think of matter and anti-matter as different when they differ in one of these respects. We get a different kind of particle depending on whether it is positively or negatively charged. While we might still claim that *gravity* might have been different, if the closest analogue to gravitational attraction were different in a cosmos, then that cosmos is very different from ours. On one (old) framework, the objects themselves interact very differently; on another (more recent) massive objects distort the fabric of space-time very differently. Insofar as it is possible to wed the physicist's concern for fundamental physical constants and laws with the philosopher's concern over essence and accident, fundamental laws and/or constants look like good candidates for informing what is essential to the cosmos, in the same way that the traditional divine attributes are essential to God.

In the wake of Lewis's counterpart theory, it is difficult to know the proper constraints for resolving this issue. Strictly numerically distinct objects in other worlds represent objects in ours so that even though Humphrey is not elected in any world, someone else sufficiently like Humphrey elsewhere makes it that he might have been elected. Given that counterparts are contextually and pragmatically related to objects in other worlds, it is not clear how to proceed. If there is a plurality of worlds, perhaps any world is a counterpart to ours and the way of any other is a way *ours* might have been.

In a single-world multiverse, one might think the same, but we should pause here. A multiverse is anchored to a quantum vacuum, which is characterized by a given set of laws. Logically and mathematically speaking, they are not necessary. There is at least some plausibility in thinking that some universes could not have come from our quantum foundation, since they require a different kind of "universe generator." Those seem to me to be distinct, contingent universes.

We are in the deepest of modal waters and it is difficult, at least for me, to see matters clearly. If the above is unpersuasive, perhaps there is a wedge to be found in the possibility of no cosmos. No quantum soup—no nothing—that is a candidate for physical theory. Only one caught in the grip of a theory, such as Lewis's plurality of worlds, would think otherwise. So, even if we ignore the *de dicto/de re* issue above, it is not even necessary that there be some cosmos or other, so ours is not necessary.

Is divine necessity any more secure? Many should think so, on methodological grounds. Those adopting theories on the basis of what is satisfying—what is the best explanation, what is more comprehensive and leaves fewer things inevitably unexplained—should think so. Given the contingency of a cosmos, God, as traditionally conceived as the most deeply perfect and complete being possible, permits things to go more smoothly than they would otherwise, theoretically speaking. Reiterating part of my reply to Welty, many philosophers are ill situated to resist this basis for thinking God necessary, since God's necessary existence is part of the most comprehensive explanatory package. Resisting at this point will undo the grounds many have for their own highest-level philosophical commitments. While I agree with Oppy that thumping the table with "God, as traditionally conceived" should carry little *philosophical* weight even among religiously committed philosophers, something like that conception provides the basis for *tu quoque* arguments. We should resist the temptation to which nearly all succumb when addressing arguments in the philosophy of religion: that arguments fail when they fail to have universal appeal. Nowhere else in philosophy do we impose this standard.

6

Abstract Objects? Who Cares!

Graham Oppy

According to naturalism, Causal Reality is entirely natural: There are none but entirely natural causal entities possessing none but entirely natural causal properties. Moreover, according to naturalism, there are none but entirely natural causal relations that hold between none but entirely natural causal states and/or none but entirely natural causal events and/or none but entirely natural causal processes.

According to theism, Causal Reality is a mix of natural and supernatural causal entities possessing a mix of natural and supernatural causal properties. On this view, there are natural and supernatural causal relations that hold between natural and supernatural states and/or natural and supernatural events and/or natural and super- natural processes. Furthermore, on this view, there is an initial part of Causal Reality that is entirely supernatural: In the beginning, Causal Reality involves no causal beings other than God and no instantiated causal properties other than the supernatural causal properties instantiated by God. However, according to this view, at some noninitial point in Causal Reality, God makes or creates Natural Reality, which—at the very least—is populated by causal entities that are not entirely supernatural and that possess causal properties that are not entirely supernatural.

When we compare the relative merits of naturalism and theism, we often focus primarily on comparison of their respective accounts of Causal Reality. Given an agreed conception of theoretical virtues—simplicity, goodness of fit with data, explan- atory breadth, predictive fruitfulness, and so forth—we can compare the theoretical virtues of naturalism and theism against a wide range of "causal" data: the global shape of Causal Reality; cosmic fine-tuning; the history of our universe; the history of the earth; the history of humanity; the suffering and flourishing of human beings and other living creatures; the nature and distribution of consciousness and reason; reports of miracles and religious experiences; the nature and distribution of religious scriptures, religious authorities, religious organizations, and religious traditions; and so forth.

However, it is not immediately obvious that a comparison of the relative merits of naturalism and theism should focus exclusively on their comparative theoretical virtues in the light of "causal" data. True enough, if Reality is exhausted by Causal

Reality, then naturalism and theism are properly construed as no more than competing theories about Causal Reality. But, if there is more to Reality than Causal Reality, then, as comprehensive theories, naturalism and theism will be properly construed as competing theories about that more extensive Reality. And then it is at least appears conceivable that it could turn out that, while one of these theories leads when only Causal Reality is taken into account, the other theory wins when all of Reality is taken into account.

The wider question that serves as background to this essay is whether there is any serious prospect that, while one of naturalism and theism leads when only Causal Reality is taken into account, the other theory wins when all of Reality is taken into account. However, our principal focus will be somewhat narrower. Suppose that we call the difference between Reality and Causal Reality "Abstract Reality." The question that will be our principal focus is this: Does either of our theories—naturalism and theism—afford a better account of Abstract Reality? Of course, it is plainly conceivable that there is no difference between Reality and Causal Reality; and, in that case, the answer to the question just framed is trivial. But there are well-known considerations that have prompted some philosophers to suppose that there is an Abstract Reality; and we shall take it that all responses to those well-known considerations are "accounts of Abstract Reality." If we conclude that there is no significant difference between the accounts that naturalism and theism can give of Abstract Reality, then we shall have a negative answer to our wider background question, and we shall be able to insist that any further comparison of the relative merits of naturalism and theism need only consider their respective accounts of Causal Reality.

In what follows, I shall (1) make some further remarks about the distinction between Causal Reality and Abstract Reality; (2) provide a taxonomy of accounts of Abstract Reality; (3) say something about the merits of competing accounts of Abstract Reality; (4) give a detailed argument for the conclusion that considerations about Abstract Reality do not differentially support either theism or naturalism; (5) explain why tokenism and conceptualism are not genuinely competitive accounts of Abstract Reality; (6) offer some critical remarks on Plantinga's sketches of arguments for the existence of God from numbers, sets, and propositions; and (7) draw some appropriate final conclusions.

Abstract and Causal Reality

There are many potential denizens of Abstract Reality: numbers, sets, classes, functions, mappings, structures, groups, rings, algebras, states, patterns, propositions, contents, intentional objects, properties, universals, attributes, characteristics, types, normative principles, values, utilities, generic objects, arbitrary objects, intensional objects, mere possibilia, impossibilia, incomplete objects, and so on. Of course, friends of Abstract Reality debate amongst themselves which of these—and other—potential denizens of Abstract Reality *are* denizens of Abstract Reality. Various questions arise.

One question concerns the distinction between Causal Reality and Abstract Reality, or the allied distinction between concrete objects and abstract objects. There are various candidates for distinguishing between concrete objects and abstract objects— e.g. that the latter are "nonmental and nonsensible," or "nonmental and nonphysical," or "nonspatial and causally inefficacious," or "generated by an abstraction function," etc. In my introductory remarks, I have taken it for granted that the right way to draw the distinction is in terms of causation: Concrete objects are denizens only of Causal Reality; abstract objects are denizens only of Abstract Reality. But not everyone is persuaded that the distinction can be drawn in these terms. Consider, for example, Rosen (2012, §3.2):

> It is widely maintained that causation strictly speaking is a relation among events or states of affairs. If we say that the rock—an object—caused the window to break, what we mean is that some event or state (or fact or condition) *involving* the rock caused the breaking. If the rock itself is a cause, it is a cause in some derivative sense. But this derivative sense has proved elusive. The rock's hitting the window is an event in which the rock 'participates' in a certain way, and it is because the rock participates in events in this way that we credit the rock itself with causal efficacy. But what is it for an object to *participate* in an event? Suppose John is thinking about the Pythagorean Theorem and you ask him to say what's on his mind. His response is an event—the utterance of a sentence; and one of its causes is the event of John's thinking about the theorem. Does the Pythagorean Theorem 'participate' in this event? There is surely *some* sense in which it does. The event consists in John's coming to stand in a certain relation to the Theorem, just as the rock's hitting the window consists in the rock's coming to stand in a certain relation to the glass. But we do not credit the Pythagorean Theorem with causal efficacy simply because it participates in this sense in an event which is a cause. The challenge is therefore to characterize the distinctive manner of 'participation in the causal order' that distinguishes the concrete entities. This problem has received relatively little attention. There is no reason to believe that it cannot be solved. But in the absence of a solution, this [characterization] must be reckoned a work in progress.

It seems to me to be entirely plausible to suppose that Rosen's challenge can be met. Suppose, for example, that we think that causation is marked by transfer of conserved quantities: wherever there is causation, there is transfer of conserved quantities between entities. When the rock hits the window, there is transfer of conserved quantities—energy and momentum— between the rock and the window. When John tells you what is on his mind, there is transfer of conserved quantities between his neural states and yours, via an intermediate chain of such transfers. John's thinking about the Pythagorean Theorem just is his being in a certain kind of neural state—that is appropriately characterized using the expression "thinking about the Pythagorean Theorem"—but there is no transfer of conserved quantities anywhere in the relevant causal chain between the Pythagorean Theorem and other entities. Whereas the rock and window "participate in the causal order in the manner that is characteristic of causal entities," the Pythagorean Theorem does not.

Now, of course, not everyone accepts that causation is marked by transfer of conserved quantities, and not everyone accepts that mental states just are neural states—but these assumptions are not essential to the meeting of Rosen's challenge. What matters is that there be some story told about causation that, on the one hand, brings the rock and the window into the causal domain *as causal entities*, in the way that the invocation of transfer of conserved quantities between the rock and the window does; and, on the other hand, invokes the Pythagorean Theorem only in roles—e.g. of characterization of the content of mental states—that do not bring *it* into the causal domain *as a causal entity*. (Perhaps it might be added here that we should be a bit cautious in accepting that there is some sense in which the Pythagorean Theorem "participates" in the event of John's thinking about the theorem. For suppose, instead, that John had been thinking about Santa Claus. Is there really a good sense in which Santa Claus "participates" in the event of John's thinking about Santa Claus? Nonexistent entities simply cannot be causal entities in the causal domain; it is *hopelessly* wrong to suppose that Santa Claus is involved in transfers of conserved quantities with other causal entities that belong to Causal Reality.)

Another question concerns allegedly distinctive properties of the denizens of Abstract Reality. It is often claimed that the denizens of Abstract Reality are distinguished by facts concerning the *necessity* of their existence and nature, the extent to which it is possible to have *a priori* knowledge of their existence and nature, and the *absolute* truth or falsity of claims made concerning their existence and nature. However, it is important not to go beyond what is properly defensible in making claims of these kinds. In particular, it is important to note that the denizens of Abstract Reality appear to divide into *two* classes. On the one hand, there are the *pure* abstracta, which: (a) exist of *necessity*; (b) have only *essential* intrinsic properties and *essential* relations to other pure abstracta; (c) can be known *a priori* to exist and to have the intrinsic properties and relations to other pure abstracta that they do have; and (d) can be described or referred to in sentences that are true or false *absolutely*, and not merely true or false relative to a certain type of theory or model. On the other hand, there are the *impure* abstracta, which (a) exist *contingently*, but whose existence is necessary given the existence of appropriate denizens of Causal Reality; (b) have *accidental* intrinsic properties and *accidental* relations to other abstracta, but only in cases where those intrinsic properties and relations are necessary given the existence of appropriate denizens of Causal Reality; (c) can only be known *a posteriori* to exist and to have the intrinsic properties and relations to other abstracta that they do have, despite the fact that it can be known *a priori* that these abstracta exist and have the properties and relations that they do given the existence of appropriate denizens of Causal Reality; and (d) may be described or referred to in sentences that are merely true or false relative to a certain type of theory or model, depending upon whether or not that theory or model adverts to the existence of appropriate denizens of Causal Reality. Putative examples of pure abstracta include numbers and pure sets (the iterative hierarchy generated from the null set); putative examples of impure abstracta include impure sets (e.g. unit sets of denizens of Causal Reality). (Cf. Yablo (2002).)

Accounts of Abstract Reality

The most obvious distinction to draw, in connection with views about Abstract Reality, is the distinction between (a) views which claim that there are some abstract objects (and hence which affirm that there is a domain of Abstract Reality), and (b) views which claim that there are no abstract objects (and hence which deny that there is any such domain as Abstract Reality). I shall refer to the former class of views as *realism* about Abstract Reality, and to the latter class of views as *anti-realism* about Abstract Reality.

Within realist views about Abstract Reality, we can distinguish between views that are full-bloodedly committed to abstract objects, and views that have a more deflationary commitment to abstract objects. Examples of what I take to be full-blooded commitments to abstract objects include the commitment of Quine (1960) to sets, the commitment of Armstrong (1978) to universals, and the commitment of Gödel (1964) to numbers. An example of what I take to be a more deflationary commitment to abstract objects is the commitment of Hale and Wright (2009) to numbers.

Within anti-realist views about Abstract Reality, we can distinguish between *struthioism*—which barefacedly denies that straightforward talk ostensibly about abstract objects brings with it commitment to the existence of any such objects—and *fictionalism*—which aims to "explain away" the apparent commitment to abstract objects in different kinds of things that we say. Struthioism is, as far as I know, a mere theoretical possibility: in particular, I do not know of any contemporary defenders of it. On the other hand, a good example of fictionalism is the general program of Yablo (2000a, 2002, 2005). There are, of course, many recent instances of fictionalism about particular abstracta—e.g. Field (1980) and Melia (1995)—but we are here interested in versions of fictionalism that treat the entire domain of Abstract Reality as fiction. (Perhaps Rosen (1990) might also have been offered as an example of fictionalism about particular abstracta; but it is debatable whether he offers a fiction about *abstracta*.)

The above taxonomy may appear to omit generalizations of traditional versions of nominalism. In particular, some may say that I have overlooked *tokenism*—which eschews commitment to abstracta in favor of commitment to "extramental" denizens of Causal Reality, such as linguistic tokens, or tokenings—and *conceptualism*—which eschews commitment to abstracta in favor of commitment to "mental" denizens of Causal Reality, such as "concepts," or "ideas in the mind," or the like. However, I deny that there are viable views that fall under either of these labels. (More about that anon.)

Merits of competing accounts of Abstract Reality

It is no part of my present project to take a stance on which is the correct view to hold about Abstract Reality. However, it will be useful for me to say something about the comparative plausibility of realism and fictionalism. (I take it that struthioism is not a view that deserves serious consideration.)

Yablo (2000a, 2002, 2005) claims that certain pieces of language that appear to commit us to abstract objects function as representational aids that boost expressive power. In particular, in Yablo (2005), he sets out a meta-myth which shows how the "myth of mathematics" might have arisen as the result of the adoption of a series of representational aids aimed at boosting the expressive powers of language. According to the meta-myth, we start out with a first-order language quantifying over concreta, and then add further resources—involving various kinds of "pretence" or "supposition" or "making as if"—in order to facilitate expression of useful claims about concreta. First comes "finite numbers of finite numbers," then "operations on finite numbers," then "finite sets of concreta," then "infinite sets of concreta," then "infinite numbers of concreta," and finally "infinite sets (and numbers) of abstracta."

The kind of idea that Yablo expresses here in connection with numbers finds application in other domains. It is commonplace in discussions of truth that the truth-predicate serves an evident need: Without it, we would need to cast around for some other means of expressing the thought that *everything that the Pope says is true*, and the like. While there are theoretical alternatives—e.g. infinite disjunction or insistence on infinitely many instances of a sentential schema—there is no alternative that admits of finite expression. (This same example demonstrates the value of propositional quantification, a value that we can exhibit using examples that have nothing to do with truth. Consider, for example: *He had nothing new to say*. This claim could also be expressed as an infinite disjunction, or via insistence on infinitely many instances of a sentential schema.) Similarly, in the discussion of universals, while it has been argued by some that sentences such as *Napoleon has all of the attributes of a great general* demonstrate that we are committed to universals, it is clear that we can understand explicit talk of attributes in this kind of case as a representational aid that serves to boost the expressive power of our language. (In this case, too, there are similar theoretical alternatives; e.g. infinite conjunction or insistence on all the instances of a sentential schema.) Of course, there are other examples of sentences alleged to demonstrate commitment to universals—consider, e.g. *Red resembles orange more than it resembles blue*, discussed in Jackson (1977) and Lewis (1983)—that raise different considerations. I'm inclined to think that this sentence is just false—but that's really a story for another occasion.

While it seems to me to be plausible to suppose that often—perhaps even always—where we feel pressure to postulate abstracta, we find representational aids that boost the expressive power of language, it is not obvious that this gives us a decisive argument against realism about abstracta. After all, it is clearly conceivable that, in finding representational aids that boost the expressive power of our language, we make discoveries about the denizens of Abstract Reality. Nonetheless, I am inclined to think that, at least, wherever we can point to connections between apparent commitments to abstracta and devices that boost the expressive powers of language, we have a powerful motivation to think that fictionalism affords the best account of the abstracta in question.

Abstract Reality does not support theism or naturalism

For each of the candidate views that might be held about Abstract Reality, there is a straightforward argument for the conclusion that that view affords no differential support to just one of theism and naturalism.

(a) **Realism**: If we are realists about abstracta, then we suppose that there is an independent domain of abstracta, with the distinctive properties of the denizens of Abstract Reality identified earlier, to which we are committed by claims that we make in connection with Causal Reality. While we noted earlier that there is room for disagreement about the thickness of the conception of object that is invoked in connection with abstracta, we shall see that this disagreement has no implications for the assessment of the comparative merits of theism and naturalism.

The key observation to make here is that, according to realism, the only connections between Abstract Reality and Causal Reality are necessary connections. If we suppose that Abstract Reality divides into Pure Abstract Reality and Impure Abstract Reality, then Pure Abstract Reality is absolutely independent of Causal Reality, and Impure Abstract Reality is dependent upon Causal Reality only in the sense that there are certain necessary connections between Causal Reality and Impure Abstract Reality. Since Pure Abstract Reality is absolutely independent of Causal Reality, and since—*ex hypothesi*—theism and naturalism differ *fundamentally* only in their accounts of Causal Reality, it is impossible for considerations about Pure Abstract Reality to favor one view over the other. Furthermore, since Impure Abstract Reality is dependent upon Causal Reality only in the sense that there are certain necessary connections between Causal Reality and Impure Abstract Reality, it is impossible for it to be the case that there are considerations about Impure Abstract Reality that favor one view over the other that do not simply mirror considerations about Causal Reality that favor that same view over the other. (It could not be, for example, that one view does better, on account of its commitments to impure unit sets unless that view also does better on account of its commitments to the causal entities that figure in those impure unit sets.)

Perhaps some might be tempted to object that it is a mistake to suppose that Abstract Reality is independent of Causal Reality, given that God belongs to Causal Reality. In particular, some might be tempted to claim that, since God is the creator, or source, or ground of all else, God is the creator, or source, or ground of Abstract Reality. But this cannot be right.

First, if God is the creator, or source, or ground of Abstract Reality, then Abstract Reality has a cause, or source, or ground—whence, Abstract Reality is part of Causal Reality, in contradiction with our initial assumption about the nature of Abstract Reality. Moreover, we cannot repair this problem by supposing that God belongs to Abstract Reality: for then God would not be the cause, or source, or ground of anything, and, in particular, would not be the cause, or source, or ground of Natural Reality.

Second, if realism requires that the denizens of Abstract Reality are either necessary, or else necessary given the mere existence of denizens of Causal Reality, then it is impossible that anything—even God—be their creator, or ground, or source. Anything that is created, or that has a ground or a source, is *dependent* upon the thing that is its creator, or ground, or source for its existence, and so is something whose existence is *contingent*, in contradiction with our assumption that it either exists of necessity, or else exists of necessity given the mere existence of other things. Dependence and contingency are asymmetric modal relationships: If A depends upon or is contingent upon B, then either it is possible not to have B, or else it is possible to have B without A—and, either way, it follows that it is possible to not have A. (True, in the *Third Way*, Aquinas writes of "necessary beings that owe their necessity to something else." But, in this context, the "necessary beings that owe their necessity to something else" are merely eternal beings whose existence is metaphysically contingent upon God's creative activities. So there is no counterexample to be found in that part of that *Summa*.)

Third, even setting the preceding two considerations aside, there seems to be a further difficulty in the idea that God might be the cause, or ground, or source of Abstract Reality that arises from the role that the denizens of Abstract Reality have in the *characterization* of the denizens of Causal Reality. If, for example, there are universals in Abstract Reality, then entities in Causal Reality *participate* in at least some of those universals; if, to take another example, there are propositions in Abstract Reality, then entities in Causal Reality *have* at least some of those propositions as *contents*; and so forth. But, on the assumption that God creates Abstract Reality, it follows that there is a part of Causal Reality—the part that is (causally) prior to the creation of Abstract Reality—that is not related to Abstract Reality by the appropriate kinds of characterization relations. On the one hand, we are to suppose that we are required to believe in Abstract Reality because of the *essential* role that it plays in "characterizing" elements of Causal Reality; and yet, on the other hand, we are to suppose that there is an entity in Causal Reality that lies beyond all of these allegedly essential "characterizing" elements: At least prior to the creation of Abstract Reality, God exists in some way and yet participates in no universals, has thoughts even though there are no contents of thoughts to be had, and so forth. I think that I will not be alone in suspecting that this overall picture is just incoherent.

(b) **Struthioism**: If we are struthioists about abstracta, then we suppose that, while some of our talk brings with it *prima facie* commitment to abstracta, there is actually no Abstract Reality, and no need for any explanation in connection with our *prima facie* commitments to abstracta. Needless to say, in the nature of the case, there is nothing in this assumption that favors either theism or naturalism. So we conclude that, on struthioism, there is no significant difference between the accounts that naturalism and theism give of Abstract Reality.

I noted earlier that struthioism appears to be a merely theoretical possibility; as far as I know, it has no actual defenders. This should not be surprising: It seems hard to resist the pull of the thought that there is *apparent* commitment to abstracta in some of the ways that we talk, and hence of the further thought that, at the very least, there is something here that requires explanation if, in fact, the commitment in question is *merely* apparent. However, these points do not affect the argument given in the previous paragraph. It is, after all, quite plain that, if struthioism were correct, it would yield no differential support to either theism or naturalism.

(c) **Fictionalism**: If we are fictionalists about abstracta, then we suppose that we can *explain* apparent commitments to abstracta by (a) appealing to the utility of adopting linguistic devices that generate the apparent commitments, and (b) adding some further story about how we take on the linguistic devices without taking on the apparently generated commitments. The further story may involve claims about the attitudes that we actually have towards the linguistic devices in question—perhaps claiming that, in fact, we view them in such a way that we take the apparent commitments that they generate to be merely apparent—or it may only involve claims about the attitudes that we could justifiably take towards the linguistic devices in question—perhaps claiming that we could justifiably view the apparent commitments that they generate as merely apparent. (Roughly, the distinction to which I am adverting here is the distinction between *hermeneutic* and *revisionary* fictionalisms. There are many other philosophical domains in which similar distinctions are drawn: consider, for example, the different ways in which contractarian political and ethical theories can be formulated.) And, of course, the further story might also involve claims to the effect that different parts of Abstract Reality are treated in different ways: "hermeneutic" fictionalism is appropriate for some abstracta (perhaps, e.g., "sakes"), while "revisionary" fictionalism is appropriate for other abstracta (perhaps, e.g., natural numbers).

The key point to note about fictionalism is that it appeals only to facts about human beings: the languages that we speak, the linguistic devices that we have invented, and the interpretations that we ourselves place upon the languages that we speak and the linguistic devices that we employ. Given that there is nothing in the data about human beings, the languages that they speak, and the linguistic devices that they employ, that favors one of theism and naturalism over the other, there is nothing in fictionalist accounts of Abstract Reality that favors one of theism and naturalism over the other.

Perhaps some may be tempted to object that facts about the evolution of human beings, or the evolution of human intellectual capacities, or the evolution of human languages actually favors one of theism and naturalism over the other. However, even if it were true that facts about the evolution of human beings, or the evolution of human intellectual capacities, or the evolution of human languages do favor one of theism and naturalism over the other, these considerations would all belong to the "causal" data that is the standard focus of traditional arguments about the existence of God. Unless there is something, about representational devices that boost the expressive power of languages at the cost of merely apparent commitments to abstracta, that *adds* to considerations about the evolution of human beings, or the evolution of human intellectual capacities, and the evolution of human languages, there is no special place for considerations about Abstract Reality in the decision between theism and naturalism.

Given that realism, struthioism, and fictionalism are the candidate views about Abstract Reality, and given that none of these views provides differential support to one of theism and naturalism, we are justified in concluding that considerations about Abstract Reality do not provide differential support to one of theism and naturalism.

Tokenism and conceptualism are not genuine accounts of Abstract Reality

As I noted above, some may think that the conclusion drawn at the end of the preceding section is premature, because there are other candidate views about Abstract Reality that have not yet been considered. I turn now to the task of arguing that these other proposed candidate views—tokenism and conceptualism—do not offer viable accounts of Abstract Reality.

(d) **Tokenism**: According to tokenism, apparent commitments to abstracta turn out to be genuine commitments to extramental denizens of Causal Reality. So, on this view, there really are abstracta—such things as numbers, sets, classes, functions, mappings, structures, groups, rings, algebras, states, patterns, propositions, contents, intentional objects, properties, universals, attributes, characteristics, types, normative principles, values, utilities, generic objects, arbitrary objects, intensional objects, mere possibilia, impossibilia, incomplete objects, and so on—but these things are extramental denizens of Causal Reality: linguistic tokens, or linguistic tokenings, or appropriately-shaped regions of space-time, or the like.

This view seems to be to be entirely misconceived. When we produce linguistic tokens, or make linguistic tokenings, those linguistic tokens or linguistic tokenings are, themselves, causal entities that belong to Causal Reality. But, when we ask what we *commit ourselves to* in producing these linguistic tokens or making these linguistic tokenings, it simply isn't part of the correct answer that we *commit ourselves* to the very linguistic tokens that we have produced, or the linguistic tokenings that we have made, and nor is it part of the correct answer—at least, in general—that we *commit ourselves* to some other linguistic tokens or linguistic tokenings (that are appropriately related to the linguistic tokens that we have produced or the linguistic tokenings that we have made). To suppose that abstracta are linguistic tokens, or linguistic tokenings, or appropriately shaped regions of space-time is just to make a kind of category error.

(e) **Conceptualism**: According to conceptualism, apparent commitments to abstracta turn out to be genuine commitments to mental denizens of Causal Reality. So, on this view, there really are abstracta but these things are mental denizens of Causal Reality: concepts, or ideas, or the like.

This view seems to me to be vitiated by an ambiguity in talk of concepts, or ideas, or the like. When we talk about concepts, or ideas, there are two different things that we might be meaning to discuss. On the one hand, we might be talking about mental tokens: causal entities that are denizens of Causal Reality. On the other hand, we might be talking about the contents of mental tokens: putative abstracta that would be denizens of Causal Reality if realism is the appropriate attitude to take towards them. And there is no third thing that we might be talking about: Either we are talking about mental tokens, or we are talking about the contents of mental tokens.

However, if we are talking about mental tokens, then conceptualism is just a variant of tokenism, in which the tokens in question are mental rather than extramental. But whether the tokens are mental or extramental makes no difference to the viability of tokenism: Either way, it is just a category mistake to suppose that putative abstracta are causal tokens.

On the other hand, if we are talking about the contents of mental tokens, then we have not been offered any account of putative abstracta: For what our theory of Abstract Reality is supposed to do is to give us an account of such things as the contents of mental tokens. If conceptualism claims only that putative abstracta are contents of mental tokens, then it simply fails to be a theory of Abstract Reality.

Either way, then, conceptualism is not a viable theory of Abstract Reality. Whatever account we might give of abstracta, we cannot say that abstracta are concepts, or ideas, or the like. What, then, of the intuition that many putative abstracta are "mind-dependent"? Well, if we are realists about Abstract Reality, we shall say that, at least for the range of cases for which there really are denizens of Abstract Reality, the intuition is simply mistaken. And if we are fictionalists about Abstract Reality, then we shall say that our fictionalist theory gives us all of the mind-dependence that we could require: for, of course, the representational aids that boost the expressive powers of our language, thereby generating apparent commitments to abstracta, are products of human minds. If Yablo's "myth of the seven" captures something important about our apparent commitment to numbers, then Yablo's "myth of the seven" establishes a significant sense in which "numbers are mind-dependent." What more could you want?

Abstract Reality and theistic arguments

Plantinga (2007) claims that there are various good arguments for the existence of God concerning denizens of Abstract Reality; in particular, he sketches arguments concerning natural numbers, sets, and intentional objects:

Argument from Numbers:

> It … seems plausible to think of numbers as dependent upon or even consti-tuted by intellectual activity…. . So, if there were no minds, there would be no numbers…. But … there are too many of them to arise as a result of human intel-lectual activity. We should therefore think of them as among God's ideas. (213)

Argument from Sets:

> Many think of sets as displaying the following characteristics … : (1) No set is a member of itself; (2) Sets … have their extensions essentially; hence sets are contingent beings and no set could have existed if one of its members had not; (3) sets form an iterated structure: at the first level, sets whose members are non-sets, at the second, sets whose members are non-sets or first-level sets, etc. Many [are] also inclined to think of sets as collections—i.e., things whose existence depends upon a certain sort of intellectual activity—a collecting or 'thinking together'. If sets were collections, that would explain their having the first three features. But

of course there are far too many sets for them to be a product of human thinking together; there are far too many sets such that no human being has ever thought their members together. That requires an infinite mind—one like God's. (211f.)

Argument from Intentionality:

Consider propositions: the things that are true or false, that are capable of being believed, and that stand in logical relations to one another. They also have another property: aboutness or intentionality ... [they] represent reality or some part of it as being thus and so.... . Many have thought it incredible that propositions should exist apart from the activity of minds.... . But if we are thinking of human thinkers, then there are far too many propositions: at least, for example, one for every real number that is distinct from the Taj Mahal. On the other hand, if they were divine thoughts, no problem here. So perhaps we should think of propositions as divine thoughts. (210f.)

I do not think that we should be quick to agree with Plantinga that these are promising routes to arguments for the existence of God. There are several reasons for this.

First, of course, there is the ambiguity in talk about "God's ideas," "divine thoughts," and the like. When Plantinga says that "we should think of numbers as among God's ideas," or that "we should think of propositions as divine thoughts," what he says is ambiguous. He could mean: We should think that numbers and propositions are God's mental state tokens—causal things that belong to Causal Reality. Or he could mean: We should think that numbers and propositions are contents of God's mental state tokens—abstracta that belong to Abstract Reality. However, as we have already noted, numbers and propositions cannot be things that belong to Causal Reality; and the observation that numbers and propositions are contents of God's mental state tokens simply fails to be an account of putative abstracta. Since there is no third construal that can be placed upon talk about "God's idea," "divine thoughts," and the like, we can conclude that there is no way that the arguments that Plantinga sketches here can be carried through.

Second, if we grant that there is some *prima facie* plausibility to the thought that numbers are "dependent upon or even constituted by" intellectual activity—and that sets are "things whose existence depends upon a certain sort of intellectual activity," and that it is "incredible that propositions should exist apart from the activity of minds"—we can explain away this *prima facie* plausibility by appealing to fictionalist accounts of numbers (and sets and propositions). We might say, for example, that our commitments to numbers—and sets and propositions—arise from our adoption of certain representational aids that boost the expressive power of our language (and advert to, say, Yablo's "myth of the seven"). Without the activity of our minds that went into developing—and goes into supporting—the use of those representational aids, we would not have any inclination or reason to suppose that we have even *prima facie* commitment to the existence of numbers (or sets or propositions), and questions about the existence of numbers (and sets and propositions) would not so much as arise.

Third, even if we were to follow Plantinga in supposing that it is literally true that the existence of, say, numbers is constituted by intellectual activity, it is not clear that the kind of argument that he tries to develop will go through. Suppose, for example, that the existence of numbers is constituted by there being people whose minds contain tokens of sentences like this one: "There are infinitely many natural numbers." If the occurrence of a token of this kind in someone's mind is enough to make it the case that there are infinitely many natural numbers, then it seems that Plantinga is simply mistaken when he claims that there are too many natural numbers for them to arise as the result of human intellectual activity. If I can have a bunch of tokens in my head that *entail* infinitely many further claims, even though it is impossible for me to have infinitely many tokens—separately representing each of those infinitely many further claims—in my head, then it is unclear why the infinite nature of mathematical domains should be thought problematic.

For these—and other—reasons, I conclude that there is no prospect of developing successful arguments for the existence of God from considerations about natural numbers, sets, propositions, or any other abstract objects, along the lines that Plantinga proposes. Of course, this conclusion dovetails nicely with the more general conclusion, argued for in the earlier parts of my essay, that considerations about abstract objects do not favor either theism or naturalism. (Perhaps it is worth noting here that there are other arguments for the existence of God—concerning our *knowledge* of matters involving putative abstracta—that would require further discussion. All that has been canvassed here is the possibility of arguments for the existence of God based upon the *metaphysics* of abstract objects. Arguments for the existence of God based upon the *epistemology* of abstract objects will have to wait for some other occasion.)

Conclusion

I took as the principal question for this essay whether theism or naturalism affords a better account of Abstract Reality. The conclusion for which I have argued is that considerations about abstracta favor neither theory. In particular, I have argued that realism and fictionalism give no differential support to either theism or naturalism, and that there are no other plausible accounts of Abstract Reality. Given this answer to my principal question, I also have an answer to the wider question whether there is any serious prospect that, while one of naturalism and theism leads when only Causal Reality is taken into account, the other theory wins when all of Reality is taken into account. My answer to that question is negative: Comparison of the relative merits of naturalism and theism need only consider their respective accounts of Causal Reality.

Response to Graham Oppy

Keith Yandell

Professor Oppy holds that if one learned that God exists, one would not be better off regarding knowing whether there are abstract objects, and if one learned that there are abstract objects, one would not be better off regarding knowing whether God exists. One probably could cook up scenarios under which this would not be true—for example, suppose God gave you an awareness of God that properly convinced you that it was God you were aware of, and as part of the authoritative revelation informed you that there are abstract objects. But presumably Professor Oppy did not have exotic revelations in mind.

A related question is whether, if we knew that one of God and abstract objects did *not* exist, that would tell us anything regarding the existence of the other. The concept of an abstract object that I work with in my essay (and continue to use here) includes neither *organizations* nor *classes* of cows. An organization depends for its existence on its members, and a class of cows owes its existence to cows, and neither workers nor cows exist with necessity. Neither organizations nor classes of cows are eternal or everlasting, and both can change in a stronger sense than that of having existed for more than two minutes. Organizations and classes can be causes, and abstract objects cannot. Organizations and classes of cows are not fundamental features of the world, but any abstract objects there may be are fundamental. Thus the notion of an abstract object with which I was (and am) concerned is much narrower than the one Professor Oppy uses. (He is, of course, right in his report that some contemporary philosophers use the term "abstract object" with the wider connotation that he describes.)

I wish to briefly investigate some of the conceptual neighborhood in which thought of both God and abstract objects dwell. If there are abstract objects, materialism is false. A material item either is in space in the usual straightforward sense, or can compose something that is in space in that sense. Abstract objects cannot play these roles. If God exists, then materialism is false, God being no more able to play the roles just described than abstract objects. (I hope no one will suppose this is any objection to divine omnipotence. God cannot become an ice-cream cone or an oak leaf, and these things are also due to the fact that an immaterial being cannot become an entirely material one.) So the claims share an interesting entailment.

Consider this argument. We can know necessary truths, and if there are abstract objects that ground those truths, knowledge of those truths cannot be caused by abstract objects which lack causal powers. So the causal theory of knowledge, at best, has exceptions. (This involves reversing Beneceraff's argument that the causal theory of knowledge is true, and on it there is no way that we can have knowledge of necessary truths by contact with items lacking causal powers.) But suppose we accept the causal theory of knowledge. Then we can affirm a doctrine of divine illumination that says that God causes us to have thoughts which have as propositional content (some of) the necessary truths. So it is possible to argue from our knowledge of necessary truths grounded in abstracta, plus the casual theory of knowledge, to the conclusion that God exists.

There are other relations between God and abstract objects that are worth noting. The question as to whether God and abstract objects can coexist is one issue. Another issue concerns whether it is coherent to think of propositions as items existing independent of any mind thinking them—distinct from being the propositional content of any thought had by any mind. If one thinks that the proposition *No one can be taller than herself* is a necessary truth and has eternally or everlastingly been such, and adds that if it is a necessary truth then it must exist to have that distinction, then it has no origin. But perhaps it must also have been thought by some mind for the entire period of its existence. Thus there is some mind that has either eternal or everlasting tenure, and that is at least a proposition that fits nicely with theism. Then one has argued from there being necessary truth to a mind that knows them, and abstract objects, having no mind, cannot ground necessary truths.

There is also this modal logic argument: a proposition ascribing a modality to a proposition (contingency, possibility, necessity) is either (narrowly or broadly) necessarily true or necessarily false. If it is true, it is necessarily true. If it is false, it is necessarily false, and so self-contradictory. Consider the following: (1) If it is possible that *Something has necessary existence*, then something does have necessary existence; (2) It is possible that something has necessary existence; (3) Something does have necessary existence. (1) is simply the fact just noted about propositions that ascribe modality to a proposition—they are necessarily true. (2) seems, upon careful examination, to be free from contradiction. (3) follows from (1) and (2).

Continuing on: (4) The only candidates for beings that have necessary existence are God and abstracta; (5) There are no abstracta; (6) God exists. The argument for (4) involves an attempt to list the promising candidates for having necessary existence, and eliminating all but two—admittedly it will be hard to show that any such list is exhaustive. (5) is stipulative, and permitted by the claim that if we knew that there are no abstracta, we'd be no better off regarding our knowledge that God exists. (6) follows from (4) and (5). For an argument for a different conclusion, one could replace (5) with (5*) God does not exist, as a different stipulation—the result, a kind of platonic atheism.

None of these arguments proceed simply from knowing whether God exists to knowledge that abstracta do not, or conversely. Nonetheless, they are arguments which, given certain added elements, make a connections between divine existence and the existence (or nonexistence) of abstracta.

Paul M. Gould and Richard Brian Davis

It is a mistake to think that abstract objects cannot enter into causal relations. Granted, this assumption is commonplace, but we think it is unwarranted. Perhaps it is natural to think, as Rodriguez-Pereyra (2011) points out, that the nonspatiotemporality of abstract objects entails their causal inertness. Indeed, if causation involves energy transfer, as Oppy suggests, it is natural to think that causation is an intrinsically temporal notion since the transfer of energy takes time. But no such entailment holds—causation is neither intrinsically temporal nor atemporal. Rather, the causal relation signifies a relation of explanation, wherein one thing is held to be the source, or ground, of another (McCann 2012, 58–62). Many theists hold that God is essentially nonspatiotemporal, yet the very font of Causal Reality, and they apparently hold this position without obvious contradiction. Granted, as nonagents, abstract objects plausibly possess no causal powers of their own, but this does not make them causally irrelevant, or unable to enter into causal relations as effects. Unless it can be shown to be logically or metaphysically impossible, we submit that it is best to think of abstract objects as (essentially) nonspatiotemporal, nonagents, yet capable of entering into causal relations.

Realism and Causal Reality

Suppose (as we maintain) that realism is true: There is an Abstract Reality. Further, suppose (as we maintain) that God is the creator of Abstract Reality. (Assume for the moment that God is the creator of all Abstract Reality, we'll refine this claim momentarily.) Oppy argues that this cannot be right for three reasons. First, "if God is the creator, or source, or ground of Abstract Reality, then Abstract Reality has a cause, or source, or ground—whence, Abstract Reality is part of Causal Reality, in contradiction with our initial assumption about the nature of Abstract Reality" (175). In response, we say, so much the worse for the initial assumption, it is unwarranted. Second, "if realism requires that the denizens of Abstract Reality are either necessary, or else necessary given the mere existence of denizens of Causal Reality, then it is impossible that anything—even God—be their creator" (175–6). The reason, according to Oppy, is that created things are dependent things, and dependent things are contingent things: "Dependence and contingency are asymmetric modal relationships: if A depends upon or is contingent upon B, then either it is possible not to have B, or else it is possible to have B without A—and, either way, it follows that it is possible to not have A" (176). The mistake here is Oppy's claim that "x is dependent" entails "x is contingent." As Kit Fine (1994) has shown, essentialist and modal facts are distinct—one does not *necessarily* fix the other. The following state of affairs is possible (we say, actual as well): Abstract object X is essentially created by God and exists of necessity. Oppy has not demonstrated how a necessary being must be independent; thus, he has not shown it to be impossible for God to create Abstract Reality.

Still, Oppy offers a third objection to the idea that God might be the cause of Abstract Reality, an objection that requires a slight modification (as we noted in our essay) regarding God's relation to Abstract Reality. One role ascribed to Abstract Reality is that of characterizing the denizens of Causal Reality. But "at least prior to the creation of Abstract Reality, God exists in some way and yet participates in no universals, has thoughts even though there are no contents of thoughts to be had, and so forth. I think that I will not be alone in suspecting that this overall picture is just incoherent" (176). We agree; this picture, as stated, is incoherent. This is why the theistic activism of Morris and Menzel (1986) is a nonstarter—it is in need of just the modifications we suggest in our essay. To wit, there is a part of Abstract Reality that exists independently of God's creative activity, namely, God's essential properties. Further (setting aside sets with contingently existing members), *created* Abstract Reality is eternal, hence eternally created—there is no temporally prior state "before" the creation of Abstract Reality. God's thoughts, as well as the content of His thoughts, are such that He is always aware of them. So too, the denizens of Plato's heaven are co-eternal with God, even as they are created by, and distinct from, God. The key point to note is that there is no part of Abstract Reality distinct from God (the divine substance) that is independent of God's creative activities. God's essential properties, while uncreated, are metaphysical parts of God. Hence, the traditional doctrines of creation and aseity is maintained: God alone exists *a se* and is the creator of all reality distinct from Himself (in addition, God is the creator of some of His constituent parts—namely, His thoughts and concepts, which are the product of divine intellectual activity).

Realism, Causal Reality, and God

If realism is true and created Abstract Reality is part of Causal Reality, then it seems we do have differential support for theism over naturalism. For theism explains *why* such entities exist and have the natures they do, whereas naturalism does not. Further, given our MTA, there is no ambiguity in talk about "God's ideas" and "divine thoughts." Propositions, as divine thoughts are mental state types—abstract objects (not concrete objects) that belong to Causal Reality; divine ideas are concepts—the contents of God's thoughts—and also abstract objects that belong to Causal Reality. God's thoughts and concepts are universals; they are capable of multiple-instanti-ation. Our thoughts and concepts, on the other hand, are tokens of the divine types. Hence, our thoughts and concepts, as instances of the divine types, are concrete members of Causal Reality. It turns out, after all, that considerations related to created Abstract Reality do make a difference in the perennial debate between theism and naturalism.

Greg Welty

Graham Oppy thinks that "the right way to draw the [abstract/concrete] distinction is in terms of causation: Concrete objects are denizens only of Causal Reality; abstract objects are denizens only of Abstract Reality" (171). Rosen contends that this distinction doesn't really do the trick, but Oppy asks us to assume "that causation is marked by transfer of conserved quantities: wherever there is causation, there is transfer of conserved quantities between entities" (171). But doesn't that preclude *God* as a cause? Don't conservation laws only apply to closed systems, when God isn't acting specially (Plantinga 2011b, 78–80, 94)? If so, then while causation in *closed* systems "is marked by transfer of conserved quantities," this observation will not apply to causation *simpliciter*. Right from the start, then, Oppy sets up his assessment of the explanatory virtues of naturalism by presupposing naturalism. Oppy says that "What matters is that there be some story told about causation" (172). Sure. But *his* story presupposes that naturalism is correct, that causation only occurs in closed systems. So Oppy needs *naturalism* to argue that "Concrete objects are denizens only of Causal Reality; abstract objects are denizens only of Abstract Reality." But if Abstract Reality is constituted by divine ideas, then since God is a causal agent *par excellence*, there is at least the prospect of such Abstract Reality entering into causal relations with us (Plantinga 1993, 121; 2011b, 291).

This is important, because when it comes time to criticize theistic proposals such as *theistic activism* (God's creating abstracta) or *theistic conceptual realism* (God's ideas constituting abstracta), Oppy explicitly appeals to *his* preferred way of articulating the abstract/concrete divide. God cannot be "the creator, or source, or ground of Abstract Reality," says Oppy, for then "Abstract Reality is part of Causal Reality, in contradiction with our initial assumption about the nature of Abstract Reality" (175). Likewise for his rebuttal of Plantinga's conceptualist arguments: "as we have already noted, numbers and propositions cannot be things that belong to Causal Reality" (180). In each case, the "assumption" presupposes naturalism. And while I agree that *if* naturalism is true then theistic activism and theistic conceptualism are false, we can't establish the latter by going in a circle.

Oppy says that "according to realism, the only connections between Abstract Reality and Causal Reality are necessary connections," and this is why "Pure Abstract Reality is absolutely independent of Causal Reality" (175). I don't see why this should be the case. Suppose A is God and B is abstracta, and that "A exists in all possible worlds, and, in every possible world in which it exists, causes B to exist in that possible world." In this case, "B will nonetheless depend upon A for its existence" (van Inwagen 1993, 108).[1] So it's not clear why "necessary connections" would require "absolute independence." Oppy then deploys this dubious point against TA, saying that "it is impossible that anything—even God—be their [i.e. abstracta's] creator, or ground, or source" (175–6). The only reason he gives for this is that dependent beings must be contingent beings. In short, Oppy treats "dependence" and "contingency" as synonyms. But "dependent" is about causal relations, whereas "contingent" is about existence in some but not all possible worlds. In a necessary dependence relation, it doesn't have to be the case that we can have A without B. What is his argument against the coherence of such a view?

Do advocates of TA offer us an overall picture that is "just incoherent" because in supposing God to be the author of Abstract Reality they "suppose that there is an entity in Causal Reality that lies beyond all of these allegedly essential 'characterizing' elements" (176) of Abstract Reality? "Modified" theistic activists such as Gould and Davis can speak for themselves, since they exempt the essential abstracta God needs from the abstracta God creates, thus avoiding the bootstrapping issues to which Oppy alludes. I'll just note that Oppy has said very little about the *kinds* of arguments realists give for "believing in Abstract Reality." Perhaps the realist arguments for propositions require us to recognize a distinction between propositional attitudes and propositions *in the human case*, but not in the divine case. If in fact the counterfactual and modal arguments for propositions deliver the conclusion that propositions necessarily exist, then these same arguments require a distinction between propositional attitudes and propositions *in the human case*. In virtue of their necessity they must be distinct from the contingently-existing attitudes humans have toward them. But since God necessarily exists, no such attitude/proposition distinction is required in the divine case. Here we can adopt a nominalistic, adverbial theory of act content. God's belief that p being about p is a feature *of the belief*. It is not a matter of the subject who has this propositional attitude being *related to* some other entity (the proposition that p). Rather, it is a matter of the subject's propositional attitude (the belief) being a certain way. In short, "we are required to believe in Abstract Reality because of the *essential* role that it plays in 'characterizing'" (176) the *contingent* elements of Causal Reality, not all Causal Reality whatsoever. Theists who are realists can infer propositions from (because they are required for) *human* engagement with language and meaning. But God takes His own cognitive content "straight up," as it were, no chaser. So theistic theories are incoherent only if the arguments for realism require that properties and propositions must exist in order to characterize or account for *divine* reality.

For conceptualism, we give an adverbial account of the content of divine mental tokens. So no platonic realism for God. Such an account won't work in the human case (their tokens fail necessity, plenitude, and objectivity conditions). So the divine ideas are Abstract Reality for us humans: necessarily existing, multiply-exemplifiable entities that have extramental existence relative to finite minds. *Our* mental tokens think God's thoughts after Him, because they are attitudes to His thoughts (whether we are aware of this or not). The contents of our mental tokens are the (adverbially characterized) contents of divine mental tokens.

William Lane Craig

Having found that Keith Yandell "just assumes" that my position is false, I am now chagrined to discover that Graham Oppy thinks that it "is not a view that deserves serious consideration," since "it has no actual defenders" (173, 176)! (I'm not exactly feeling the love here!) Oppy calls the view I defend "struthioism." The reader should not be surprised that he has never heard this term, since it is a satirical label coined by Oppy himself.[2] As he defines it, struthioism "barefacedly denies that straightforward talk ostensibly about abstract objects brings with it commitment to the existence of any such objects" (173). It is evident that struthioists comprise anti-realists who reject the customary criterion of ontological commitment underlying the Indispensability Argument for platonism (or deny its applicability to such discourse). Among the many defenders of this position are neutralists, neo-Meinongians, advocates of quantifier variance, constructibilists, figuralists, certain proponents of free logic, and so on.

Some terminological clarification may be helpful in understanding Oppy's essay. First, the realism/anti-realism divide (recall Figure 1 on p. 40) should not be seen as a distinction drawn with respect to *abstracta*, but with respect to specific entities like numbers, sets, propositions, and so on (cf. pp. 100–1 [response to Welty]). Anti-realists deny that such things exist. Realists hold that they do. Arealists say that there is no fact of the matter. Among realists there is a further distinction between those who take such entities to be abstract and those who take them to be concrete, either physical or mental. Oppy launches overly easy critiques of these latter views simply because they do not agree that the relevant objects are, in fact, *abstracta*.

Now within platonism there is a further distinction between what has been called "lightweight platonism" and "heavyweight platonism". Oppy calls the former "deflationary" and the latter "full-blooded." This is potentially misleading, since "full-blooded platonism" is widely used in the literature to denominate the controversial view that the *abstracta* posited in *any* mathematical theory exist, a view most heavyweight platonists reject. Oppy is really talking about heavyweight (not full-blooded) platonism in contrast to lightweight platonism (which may actually be neo-Meinongianism in disguise).

Within anti-realist views Oppy distinguishes fictionalism from struthioism. Unfortunately, Oppy's characterization of fictionalism is idiosyncratic. What distinguishes fictionalism from other anti-realist views is that while it agrees with platonism that the truth of abstract talk is ontologically committing, it denies that such talk is true. By this definition, Yablo's figuralism is not, *pace* Yablo, a species of fictionalism, for it holds that abstract object talk is figurative language and therefore the customary criterion of ontological commitment does not apply to it (cf. p. 161 [response to Shalkowski]). So, contrary to the fictionalist, mathematical statements like "2+2=4" are true without commitment to numbers, just as "It's raining cats and dogs!" may be true without commitment to animals falling from the sky.

Figuralism is really a sort of struthioism in that it holds that abstract object talk, properly understood, makes no ontological commitments to *abstracta*. As Yablo presents it, figuralism is a kind of hermeneutic nominalism which claims that the literal, *prima facie* reading of mathematical statements is not the correct interpretation. But figuralism could also be presented as a revolutionary (or in Oppy's terminology, revisionary) nominalism that seeks to replace the customary interpretation with a figurative interpretation.

It must be said, however, that the common distinction between hermeneutic and revolutionary nominalism is a false dichotomy, for, as thinkers like Charles Chihara and Geoffrey Hellman emphasize, the nominalist need not take any stand at all on what the customary or normal interpretation of mathematical sentences is, being agnostic on the question. Chihara's constructibilism and Hellman's modal structuralism may be regarded simply as undercutting defeaters of the Indispensability Argument for platonism by showing that mathematically adequate paraphrases are available which do not commit their users to abstract objects.

With respect to Oppy's principal question, "Does either of our theories—naturalism and theism—afford a better account of Abstract Reality?" he anticipates my answer when he says that if "there is no difference between Reality and Causal Reality," then, "in that case, the answer to the question just framed is trivial" (170). That is to say, on my view, there just is no abstract reality, and so there is nothing to explain. So with regard to *abstracta* naturalism is not explanatorily superior to theism nor theism to naturalism. But the more fundamental question remains whether abstract objects are even compatible with theism and naturalism. That will depend on how these views are understood. I have argued that the existence of uncreated objects (in a metaphysically heavy sense) is incompatible with classical theism. If, as is customary, naturalism is defined as the view that only the natural world, that is to say, space-time and its contents, exists, then abstract objects are just as incompatible with naturalism as with theism. Oppy achieves compatibility only by watering down theism and naturalism to less robust claims. Oppy's attenuated naturalism is the analogue of Yandell's attenuated (plain) theism. The interesting question is not whether platonism is compatible with these watered down claims but with classical theism and naturalism.

Scott A. Shalkowski

Graham Oppy gives us a useful framework within which to think about abstract objects in terms of causation. I wonder how many can be as sanguine as he is regarding some answer to Rosen's (2012) challenge. Oppy agrees with Rosen that the lack of causal involvement is the key to abstracta but he thinks that the transfer of some conserved quantity is the key to causal involvement. This answer, though, must be one that can be integrated within one's larger theological or naturalistic framework, for it to be any use to us here. I have doubts that either theists or (many) naturalists can adopt Oppy's proposal.

God could not have caused the universe by transferring (physical) energy and momentum, having neither. Moreover, there being no universe, its creation could not be the result of *transferring* those quantities *to* anything. This problem is not unique to the supernaturalist, however. Those inclined to think that the story of physics provides an explanation of the Big Bang in terms of something like quantum field theory must also find a different account of causal involvement, at least to the degree that transfers are spatiotemporal processes. "Prior" to the Big Bang, the Quantum Soup "was" not spatiotemporally located and there "was" nothing spatiotemporally located to which any conserved quantity could be transferred.

Each is entitled to think that it is of the essence of causes to transfer conserved quantities to affected objects, but that the real concern about origins is not a causal concern. Perhaps, the question of origins is really an explanatory concern. In isolation, this may be fine and it gives us some framework within which to formulate the idea that space-time was created by God or arose from quantum fields, but then on Oppy's characterization of the issues of this volume each is saddled with the uncomfortable consequence that both God and the Quantum Soup are abstract objects since neither is part of Causal Reality. So, while some can adopt Oppy's solution to Rosen's challenge, I don't yet see that traditional theists or those invested in contemporary cosmology can.

I welcome some elaboration on the arguments that the standing of abstracta as noncausal and necessary existents would be impugned were they dependent upon God. So long as there is an applicable respect in which dependence may be noncausal, the dependence does not impugn the initial separation of Causal Reality from Abstract Reality. Though it is not an applicable sense of noncausal dependence, a whole depends for its existence on its parts, even though it is quite awkward to make that dependence into causation as the transfer of conserved quantities. Even if the parts transfer conserved quantities to something(s) or other when they come together, they do not transfer them to the item they corporately compose, since it does not exist to receive the transfer until the composition process is complete. Certainly, the expressions "depends upon" and "is contingent upon" diverge in their informal implications, even if not in their strict implications. The necessity of abstracta is not impugned simply because they depend upon God. God must merely exist necessarily and necessarily be that upon which abstracta depend. They may, then, be contingent upon what is not contingent and what does not contingently explain their existence.

In the taxonomy, struthioism should receive a rather longer shrift than Oppy gives it. Craig and some of his sources, such as Azzouni, seem to maintain that such swift rejection of struthioism concedes too much to platonists. They should maintain that "our" inclination to think that the very use of singular terms or existential quantificational expressions brings with them ontological commitments is due, at least in part, to a philosophically contentious education—one that intellectually bludgeoned us into ignoring uses of such expressions that are perfectly straightforward but not plausibly ontologically committing. Given the current philosophical climate, it is hard to see how one could faithfully exhibit one's struthioism. If nearly all are in thrall to the current received view that the presumptive function of such expressions is to signal ontological commitments, the philosophical masses will demand some accounting of why, contrary to what *they* take the appearances to be, some uses do not signal such commitments. Simply insisting on one's struthioism and doing no more will make one appear philosophically unserious. The considerations espoused by Craig and others seem to lead in the direction that even when dealing with truths, there is no presumption in favor of commitments, based on the grammar of the expressions used. Only when extralinguistic considerations are invoked do commitments come on to the scene. I welcome some comment regarding why this is not sufficient for struthioism.

It would, also, be worth a few further remarks regarding Field's and Melia's fictionalisms, which are quite different from Yablo's. Field's seems more like an error theory than fictionalism (regardless of his use of the term "fictionalism"), since all nontrivial mathematical claims are false. I also wonder whether Melia's is happily described as fictionalism and one only about particular abstracta. He does give some specific accounts of the functions of expressions like "the average mother," but his seems to me to be a generalizable strategy, even if he himself did not generalize it. My own preference is to do just that. Pretense seems an ill-fitting characterization of the use of representational aids, since almost none seem to recognize their own pretenses regarding abstracta. Oppy is quite right that the use of such aids does not entail that no discovery of objects represented occurs. The questions, though, are (i) whether there was ever the development of such aids that strays beyond a kind of expressive short-hand with which nominalists can be comfortable and (ii) how to integrate claims to discovery into one's wider epistemological framework. I think the answer to (i) is "no" and without a satisfactory answer to (ii), I cannot see much more in the discovery claim than whistling while walking past what some see as a metaphysical graveyard.

Notes

1   See also Leftow 1989, 137 and 1990, 194.
2   In response to my inquiry, Oppy writes, "On 'struthioism,' I confess: I made up the word! It is a joke that plays with David Armstrong's characterization of Michael Devitt's view as 'ostrich nominalism.' The common ostrich's scientific name is 'struthio camelus'" (personal communication, 13 November 2012). In debates over nominalism about universals, "ostrich nominalism" is the uncharitable characterization on the part of its opponents of the view that there need be no explanation of why, for example, something is red beyond the customary scientific explanation—no need, in particular, of positing metaphysical entities like redness to explain it. Such nominalists hold to a criterion of ontological commitment according to which "The fire truck is red" commits its user to the existence of the fire truck but not to the existence of the property redness. Analogously, in debates over nominalism about abstract objects, Oppy wants to identify a position parallel to ostrich nominalism—hence, "struthioism." Such a view would hold that "2+2=4" does not commit the person asserting it to the existence of mathematical objects like "4." Oppy apparently thinks that all nominalists about *abstracta* are fictionalists, who agree with platonists that such mathematical statements are ontologically committing. But, in fact, there are plenty of so-called struthioists running about!

Response to Critics

Graham Oppy

Thanks to everyone who participated in this project. Special thanks to Paul Gould for making it all happen. I am grateful for the comments on my initial paper; I have learned much from those responses. Given the limited space available, my replies below are terse. I have not focused at all on areas of agreement; however, it is worth noting that I find myself in pretty broad sympathy with much that everyone else says.

⌐   1. Gould and Davis say that transfer of conserved quantities takes time, whence, if causation involves transfer of conserved quantities, causation is intrinsically temporal. Shalkowksi says much the same: Because transfer of conserved quantities is a spatiotemporal process, those who appeal to quantum field theory to explain the Big Bang
└ cannot suppose that all causation involves transfer of conserved quantities. I disagree. I think it quite attractive to suppose that parts of Causal Reality are nontemporal: those parts of Causal Reality have an asymmetrical ordering but no metric. If this is right, then there is no problem talking about what happened before there was time: We are talking about what was prior in the causal order, even though there was no prior temporal order. Said differently (and with a distinctively naturalistic slant): our *manifold* is globally causal, but only locally temporal, in those parts with sufficient structure to sustain a metric.

⌐   Welty says that I argue in a circle: I rule out some views by appealing to my preferred way of articulating the abstract/concrete divide, but that way of articulating the abstract/contract divide depends upon my naturalistic assumptions that causation is marked by transfer of conserved quantities and that mental states are just neural
⟶ states. This isn't quite right, though there is some justice to the complaint. True enough, my *preferred* view of causation and mental states is naturalistic; but, at the very least, I insist that it is an open question whether *other*—non-naturalistic—views can find analogous ways of meeting Rosen's challenge. And I would add—though perhaps at the cost of begging certain questions—if they cannot, so much the worse
└ for them!

⌐   Gould and Davis argue for a view on which abstract objects are "causally relevant"—even though they have no causal powers of their own and are incapable of being causes—because they can enter into causal relations as effects. I suspect that causally epiphenomenal abstract objects are no more attractive than noncausal
⟶ abstract objects. If you are bothered by the suggestion that the contentfulness of our words and thoughts depends upon the existence of objects that cannot possible have any causal influence upon us, you are hardly likely to be less bothered by the suggestion that the contentfulness of our words and thoughts depends upon whether
└ God made some things that cannot possibly have any causal influence upon us.

   2. Gould and Davis say that I mistakenly claim that "x is dependent" entails "x is contingent," when essentialist and modal facts are, in fact, distinct. Welty says that I mistakenly treat "dependence" and "contingency" as synonyms, when, in fact,

"dependence" is about causal relations, and "contingency" is about existence in some but not all possible worlds. Shalkowski says that "depends upon" and "is contingent upon" diverge in their informal implications, even if not in their strict implications: the necessity of abstracta is not impugned simply because they depend upon God. I deny pretty much all of this. I'm inclined to think that "A depends upon B" and "A is contingent upon B" require, at least, that A and B are actual, that nearest B-worlds are A-worlds, that nearest non-B-worlds are non-A-worlds, and that there are some non-A-worlds; I'm inclined to think that "A is dependent" and "A is contingent" require only that A is actual and there are some non-A-worlds; and I'm inclined to think that "A is dependent" and "A is contingent" entail "There is something upon which A is dependent" and "There is something upon which A is contingent." We do have synonymy; we do have mutual entailment; we do not have anything here that particularly concerns causation; we do not have dependence relations between necessary existents. I grant that what I'm inclined to think is controversial; I hope to find an occasion to do more to defend these inclinations at some point in the future.

3. Craig and Shalkowski both take issue with my claim that there are no actual struthioists: Craig self-identifies as a struthioist, and Shalkowski insists that Craig and Azzouni—among others—are surely entitled to self-identify as struthioists. This seems right. I followed Yablo's own lead in classifying his figuralism as fictionalism; it seemed clear enough that Yablo seeks to "explain away apparent commitment to abstract objects in different kinds of things that we say." But, even if this is right about Yablo, it isn't right about those theorists—such as Craig—who reject the underlying theory of commitment. Of course, disagreements about whether to locate theorists as struthioists or fictionalists makes no difference to the main argument that I ran: neither struthioism nor fictionalism offers stronger support to one of theism and naturalism.

4. Craig complains that I understand naturalism in a "watered down" sense: in his view, naturalism is to be defined as the view that only the natural world exists. I disagree. I self-identify as a naturalist, and I insist that what I mean by "naturalism" is the view that Natural Reality exhausts Causal Reality. If it turns out that Abstract Reality is nonempty, then fine: paradigm naturalists such as Quine will be vindicated. And if it turns out that Abstract Reality is empty, no less fine: in that case Natural Reality exhausts Reality, and we can consequently redefine "naturalism" in accordance with Craig's stipulation. As it happens, my sympathies lean more towards fictionalism: I lean towards the view that Abstract Reality is empty. But I am much more strongly of the view that Natural Reality exhausts Causal Reality than I am of the view that Abstract Reality is empty: debate about the nature of Causal Reality grips my imagination in a way that debate about the emptiness—or otherwise—of Abstract Reality does not.

5. Yandell seeks to articulate various connections between God and abstract objects. In his "modal logic argument," he claims that the only candidates for beings that have necessary existence are God and abstracta. I deny this. In my view, it is most attractive to suppose that Natural Reality is a necessary existent: It is most attractive to suppose that all possible worlds share an initial segment with actual Natural

Reality, and diverge from actual Natural Reality only as a result of the outworkings of objective chance. It is a consequence of what I take to be the most attractive view that it is possible that something has necessary existence; however, there are what I take to be less attractive, but nonetheless perfectly entertainable, views on which it is not possible that something has necessary existence. If there is an initial state of Natural Reality, and that initial state has contingent properties, then it isn't true that all possible worlds share an initial segment of actual Natural Reality; and it also isn't true that there is something that exists of necessity, unless there is something—"the initial singularity"—that exists in each possible world as part of the contingent initial state of Natural Reality in each world.

6. Gould and Davis say that God's thoughts are mental state types and God's ideas are concepts, and that our thoughts and concepts are instances of God's thoughts and concepts; and they insist that these claims give theism an explanatory advantage over naturalism when it comes to the existence of entities in Abstract Reality. But, if God's thoughts and concepts are abstract, and if abstract entities can only be effects and not causes, then it turns out that God's thoughts and concepts play no causal role in God's creative endeavors: God causes our universe to come into existence, and God has thoughts and concepts, but those thoughts and concepts have no causal involvement in God's bringing our universe into existence. Perhaps even worse, I think, if our thoughts and concepts are tokens of God's thoughts and concepts, then God has all of the thoughts that we have: Wicked thoughts, mundane thoughts, bawdy thoughts, contradictory thoughts, and so forth. It seems to me improbable that this is consonant with orthodox conceptions of God. In any case, it seems to me that views that hold that thought and concepts play a causal role in the production of behavior should be favored above views that deny that thoughts and concepts play a causal role in the production of behavior.

7. Welty claims that we can have an adverbial account of the content of divine mental tokens: God's thinking p-ly is plenitudinous, and, in every case, God's thinking p-ly provides an appropriate object for any of us who thinks that p. ("Our mental tokens think God's thoughts after Him, because they are attitudes to His thoughts" 187.) I take it that "thinking" is a generic term that covers a wide range of propositional attitudes: believing, desiring, wondering, hoping, and so forth. So, it seems, the proposal here is that God's Φ-ing p-ly—for some appropriate attitude Φ—provides an appropriate object for any of us who Ψ's that p, for any Ψ. A question that then arises is whether it is true that there is an attitude Φ for which it is true that God Φ's p-ly whenever it is true that one of us Ψ's that p. Suppose that Richard says—because he believes—that the Pope is a #@!&*$ bigot. What attitude is it here appropriate to attribute to God? God Φ's the-Pope-is-a-#@!&*$-bigot-ly for which Φ? Does God believe the-Pope-is-not-a-#@!&*$-bigot-ly? Well, even if so, that doesn't give you the right object for Richard's attitude; and, in any case, it's not clear that it is *seemly* to attribute this belief to God. It won't do to say that God *disbelieves* the-Pope-is-a-#@!&*$-bigot-ly: for, despite superficial appearances, we don't have here an attitude to a proposition. (What we have here is rather: It is not the case that God believes the-Pope-is-a-#@!&*$-bigot-ly; and that just isn't an instance of God's Φ-ing p-ly.) It's even worse to offer that God

knows that Richard believes that the Pope is a #@!&*$ bigot: for, even if it is true that God knows Richard-believes-that-the-Pope-is-a-#@!&*$-bigot-ly, that clearly doesn't give you the right object for *Richard's* attitude. While I can hardly claim to have exhausted all of the possibilities in this brief discussion, it does seem to me that, if I were a theist, I would think that we are here being committed to an excessively anthropomorphic conception of God.

8. Yandell suggests that the claim, that God might reveal to you that there are abstract objects, is a counterexample to my alleged claim that, if one learned that God exists, one would not be better off regarding knowing whether there are abstract objects. I can't see that I anywhere committed myself to the claim that Yandell attributes to me. I take it that no one thinks that God has actually made such a revelation; whence it is clear that the claim that there has been such a revelation does not feature in the best formulations of theism. But, in any case, it seems that, even given such a revelation, it would still be true that your learning that God exists did not, *on its own*, make you any better off regarding knowing whether there are abstract objects.

9. Craig complains that my critiques of tokenism and conceptualism are "overly easy" because they amount to nothing more than the complaint that tokenism and conceptualism suppose that "the relevant objects" are not really *abstracta*. I demur; I say that my objections are clearly more than this. I argue that linguistic tokens and linguistic tokenings cannot play the theoretical roles for which abstracta are typically invoked: Linguistic tokens and linguistic tokenings *cannot be the contents of* linguistic tokens and linguistic tokenings (nothing can be a proper content of itself). And I argue that, when we disambiguate, we find that there is no sense in which concepts or ideas can play the theoretical roles for which abstracta are typically invoked: as before, linguistic tokens and linguistic tokenings *cannot be the contents of* linguistic tokens and linguistic tokenings; and the *contents* of linguistic tokens and linguistic tokenings are that which is to be explained, rather than that which is invoked in the giving of explanation, in theories of those things that fill the theoretical roles for which abstracta are typically invoked.

Bibliography

Adams, Robert. 1983. "Divine Necessity." *The Journal of Philosophy* 80:741–52. Reprinted in *The Virtue of Faith*, by Robert M. Adams. Oxford: Oxford University Press, 1987. All page numbers are to this reprint.

Anderson, James and Greg Welty. 2011. "The Lord of Noncontradiction: An Argument for God from Logic." *Philosophia Christi* 13: 321–38.

Aquinas, Thomas. 1995. *Summa Contra Gentiles*, ed. Anton C. Pegis. New York: Image.

Armstrong, David. 1978. *Universals and Scientific Realism*, 2 vols. Cambridge: Cambridge University Press.

—1997. *A World of States of Affairs*. Cambridge, New York: Cambridge University Press.

Azzouni, Jody. 1998. "On 'On what There Is." *Pacific Philosophical Quarterly* 79: 1–18.

—2004. *Deflating Existential Consequence: A Case for Nominalism*. Oxford: Oxford University Press.

—2007. "Ontological Commitment in the Vernacular." *Noûs* 41: 204–26.

—2010. "Ontology and the Word 'Exist': Uneasy Relations." *Philosophia Mathematica* 18:74–101.

Baggett, David and Jerry Walls. 2011. *Good God: The Theistic Foundations of Morality*. Oxford: Oxford University Press.

Balaguer, Mark. 1998. *Platonism and Anti-Platonism in Mathematics*. Oxford: Oxford University Press.

—2004. "Platonism in metaphysics," in *Stanford Encyclopedia of Philosophy*, ed. Edward N. Zalta. http://plato.stanford.edu/entries/platonism/

Båve, Arvid. 2006. *Deflationism: A Use-Theoretic Analysis of the Truth-Predicate*, Stockholm Studies in Philosophy 29. Stockholm: Stockholm University.

—2009. "A Deflationary Theory of Reference." *Synthèse* 169: 51–73.

Bealer, George. 1998a. "A Theory of Concepts and Concept Possession." *Philosophical Issues* 9: 261–301.

—1998b. "Propositions." *Mind* 107: 1–32. Reprinted in *Philosophy of Logic: An Anthology*, ed. Dale Jacquette. Oxford: Wiley-Blackwell, 2002. All page numbers are to this reprint.

Bergmann, Gustav. 1967. *Realism: A Critique of Brentano and Meinong*. Madison: University of Wisconsin Press.

Bergmann, Michael and Jeff Brower. 2006. "A Theistic Argument against Platonism (and in Support of Truthmakers and Divine Simplicity)." In *Oxford Studies in Metaphysics*, vol. 2, ed. Dean Zimmerman, 357–86. Oxford: Clarendon Press.

Bergmann, Michael and Jan Cover. 2006. "Divine Responsibility without Divine Freedom." *Faith and Philosophy* 23: 381–408.

Carroll, John. 2010. "Anti-reductionism." In *The Oxford Handbook of Causation*,. Helen Beebee, Christopher Hitchcock, and Peter Menzies (eds), 279–98. Oxford: Oxford University Press.

Chihara, Charles. 1973. *Ontology and the Vicious Circle Principle*. Ithaca, NY: Cornell University Press.

—1990. *Constructibility and Mathematical Existence*. Oxford: Clarendon Press.

Chisholm, Roderick. 1989. *On Metaphysics*. Minneapolis: University of Minnesota Press.

→ Colyvan, Mark. 2001. *The Indispensability of Mathematics*. New York: Oxford University Press.

Copan, Paul and William Lane Craig. 2004. *Creation out of Nothing*. Grand Rapids: Baker Academic.

Craig, William Lane. 2011a. "A Nominalist Perspective on God and Abstract Objects." *Philosophia Christi* 13: 305–18.

—2011b. "Nominalism and Divine Aseity." *Oxford Studies in Philosophy of Religion* 4: 44–65.

—2012. "Truth—Who Needs it?" Paper presented at the *Evangelical Philosophical Society National Meeting*, Milwaukee, WI.

—Forthcoming. "Is Faith in God Reasonable? Opening Speech." In *Is Faith in God Reasonable? Debates in Philosophy, Science, and Rhetoric*, Corey Miller and Paul Gould (eds). London: Routledge.

Crane, Tim. 1998a. "Intentionality as the Mark of the Mental." In *Current Issues in Philosophy of Mind*, ed. A. O'Hear. Cambridge: Cambridge University Press.

—1998b. "Intentionality." In *The Routledge Encyclopedia of Philosophy*, ed. Edward Craig. London: Routledge.

—2001. *Elements of Mind*. Oxford: Oxford University Press.

Davidson, Matthew. 1999. "A Demonstration against Theistic Activism." *Religious Studies* 35: 277–90.

Davis, Richard Brian. 2001. *The Metaphysics of Theism and Modality*. New York: Peter Lang.

—2006. "God and Counterpossibles." *Religious Studies* 42: 371–91.

—2011. "God and the Platonic Horde: A Defense of Limited Conceptualism." *Philosophia Christi* 13: 289–303.

Davison, Scott. 1991. "Could Abstract Objects Depend Upon God?" *Religious Studies* 27: 485–97.

Divers, John. 2002. *Possible Worlds*. London and New York: Routledge.

Dummett, Michael. 1991. *Frege: Philosophy of Mathematics*. Cambridge, MA: Harvard University Press.

Field, Hartry. 1980. *Science without Numbers*. Princeton: Princeton University Press.

Fine, Kit. 1994. "Essence and Modality." *Philosophical Perspectives* 8: 1–16.

Frege, Gottlob. 1919. "Der Gedanke: Eine Logische Untersuchung." *Beiträge zur Philosophie des deutschen Idealismus* 1. In *Logical Investigations*, Part I: 351–72, trans. Peter Geach and R. H. Stoothoff.

—1997. "Thought." In *The Frege Reader*, ed. Michael Beaney. Malden, MA: Blackwell.

Gale, Richard M. 1967. "Propositions, Judgments, Sentences, and Statements." In *The Encyclopedia of Philosophy*, ed. Paul Edwards. New York: Macmillan.

Gödel, Kurt. 1964. "What is Cantor's Continuum Problem?" In *Philosophy of Mathematics: Selected Readings*, Paul Benacerraf and Hilary Putnam (eds). Englewood Cliffs: Prentice-Hall.

Gould, Paul. 2010. "A Defense of Platonic Theism." PhD diss., Purdue University.

—2011a. "Theistic Activism: A New Problem and Solution." *Philosophia Christi* 13: 127–39.

—2011b. "The Problem of God and Abstract Objects: A Prolegomenon." *Philosophia Christi* 13:255–74.

—2012. "The Problem of Universals, Realism, and God." *Metaphysica* 13:2: 183–94.
—2013. "Can God Create Abstract Objects? A Reply to Peter van Inwagen." *Sophia*, published online on August 24, 2013.
—2013. "How Does an Aristotelian Substance Have its Platonic Properties? Issues and Options." *Axiomathes* 23 (2): 343–64.
Grayling, A. C. 1997. *An Introduction to Philosophical Logic*, 3rd edn. Oxford: Blackwell.
Grossmann, Reinhardt. 1992. *The Existence of the World: An Introduction to Ontology*. London and New York: Routledge.
Hale, Bob. 1987. *Abstract Objects*. Oxford: Blackwell.
Hale, Bob and Crispin Wright. 2001. *The Reason's Proper Study: Essays Towards a Neo-Fregean Philosophy of Mathematics*. Oxford: Clarendon Press.
—2009. "The Metaontology of Abstraction." In *Metametaphysics: New Essays on the Foundations of Ontology*, ed. David Chalmers. Oxford: Oxford University Press.
Hofweber, Thomas. 1999. "Ontology and Objectivity." PhD diss., Stanford University.
Hornsby, Jennifer. 1997. "Truth: The Identity Theory." *Proceedings of the Aristotelian Society* (1): 1–24.
Hrbacek, Karel and Thomas Jech. 1999. *Introduction to Set Theory*, 3rd edn. New York: Marcel Dekker.
Huemer, Michael and Ben Kovitz. 2003. "Causation as Simultaneous and Continuous." *The Philosophical Quarterly* 53: 556–65.
Jackson, Frank. 1977. "Statements about Universals." *Mind* 86: 427–9.
Jubien, Michael. 1997. *Contemporary Metaphysics: An Introduction*. Malden, MA: Wiley-Blackwell.
—2001. "Propositions and the Objects of Thought." *Philosophical Studies* 104: 47–62.
Kaplan, David. 1989. "Demonstratives." In *Themes From Kaplan*, Joseph Almog, John Perry, and Howard Wettstein (eds). New York: Oxford University Press.
Katz, Jerrold. 1998. *Realistic Rationalism*. London: MIT Press.
Kittel, Gerhard. 1967. *Theological Dictionary of the New Testament*, ed. and trans. Geoffrey W. Bromiley. Grand Rapids, MI: Eerdmans.
Korhonen, Anssi. 2009. "Russell's Early Metaphysics of Propositions." *Prolegomena* 8 (2): 159–92.
Kripke, Saul. 1976. "Is There a Problem about Substitutional Quantification?" In *Truth and Meaning: Essays in Semantics*, Gareth Evans and John McDowell (eds). Oxford: Clarendon Press.
Leftow, Brian. 1989. "A Leibnizian Cosmological Argument." *Philosophical Studies* 57: 135–55.
—1990. "Is God an Abstract Object?" *Noûs* 24: 581–98.
—2006. "God and the Problem of Universals." In *Oxford Studies in Metaphysics*, vol. 2, ed. Dean Zimmerman, 325–56. Oxford: Clarendon Press.
—2009. "Necessity." In *The Cambridge Companion to Christian Philosophical Theology*, Charles Taliaferro and Chad Meister (eds), 15–30. Cambridge: Cambridge University Press.
—2012. *God and Necessity*. Oxford: Oxford University Press.
Leonhardt-Balzer, Jutta. 2004. "Der Logos und die Schöpfung: Streiflichter bei Philo (Op 20–5) und im Johannesprolog (Joh 1, 1–18)." In *Kontexte des Johannesevangelium*, Jörg Frey and Udo Schnelle (eds). Tübingen: Mohr-Siebeck.
Lewis, C. S. 1947. *Miracles*. New York: MacMillan.
Lewis, David. 1973. *Counterfactuals*. Oxford: Blackwell.
—1979. "Attitudes De Dicto and De Se." *The Philosophical Review* 88.4: 513–43.
—1983. "New Work for a Theory of Universals." *Australasian Journal of Philosophy* 61: 343–77.

—1986. *On the Plurality of Worlds*. Oxford: Blackwell.

Linnebo, Øystein. 2011. "Platonism in the Philosophy of Mathematics," in *Stanford Encyclopedia of Philosophy*, ed. Edward N. Zalta. http://plato.stanford.edu/entries/platonism-mathematics/

Locke, John. 2004. *An Essay Concerning Human Understanding*, ed. Roger Woolhouse. New York: Penguin.

Loux, Michael. 1978. *Substance and Attribute*. Dordrecht: D. Reidel.

—1979. "Introduction: Modality and Metaphysics." In *The Possible and the Actual: Readings in the Metaphysics of Modality*, ed. Michael Loux. Ithaca, NY: Cornell University Press.

—1986. "Toward An Aristotelian Theory of Abstract Objects." In *Midwest Studies in Philosophy, vol. 11: Studies in Essentialism*, P. French, T. Uehling, and H. Wettstein (eds). Minneapolis: University of Minnesota Press.

—1998. *Metaphysics: a Contemporary Introduction*. London: Routledge.

—2006. *Metaphysics: A Contemporary Introduction*, 3rd edn. New York: Routledge.

Lycan, William. 1979. "The Trouble with Possible Worlds." In *The Possible and the Actual: Readings in the Metaphysics of Modality*, ed. Michael Loux. Ithaca, NY: Cornell University Press.

—1998. "Possible Worlds and Possibilia." In *Contemporary Readings in the Foundations of Metaphysics*, Stephen Laurence and Cynthia Macdonald (eds). Oxford: Blackwell.

Mackie, J. L. 1955. "Evil and Omnipotence." *Mind* 64 (254): 200–12.

McCann, Hugh. 2012. *Creation and the Sovereignty of God*. Bloomington, IN: Indiana University Press.

McDowell, John. 1994. *Mind and World*. Cambridge, MA: Harvard University Press.

McGrath, Matthew. 2012. "Propositions," in *Stanford Encyclopedia of Philosophy*, ed. Edward N. Zalta. http://plato.stanford.edu/entries/propositions/

Melia, Joseph. 1995. "On What There's Not." *Analysis* 55: 223–9.

—2005. "Truthmaking Without Truthmakers." In *Truthmakers: The Contemporary Debate*, Helen Beebee and Julian Dodd (eds), 67–84. Oxford: Clarendon Press.

Menzel, Christopher. 1987. "Theism, Platonism, and the Metaphysics of Mathematics." *Faith and Philosophy* 4(4): 365–82.

Merricks, Trenton. 2007. *Truth and Ontology*. Oxford: Clarendon Press.

—2009. "Propositional Attitudes?" *Proceedings of the Aristotelian Society* 109: 207–32.

Moore, G. E. 1953. "Propositions." In *Some Main Problems of Philosophy*. London: George Allen & Unwin.

Moreland, J. P. 2001. *Universals*. Montreal & Kingston: McGill-Queen's University Press.

—2013. "Exemplification and Constituent Realism: A Clarification and Modest Defense." *Axiomathes* 23 (2): 247–59.

Moreland, J. P. and Timothy Pickavance. 2003. "Bare Particulars and Individuation: Reply to Mertz." *Australasian Journal of Philosophy* 81 (1): 1–13.

Morris, Thomas and Christopher Menzel. 1986. "Absolute Creation." *American Philosophical Quarterly* 23: 352–62. Reprinted in *Anselmian Explorations: Essays in Philosophical Theology*, by Thomas Morris. Notre Dame: University of Notre Dame Press, 1987. All page numbers are to this reprint.

Oliver, Alex. 1996. "The Metaphysics of Properties." *Mind* 105: 1–80.

Pelham, Judy and Alasdair Urquhart. 1994. "Russellian Propositions." In *Logic, Methodology and Philosophy of Science 9*, D. Prawitz, B. Skyrms, and D. Westerståhl (eds). Amsterdam: Elsevier Science B.V.

Pickavance, Timothy. 2009. "In Defence of 'Partially Clad' Bare Particulars." *Australasian Journal of Philosophy* 87 (1): 155–8.

Plantinga, Alvin. 1973. "Transworld Identity or Worldbound Individuals?" In *Logic and Ontology*, ed. Milton Munitz. New York: New York University Press. Reprinted in *The Possible and the Actual: Readings in the Metaphysics of Modality*, ed. Michael Loux. Ithaca, NY: Cornell University Press, 1979. All page numbers are to this reprint.

—1974. *The Nature of Necessity*. Oxford: Clarendon Press.

—1976. "Actualism and Possible Worlds." *Theoria* 42: 139–60. Reprinted in *The Possible and the Actual: Readings in the Metaphysics of Modality*, ed. Michael Loux. Ithaca, NY: Cornell University Press, 1979. All page numbers are to this reprint.

—1978. *God, Freedom, and Evil*. Grand Rapids, MI: Eerdmans.

—1980. *Does God Have A Nature?* Milwaukee: Marquette University Press.

—1982. "How to be an anti-realist." *Proceedings and Addresses of the American Philosophical Association* 56: 47–70.

—1985. "Self-Profile" and "Replies." In *Alvin Plantinga*, James E. Tomberlin and Peter van Inwagen (eds). Dordrecht: D. Reidel.

—1987. "Two Concepts of Modality: Modal Realism and Modal Reductionism." In *Metaphysics*, Philosophical Perspectives 1, ed. James Tomberlin. Atascadero, CA: Ridgeview.

—1992. "Augustinian Christian Philosophy." *The Monist* 75 (3): 291–320.

—1993. *Warrant and Proper Function*. Oxford: Oxford University Press.

—1998. "God, Arguments for the Existence of." In *The Routledge Encyclopedia of Philosophy* (Vol. 4), ed. Edward Craig. London: Routledge.

—2006. "Against Materialism." *Faith and Philosophy* 23 (1): 3–32.

—2007. "Appendix: Two Dozen (or so) Theistic Arguments." In *Alvin Plantinga*, ed. Deane-Peter Baker. Cambridge: Cambridge University Press.

—2011a. "Theism and Mathematics." *Theology and Science* 9 (1): 27–33.

—2011b. *Where the Conflict Really Lies*. Oxford: Oxford University Press.

Potter, Michael. 2004. *Set Theory and its Philosophy*. Oxford: Oxford University Press.

Prestige, George. 1964. *God in Patristic Thought*. London: SPCK.

Prior, Arthur Norman. 1971. *Objects of Thought*, Peter Geach and Anthony Kenny (eds). Oxford: Clarendon Press.

Putnam, Hilary. 1971. *Philosophy of Logic*. New York: Harper & Row.

Quine, W. V. 1951. "Ontology and Ideology." *Philosophical Studies* 2: 11–15.

—1960. "Ontic Decision." In *Word and Object*, by W. V. Quine, 233–76. Cambridge, MA: MIT Press.

Rescher, Nicholas. 1973. "The Ontology of the Possible." In *Logic and Ontology*, ed. Milton Munitz. New York: New York University Press. Reprinted in *The Possible and the Actual: Readings in the Metaphysics of Modality*, ed. Michael Loux. Ithaca, NY: Cornell University Press, 1979. All page numbers are to this reprint.

Robson, Eleanor. 2008. *Mathematics in Acient Iraq*. Princeton, New Jersey: Princeton University Press.

Rodriguez-Pereyra, Gonzalo. 2011. "Nominalism in Metaphysics," in *Stanford Encyclopedia of Philosophy*, ed. Edward N. Zalta. http://plato.stanford.edu/entries/nominalism-metaphysics

Rosen, Gideon. 1990. "Modal Fictionalism." *Mind* 99: 327–54.

—2012. "Abstract Objects" in *Stanford Encyclopedia of Philosophy*, ed. Edward N. Zalta. http://plato.stanford.edu/entries/abstract-objects

Rowe, William. 2004. *Can God Be Free?* Oxford: Clarendon Press.
Runia, David T. 1983. *Philo of Alexandria and the "Timaeus" of Plato.* Amsterdam: Free
    University of Amsterdam.
Russell, Bertrand. 1903. *Principles of Mathematics*, 2nd edn. New York: W.W. Norton.
—1984. *Theory of Knowledge: The 1913 Manuscript.* London: Routledge.
—1997. *The Problems of Philosophy.* Oxford: Oxford University Press.
Searle, John. 1983. *Intentionality.* Cambridge: Cambridge University Press.
—1998. *Mind, Language, and Society: Philosophy in the Real World.* New York: Basic
    Books.
Sellars, Wilfrid. 1963. "Abstract entities." *Review of Metaphysics.* Reprinted in *Universals
    and Particulars: Readings in Ontology*, 2nd edn, ed. Michael Loux. Notre Dame, IN:
    University of Notre Dame Press, 1976.
—1975. "The structure of knowledge II." In *Action, Knowledge, and Reality: Critical
    Studies in Honor of Wilfrid Sellars*, ed. H. N. Castaneda. Indianapolis, IN: Bobbs-Merrill.
Shalkowski, Scott. 1994. "The Ontological Ground of the Alethic Modality." *Philosophical
    Review* 103: 669–88.
—1997. "Theoretical Virtues and Theological Construction." *International Journal for
    Philosophy of Religion* 41: 71–89.
Sider, Theodore. 1999. "Presentism and Ontological Commitment." *Journal of Philosophy*
    96: 325–47.
—2006. "Bare Particulars." *Philosophical Perspectives* 20 (1): 387–97.
Stalnaker, Robert. 1968. "A Theory of Conditionals." In *Studies in Logical Theory,
    American Philosophical Quarterly* Monograph Series, 2, 98–112. Oxford: Blackwell.
Swinburne, Richard. 1994. *The Christian God.* Oxford: Oxford University Press.
Vallicella, William. 2000. "Three Conceptions of States of Affairs." *Noûs* 34 (2): 237–59.
van Inwagen, Peter. 1983. *An Essay on Free Will.* Oxford: Oxford University Press.
—1986. "Two Concepts of Possible Worlds." In *Midwest Studies in Philosophy, vol. 11:
    Studies in Essentialism*, ed. P. French, T. Uehling, and H. Wettstein. Minneapolis:
    University of Minnesota Press.
—1993. *Metaphysics.* Boulder, CO: Westview Press.
—2004. "A Theory of Properties." In *Oxford Studies in Metaphysics*, vol. 1, ed. Dean
    Zimmerman, 107–38. Oxford, Clarendon.
—2009. "God and Other Uncreated Things." In *Metaphysics and God; Essays in Honor of
    Eleonore Stump*, ed. Kevin Timpe, 3–20. London: Routledge.
—2011. "Relational vs. Constituent Ontologies." *Philosophical Perspectives* 25: 389–405.
Vision, Gerald. 1986. "Reference and the Ghost of Parmenides." In *Non-Existence
    and Predication*, ed. Rudolf Haller, Grazer Philosophische Studien 25–6: 297–336.
    Amsterdam: Rodopi.
Walton, Kendall. 1990. *Mimesis as Make-Believe: On the Foundations of the
    Representational Arts.* Cambridge, MA: Harvard University Press.
—2000. "Existence as Metaphor" In *Empty Names, Fiction, and the Puzzles of
    Non-Existence*, Anthony Everett and Thomas Hofweber (eds), 69–94. Stanford: Center
    for the Study of Language and Information.
Weaver, Richard. 1984. *Ideas Have Consequences.* Chicago: University of Chicago Press.
Welty, Greg. 2004. "Truth as Divine Ideas: A Theistic Theory of the Property 'Truth.'"
    Southwestern Journal of Theology 47: 57–70.
—2006. "Theistic Conceptual Realism: The Case for Interpreting Abstract Objects as
    Divine Ideas." DPhil diss., University of Oxford.

Willard, Dallas. 1999. "How Concepts Relate the Mind to its Objects." *Philosophia Christi* 1: 5–20.

Wittgenstein, Ludwig. 2001. *Tractatus Logico-Philosophicus*, 2nd edn. Translated by Brian McGuiness and David Pears. London: Routledge.

Wolfson, Harry Austryn. 1966. "Plato's Pre-existent Matter in Patristic Philosophy." In *The Classical Tradition*, ed. Luitpold Wallach. Ithaca, NY: Cornell University Press.

—1970. *The Philosophy of the Church Fathers*, vol. 1: *Faith, Trinity, and Incarnation*, 3rd edn. Cambridge, MA: Harvard University Press.

Wolterstorff, Nicholas. 1970. *On Universals*. Chicago: University of Chicago Press.

—1991. "Divine Simplicity." *Philosophical Perspectives* 5: 531–52.

Woodin, W. Hugh. 2011. "The Realm of the Infinite." In *Infinity: New Research Frontiers*, Michael Heller and W. Hugh Woodin (eds), 89–118. Cambridge: Cambridge University Press.

Woodward, James. 1990. "Supervenience and Singular Causal Statements." In *Explanation and Its Limits*, ed. Dudley Knowles, 211–46. Cambridge: Cambridge University Press.

Yablo, Stephen. 2000a. "A Priority and Existence." In *New Essays on the A Priori*, Peter Boghossian and Christopher Peacocke (eds). Oxford: Oxford University Press.

—2000b. "A Paradox of Existence." In *Empty Names, Fiction, and the Puzzles of Non-Existence,* Anthony Everett and Thomas Hofweber (eds). Stanford: Center for the Study of Language and Information.

—2002. "Abstract Objects: A Case Study." *Philosophical Issues* 12: 220–40.

—2005. "The Myth of the Seven." in *Fictionalism in Metaphysics*, ed. Mark Kalderon. Oxford: Oxford University Press.

Yandell, Keith. 1984. *Christianity and Philosophy*. Grand Rapids, MI: Eerdmans.

—1993. *The Epistemology of Religious Experience*. Cambridge: Cambridge University Press.

—1994. "The Most Brutal and Inexcusable Error in Counting?: Trinity and Consistency." *Religious Studies* 30: 201–17.

—1999. *Philosophy of Religion: A Contemporary Introduction*. London: Routledge.

—2011. "God and Propositions." *Philosophia Christi* 13: 275–87.

Zagzebski, Linda. 1990. "What if the Impossible Had Been Actual?" In *Christian Theism and the Problems of Philosophy*, ed. Michael Beaty, 165–83. Notre Dame: Notre Dame Press.

Contributors

William Lane Craig is a Research Professor of Philosophy at Talbot School of Theology in La Mirada, California. He earned a doctorate in philosophy at the University of Birmingham, England, before taking a doctorate in theology from the Ludwig-Maximilians-Universität München, Germany, where he was for two years a Fellow of the Alexander von Humboldt-Stiftung. Prior to his appointment at Talbot he spent seven years at the Higher Institute of Philosophy of the Katholike Universiteit Leuven, Belgium. He has authored or edited over 30 books, including *The Kalam Cosmological Argument*; *Divine Foreknowledge and Human Freedom*; *Theism, Atheism, and Big Bang Cosmology*; and *God, Time, and Eternity*, as well as over a hundred articles in professional journals of philosophy and theology, including *The Journal of Philosophy, American Philosophical Quarterly, Philosophical Studies, Philosophy*, and *British Journal for Philosophy of Science*.

Richard Brian Davis is Professor and Chair of Philosophy at Tyndale University in Toronto, Canada. He is the author or editor of four books, including *The Metaphysics of Theism and Modality* (Peter Lang, 2001). He has published numerous articles in metaphysics and philosophy of religion in such places as *Australasian Journal of Philosophy, Religious Studies, Acta Analytica, Philosophia Christi, The Modern Schoolman*, and *Axiomathes*.

Paul M. Gould is an Assistant Professor of Philosophy and Christian Apologetics at Southwest Baptist Theological Seminary in Fort Worth, Texas. He is the editor of four books, including *Is Faith in God Reasonable? Debates in Philosophy, Science, and Rhetoric* (Routledge, forthcoming). He has published articles in metaphysics and philosophy of religion in such places as Philo, Faith and Philosophy, Philosophia Christi, Axiomathes, and Metaphysica.

Graham Oppy is Professor of Philosophy at Monash University. He is author of: *Ontological Arguments and Belief in God*; *Philosophical Perspectives on Infinity*; *Arguing about Gods*; *Reading Philosophy of Religion* (with Michael Scott); and *The Best Argument against God*; and editor (with Nick Trakakis) of *The History of Western Philosophy of Religion*.

Scott A. Shalkowski teaches at the University of Leeds. His work has been largely in metaphysics, including the philosophy of logic and mathematics, and the philosophy of religion. He has published in journals such as *Philosophy and Phenomenological Research, Synthese, Mind, Journal of Philosophy*, and *The Philosophical Review*.

Greg Welty received his DPhil. in Philosophical Theology from Oriel College, University of Oxford, focusing on the relation between God and abstract objects. He serves at Southeastern Baptist Theological Seminary (Wake Forest, NC) as both associate professor of philosophy and coordinator for the MA program in philosophy of religion.

Keith E. Yandell (BA, MA, Wayne State University; PhD Ohio State University); Lecturer (OSU, 1965); Assistant Professor (1966–71), Associate (1971–4), Professor (1975–2010) at University of Wisconsin. He is Julius R. Weinberg Professor of Philosophy Emeritus at UW and Adjunct Professor of Philosophy of Religion at TEDS (2000-present). He has written *Basic Issues in the Philosophy of Religion* (Allyn and Bacon), *Christianity and Philosophy* (Eerdmans), *Hume's "Inexplicable Mystery"* (Temple University Press), *The Epistemology of Religious Experience* (Cambridge University Press), and *Buddhism: A Christian Exploration* (Inter Varsity Press), in *Great Britain Spirituality Without God* (Paternoster), as well as numerous articles and book chapters.

Index

absolute creationism 8–11, 40, 68–9, 115, 128, 137
abstract objects
  arguments to God from abstract objects 94, 179–81, 182–3, 185
  co-eternal with God 9, 129, 185
  created 6–7, 9–10, 26–7, 61–2, 99–100
  nature of 1–2, 3, 21, 51, 172
abstract/concrete distinction 65, 94–5n. 2, 97, 100, 107, 108, 170–2, 186, 188, 192
Adams, Robert 94, 124n. 7
adverbial theory 187, 194–5
Anderson, James 88
Aquinas, Thomas 57, 123n. 1, 176
Armstrong, David 144, 173
aseity-sovereignty doctrine 1–4, 7–8, 15, 38–9, 65, 81, 143–4, 161 see also God, aseity; God, creator of abstract objects
Augustine 2, 32, 65
Azzouni, Jody 119–20, 132, 139, 190

Baggett, David 8
Balaguer, Mark 116, 127–8, 138
Båve, Arvid 122–3, 139
Bealer, George 12, 60, 95n. 11
Beneceraff, Paul 182
Biggest Bang 9, 77
bootstrapping worry 4, 10–11, 32, 62–3, 68–9, 75–7, 176, 185, 187
Brentano, Franz 69

causal theory of knowledge 182–3
causation 61–2, 171–2, 184, 186, 189–90, 192
Chihara, Charles 125n. 14, 188–9
Chisholm, Roderick 144–5
conceptualism 173, 178–9
concretism 116

Copan, Paul 9–10
cosmological argument 150–1, 163, 166–8
counterpossibles 36–7, 45, 46
Craig, William Lane 9–10, 14–15, 158
Crane, Tim 90–1
creation, doctrine of
  biblical passages on creation 7–8, 18n. 13, 23–4, 40, 44, 113–15, 127, 134, 137, 152–3, 162
  rationality of 92–3

Davidson, Matthew 7, 68
Davison, Scott 8
deflationary theory of reference 122–3, 139–40
deflationary theory of truth 41, 48, 69–70, 101, 109, 110, 121–2, 147–8, 157–8, 165
deity theories 105, 106nn. 1, 2, 108
dependency problem 3–4, 6–7, 11, 26–7, 44, 48, 51, 190, 192–3
Divers, John 84
divine conceptualism see theistic activism; possible worlds, as divine thoughts/ideas; and propositions, as divine thoughts/ideas
Dummett, Michael 121

emanation 26, 31, 43, 44, 66, 108
exemplification 54, 60, 69, 75–6, 137

fictionalism 13, 117–18, 127–8, 131–2, 133, 135, 138–9, 173, 174, 177, 179, 180, 188–9, 190–1, 193
Field, Hartry 116, 125n. 9, 131–2, 138, 173, 190
figuralism 161, 162, 166, 188, 193
Fine, Kit 42, 184
Frege, Gottlob 58, 87, 116

God
  aseity 113–15, 127, 132–3, 134, 137,
    152–3, 160, 161–2, 166 *see also*
    aseity-sovereignty doctrine
  creator of abstract objects 2–4, 6–7,
    8–10, 61–2, 175–6, 184, 186–7
    see also creation, doctrine of;
    dependency problem
  creator of His own nature 8, 10–11, 62
  freedom in creating 9–10, 31, 151 *see
    also* emanation
  necessary existence 1–2, 3, 22–3,
    44, 48, 97, 160, 168, 183 *see also*
    ontological argument
  omnipotence 25–6
  omniscience 32–3, 43, 65
  worthy of worship 1 *see also* ultimacy
    problem
Gödel, Kurt 173
Gould, Paul 11
Grayling, A. C. 109

Hellman, Geoffrey 189
Hofweber, Thomas 120

Inconsistent Triad 2–15, 81–2, 97, 100,
  107
indispensability argument 101, 116–23,
  130, 131–2, 134, 138–40, 144–6,
  148–9, 160–1
Inwagen, Peter van 6–7, 12–13, 49, 61, 83,
  145, 186

Jackson, Frank 174
Jubien, Michael 55, 63n. 12

Katz, Jerrold 135–6n. 3
Korhonen, Anssi 53
Kotarbiński, Tadeusz 116
Kripke, Saul 119–20

Leftow, Brian 2, 3, 13–14, 99, 105, 106n. 1,
  108, 154n. 4
Lewis, C. S. 78
Lewis, David 83, 85, 91, 95n. 6, 95n. 8,
  107, 109, 145, 154nn. 2–4, 174
Locke, John 56, 57, 58
Loux, Michael 60, 86, 89, 144

Lycan, William 83–4

mathematical objects 40, 117–18, 131–2,
  133, 135, 138–9, 145, 149, 179–80,
  188–9
McGrath, Matthew 63n. 7
Meinong, Alexius 69
Melia, Joseph 154n. 7, 173, 190–1
Menzel, Christopher 8–11, 18n. 14, 51, 59,
  93, 185
Merricks, Trenton 108–9
Moore, G. E. 52
Moreland, J. P. 63n. 13
Morris, Thomas 8–11, 18n. 14, 51, 59, 93,
  185
multiverse 168

naturalism 105, 163–4, 169–70, 186, 189,
  193–4
necessary beings 1–4, 9, 113, 151–2, 176
necessary truths 27, 38–9, 97–8, 182–3 *see
  also* ontological argument
necessity, conventional 24–5, 42
Nelson, Everett 49
Nicene Creed 49, 114
nominalism 12–15, 89–90 *see also*
  deflationary theory of reference;
  deflationary theory of truth;
  fictionalism; ontological economy;
  possible worlds; proposition

ontological argument 28–30, 39, 41, 48,
  97, 107
ontological commitment 13, 101, 119–23,
  133, 134, 139–40, 166, 188, 190
ontological economy 13–14, 19n. 23,
  87–8, 91

perfect being theology 28–9, 150–3
Philo 114, 123–4n. 3, 134, 162
Pickavance, Timothy 63n. 13
Plantinga, Alvin 6, 7, 8, 9, 11, 17n. 6,
  28–9, 48, 51, 52, 64n. 17, 82, 86,
  87–8, 94, 95n. 5, 95n. 7, 102, 106n.
  3, 108, 110, 179–81
Plato 32, 115, 134
platonic theism 5–8, 11–12, 61–2
platonism 2, 4, 10, 17n. 5, 90 *see also*

platonic theism; possible worlds;
    problem of universals; proposition;
    realism
    argument for 29–30, 41–2,
        lightweight 124n. 7, 131, 188
    theological objections to 14, 40, 42,
        115
possible worlds
    arguments for/against 83–4, 89–90,
        101–2, 104–5, 109, 110
    as divine thoughts/ideas 89, 105
    intentionality 85–6
    necessity 85
    objectivity 85
    plenitude 86–7
    relevance 86, 92–3
Potter, Michael 125n. 10
Prior, A. N. 101, 108–9
problem of universals 2, 115–16, 129–30,
    131, 140, 144–5, 191n. 2
properties 6, 12, 32, 60–1 *see also*
    bootstrapping worry; theistic
    activism
propositionalism 21–3, 32, 40, 42, 45,
    65–6 *see also* platonism
propositions
    arguments for/against 41–2, 72, 82–3,
        101, 103–4, 109, 147–8, 155–6,
        158–9, 187
    as divine thoughts/ideas 6, 8, 9, 11,
        31–2, 44–5, 49–50, 58–9, 60–1, 70,
        72, 74, 77–9, 87–9, 105, 185, 194
    intentionality 23, 52–9, 67–8, 69, 70–1,
        72–4, 85–6, 98
    necessity 85
    objectivity 85
    plenitude 86–7
Pythagoras 115

Quine, W. V. O. 13, 101, 120, 134–5, 173,
    193

realism 19n. 19, 90–2, 100, 108, 127–8,
    175–6, 184–5, 187, 188 *see also*
    platonism; problem of universals
reism 116

Rodriquez-Pereyra, Gonzalo 184
Rosen, Gideon 90, 171, 173, 189
Runia, David 124n. 3
Russell, Bertrand 1, 52, 53

Searle, John 91, 95n. 13
Shalkowski, Scott 17n. 13, 84
struthioism 173, 176–7, 187–8, 190, 193
substance
    Aristotelian 11, 60–1, 62, 76
    bare particular theory 60
    bundle theory 59–60
Swinburne, Richard 96n. 14

theism 2–5, 22, 33–4, 94, 169–70, 189
theistic activism 5, 8–11, 18n. 14, 21, 22,
    30–3, 36, 42–3, 51–2, 59–63, 185,
    186
theistic ideaism 21–2, 33–4, 38, 40 *see also*
    divine conceptualism
theistic propositionalism 22, 33–4, 38, 40
theory evaluation 84–7, 102–3
tokenism 173, 178, 195
truthmaker principle 144, 146, 158
Twardowski, Kazimierz 116

ultimacy problem 3, 43–4, 62, 74n. 2, 100,
    185

Vallicella, William 54

Walls, Jerry 8
Walton, Kendall 118
Weaver, Richard 2
Welty, Greg 11, 88
Willard, Dallas 63n. 14
Wittgenstein, Ludwig 56
Wolfson, Harry Austryn 115
Wolterstorff, Nicholas 6–7, 49, 79n. 1

Yablo, Steven 161, 162, 166, 173, 174, 179,
    180, 188, 190, 193
Yandell, Keith 37

Zagzebski, Linda 37